# A TIME TO SERVE

*Bertie County during World War I*

SIGNAL DETAIL.
BAT. D—316 H.F.A.

## GERALD W. THOMAS

NORTH CAROLINA DEPARTMENT OF NATURAL AND CULTURAL RESOURCES

SUSI H. HAMILTON
*Secretary*

OFFICE OF ARCHIVES AND HISTORY
KEVIN CHERRY
*Deputy Secretary*

DIVISION OF HISTORICAL RESOURCES
RAMONA BARTOS
*Director*

FRONT COVER: The identities of the individuals on the front cover are (left to right): Edmund J. Pruden, John Hilary Matthews, William Haywood Farless. Credit: Angie White furnished the photos of Pruden and Farless. Photo of John Hilary Matthews furnished by the State Archives of North Carolina.

The men in the bottom photograph served as part of a signal detail of Battery D, 316th Field Artillery Regiment. Pvt. Edmund J. Pruden of Aulander, Bertie County is in the center of the back row. This photo is also on p.61. Credit: Angie White

Distributed by the University of North Carolina Press, Inc.
www.uncpress.org

# Contents

# IMAGES AND TABLES

# FOREWORD

With this book Gerald W. Thomas completes a four-volume set dedicated to analyses of the roles played by residents of Bertie County, North Carolina, in four wars: the Revolutionary War, the War of 1812, the Civil War, and World War I. Bertie is a mostly rural county in northeastern North Carolina; its county seat is Windsor. Mr. Thomas, a native of Bertie, is a retired federal executive now residing in Maryland. With ready access to the National Archives, the author performed exhaustive research in pursuit of his goal of paying tribute to the people of Bertie County. Such localized history, telling the story of a single county over the course of several generations, is rare. The books, which include soldier-by-soldier rosters, should have value to genealogists as well as those interested in the history of North Carolina.

Mr. Thomas's series opened in 1996 with *Divided Allegiances: Bertie County during the Civil War*, detailing the fact that Bertie County in 1861–1865 was a no-man's-land with less-than-unanimous support for the Confederate cause. Mr. Thomas had co-authored, with Weymouth T. Jordan Jr., in 1995 an article in the *North Carolina Historical Review* entitled "Massacre at Plymouth: April 20, 1864," dealing with a tragic episode growing out of internal divisions in a neighboring county.

In 2012 a companion study, *Destitute Patriots: Bertie County in the War of 1812*, appeared, followed one year later by *Rebels and King's Men: Bertie County in the Revolutionary War*. Whereas Bertie County residents were deeply divided during the Civil War and the Revolution, this was not the case during the First World War. The story that Mr. Thomas tells in the pages that follow is one of unity, duty, and resolve, in Europe and at home.


Michael Hill, *Supervisor*
Historical Research Office

# PREFACE

Webster's defines *patriotism* as "love and devotion to one's country" and *service* as "an act of assistance or benefit to another or others." The two attributes forthrightly convey the overall character and bearing of the citizens of Bertie County in northeastern North Carolina during World War I, or the "Great War" as it was termed at the time. The conflict united the citizens behind a focused cause for which they generously contributed their resources and time to support the nation's war efforts. During the entirety of the United States' involvement in the war—from the declaration of war against Germany on April 6, 1917 until the cessation of combat on November 11, 1918—the people of Bertie County strongly stood behind the federal government by unequivocally supporting the wide-ranging measures implemented to prosecute the war.

Bertie County residents—the majority of whom derived their livelihoods through farming in the early twentieth century—lived in a "little world." Many rarely ventured beyond the county's boundaries. Most of the citizens had never heard of the places in Europe where the Allied and Central Powers' militaries had, since the summer of 1914, slaughtered their opposition in horridly astounding numbers: places such as Tannenberg, Marne, Ypres, Champagne, Verdun, and the Somme. The county's citizens, defined by their simple yet peaceful and enjoyable lives, during the spring of 1917 overwhelmingly supported the nation's war effort.

During the early days of May 1917, the United States Congress was nearing completion of deliberations and passage of a legislative bill that would drastically impact the lives of millions of young American men. President Woodrow Wilson signed the final bill, the Selective Service Act, into law on May 18, 1917. Six weeks earlier the United States had declared war on Germany. A "Great War" had been raging in Europe for thirty-three months, and by the time the American nation moved to enter the conflict, millions of Europeans had been killed and maimed, both as military combatants and civilians. The United States would be sending substantial military forces to Europe to fight—forces the magnitude of which did not exist in the spring of 1917 and which would have to be raised through selective service, or the draft. Almost 4,300 Bertie County men registered for the draft in 1917 and 1918, and more than 570 were subsequently called into active military service (of whom thirty-one were later rejected by military authorities).

Additionally, ninety-three people—men and women—from the county volunteered to serve and enlisted in the Army, the Navy, and the Marine Corps after the nation declared war. During the nation's involvement in Europe, twenty-six Bertie County men, whites and African Americans, gave their lives while serving in the Army and Navy. The majority (twenty-two individuals) died of disease and illness; only four soldiers were killed in combat.

Military service, while a major component of Bertie County's citizens' involvement in the war efforts, was not their only significant contribution. The residents provided substantial amounts of commodities and foodstuffs, derived from the agricultural fields and gardens throughout the county. They purchased war bonds and war saving stamps, furnishing funds to the federal government's war coffers. They made items of clothing and various amenities that were given to county men as they boarded trains at the railway station in Windsor to be transported to various army training camps across the nation. They formed a chapter of the American Red Cross, which was active in a number of service and war-supportive initiatives.

This book recounts the service and sacrifices made by the citizens of Bertie County in their unwavering support of the nation's war efforts. The United States' participation in the war lasted slightly more than nineteen months. That relatively short, but critical, period in the nation's history proved for Bertie County citizens to be a time to serve humanity. Motivated by both their patriotic sentiment and commitment to serve their country in varying capacities, the citizens contributed on the front in Europe and at home.

This study seeks to recognize and acknowledge the services performed by Bertie County citizens during the war. Chapter 1 surveys both the major events that ignited the conflict and certain principal military actions and campaigns carried out by the Allies and Central Powers from the summer of 1914 until the United States entered the war in April 1917. Chapter 2 documents the federal government's actions to rapidly enlarge the nation's military forces to a level sufficient to wage war in Europe effectively. Primary among those actions was enactment of the Selective Service Act, under whose provisions the majority of Bertie County's military personnel served. Chapter 3 presents the major contributions, such as fundraising and food production, made by county residents to support national war measures from the home front. Chapter 4 documents the overall military service—Army, Navy, and Marine Corps—of Bertie County's men and women who enlisted or were inducted into the armed forces. Appendix 1 is a roster of the county's military service personnel. Appendix 2 is a listing of county residents who performed services and functions at home, primarily under the auspices of the Bertie County Council of Defense.

This book is dedicated to the memory of the Bertie County residents who served and sacrificed in their various capacities, both military and civilian, during the "Great War."

GERALD W. THOMAS

# 1

## PISTOL SHOTS AND WAR

G avrilo Princip—a radical Bosnian Serb student—anxiously waited in a crowd of people gathered along a street in Sarajevo, Bosnia
(then an Austrian province) during the late morning of Sunday,
June 28, 1914. Princip, along with the other members of the gathered
throng, awaited the arrival of Archduke Franz Ferdinand, heir to the Austria-
Hungary throne, and his wife, Sophie. Princip, almost twenty years of age
and an ardent member of a clandestine Serbian extremist organization, the
Black Hand, was not present there to applaud and cheer the archduke and
his wife. Rather, he viewed the future monarch contemptuously and held
the most sinister of intentions—the assassination of Ferdinand. Princip, as
an agent of the Black Hand, was dedicated to furthering the organization's
cause, the creation of a Greater Serbia. That cause necessitated that Austria-
Hungary's rule over Bosnia-Herzegovina be terminated, through violence
or other means.

Seven members of the Black Hand, including Princip, were positioned
at various locations along Ferdinand's route, all focused on ending his life.
Earlier in the morning one of the members had attacked the archduke's
entourage with a small bomb but failed to kill or injure the intended future
monarch, who warded off the projectile with his arm. The thrown explo-
sive device bounced off Ferdinand's vehicle and exploded behind it in the
street, severely wounding the archduke's aide-de-camp, who was riding in

Archduke Franz Ferdinand. *Credit:* Library of Congress.

Gavrilo Princip. *Credit:* Wikipedia.

the trailing car. The attempt generated confusion and anxiety among the procession and the crowd but, astoundingly, failed to lead the archduke to change or terminate his morning's schedule. Following a reception at the Sarajevo city hall, the royal entourage—despite the earlier failed assassination attempt—began to trace a predetermined route through the city. Ferdinand had directed his entourage to travel to the hospital so that he could check the condition of the wounded member of his suite. His automobile soon approached the corner of Franz Josef and Rudolph Streets, where Princip lay in wait. As fate seemingly intervened, Ferdinand's vehicle, an open-top touring car, slowed or stopped within mere feet of Princip, who leaped from the crowd onto the running board of the car and at point-blank range fired two shots from a semi-automatic pistol into the archduke and his wife. Within minutes both were dead.[1]

Princip's two deadly shots ignited a calamitous war on the European continent. Austrian-Hungarian officials suspected that their small neighbor, Serbia, had approved the plot to kill Ferdinand. Austria-Hungary responded on July 28 by declaring war on Serbia. On August 1—only five weeks following the assassination of Ferdinand—Germany declared war on Russia. Two days later Germany declared war on France. German military forces invaded Belgium on the fourth prompting the United Kingdom to declare war on Germany on the same day. On the sixth Austria-Hungary declared war on Russia and Serbia declared war on Germany. Two days later Great Britain launched an incursion into Togoland and East Africa. During the first week of August, the European continent plunged into chaos and hostilities, as massive military forces began mobilizing and marching to meet declared enemies. The local conflict between the Balkan countries within so very few days had escalated to a "Great War," subsequently termed the "First World War."[2]

The outbreak of war culminated decades of tensions, issues, and conflicts among various European nations. For almost forty years European powers had seized large portions of the Ottoman Empire: Great Britain had taken Egypt and Cyprus; France acquired Morocco and Tunisia; Italy controlled Tripoli (Libya); and Austria-Hungary took Bosnia-Herzegovina. Balkan wars in 1912-1913 had not ended nationalistic aspirations; Russia, Serbia, and the Habsburgs still contended for their share of dominance and influence. Germany, with its established formidable military capability, occupied a pivotal geographic and political position in Europe as an emerging economic power. Germany's strength would prompt Great Britain and France to align with Russia in order to deter and intimidate Germany. The European nations affiliated themselves into political and military alliances as the tensions among those nations grew.[3]

American politicians overwhelmingly desired that the nation not become embroiled in the conflict. Indeed, during the half-century following the Civil War the United States had maintained a predominantly isolationist posture in regard to the feuding European monarchs and governments. Early on during the postwar period, Americans were preoccupied with mending the divisions that had permeated their nation as a consequence of the Civil War. Still, before the turn of the century, the United States emerged as a world power by declaring war on Spain. The ensuing conflict, the Spanish-American War, lasted only four months (April-August 1898) and resulted in Spain's capitulation to the Americans. Despite the brief but decisive venture into international military action, American leaders continued the United States' isolationist policies in dealing with the European countries during the early 1900s.[4]

The eruption of hostilities across the Atlantic Ocean shocked Americans. President Woodrow Wilson declared that the United States would remain neutral, supporting neither of the warring sides—the Allies or the Central Powers—militarily or economically.[5] On August 4, 1914, Wilson issued a "Proclamation of Neutrality," decreeing that the nation would remain "impartial in thought as well as in action." Fifteen days later the president appealed to American citizens to be neutral in their thoughts, speech, and actions. A central point in Wilson's appeal was the attempt to cool and soothe the passions of those immigrant groups throughout the nation who identified with the belligerents. Most Americans felt that the outbreak of war in Europe was quite senseless.[6]

Bertie County's residents were largely detached from the European troubles and chaos. The county's citizenry predominantly comprised British- and African-descent persons, with most of the residents' ancestral lineages dating back multiple generations. Therefore, ancestral ties to the citizens' home lands were quite diluted and noncommittal. Bertie County was a thoroughly rural community, a large majority of whose inhabitants earned their livelihoods by farming or laboring on farms. The county was not affluent, with per capita wealth of only $327. Land values, largely farm and forest lands, were estimated to be only about $3 million in 1917. Logging enterprises and railroads employed substantially smaller contingents of the county's male workforce.[7] The European war had little, if any, impact on the daily lives and existence of the county's citizens.

By late August German forces had launched a formidable military offensive against the Allies by invading Belgium and France. The Germans slammed into two Russian armies in a ferocious four-day affair, known today as the Battle of Tannenberg. The Germans completely destroyed Russia's Second Army and demolished much of the First Army. By the end of September, a massive war front extended from the Baltic Sea on the west to Minsk to the east, Saint Petersburg to the north, and the Black Sea to the south.[8]

On September 5, the Battle of the Marne River (near Paris) opened. The battle concluded one week later as a strategic Allied victory when French and British armies compelled German forces to retreat to the northeast from the outskirts of Paris.[9] The victorious Allies had curtailed Germany's month-long, war-opening offensive in Belgium and France. From this point throughout the remainder of the conflict, the warring armies situated themselves along trench lines which snaked through the Belgian and French country sides. The belligerents engaged in predominantly static "trench warfare" as soldiers on both sides dug in, oftentimes

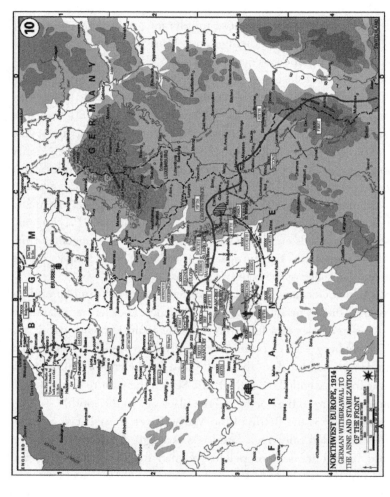

The above map depicts the 400-plus miles of stabilized battle lines which coursed through Belgium and France by the fall of 1914. The entrenched lines became commonly known as the "Western Front." *Credit:* Courtesy of the Department of History, United States Military Academy, West Point, New York.

within a mere hundred yards of each other.[10] Trench warfare was a new method of combat to the Germans and Allies, but the Germans quickly adapted their artillery and other offensive weaponry (mortars, rifle grenades, and hand grenades) to inflict substantial casualties on the Allied troops, particularly the British. The belligerents continuously attempted to outflank each other as they drew progressively nearer to the North Sea. Soon heavily fortified trench lines extended more than 450 miles from the North Sea to the French-Swiss border, battle lines commonly known as the Western Front.[11]

The ground war had quickly exploded across the European continent, but by late autumn 1914, the naval war had likewise escalated significantly. Great Britain—whose navy was vastly superior to Germany's—on November 3 proclaimed that the North Sea was a military area and effectively established a blockade to prevent delivery of goods by seagoing vessels destined for Germany. Any commander who took his ship into the North Sea did so at extreme risk of having the vessel attacked and sunk. The British blockade targeted ships carrying provisions and foodstuffs for the German people, determined by the British authorities to be legitimate contrabands of war. Germans viewed the British measure as an outright attempt to starve them into submission.[12]

In early February 1915 Germany reciprocated by declaring that a war zone existed around Great Britain, thereby effectuating a submarine (U-boat) blockade in which neutral merchant vessels were deemed viable targets and any ship approaching Great Britain a legitimate war asset subject to destruction. Britain relied heavily on imports to feed its people and to provide raw materials for its war efforts and machinery. Since the British navy was recognized as clearly superior to the German in numbers of vessels and war-fighting capabilities, Germany's only avenue to effectively deter merchant ships from entering British ports was submarine warfare. German warships had sunk a number of Allied vessels in 1914 and early 1915, but the declaration issued on February 4 marked an all-out assault on shipping bound for the British nation. Subsequently, German submarines steadily increased their attacks, eventually averaging almost two ships sunk per day by the summer of 1915. Germans discovered their submarines could operate more effectively against merchant shipping than against Allied warships. Thereafter, German mines laid in the North Sea began sinking and damaging merchant vessels.[13]

American vessels soon became targets for German submarines' torpedoes and mines. From mid-February until early May German naval forces sank three American merchant ships, killing seven crew members.[14] The escalation of German submarine attacks and the resulting loss of life raised the concern and ire of Americans. Indeed, the issue of such attacks on American-registered vessels, whether inadvertent or intentional, had worried United States government officials since the inception of the conflict. On several occasions American governmental representatives strongly protested to their German counterparts. In response German officials assured the Americans that its navy would be respectful of the rights of neutral countries.[15]

On May 7, 1915, a German submarine operating in waters south of Ireland near the British homeland launched a single torpedo into the hull of the *Lusitania*, a large British ocean liner carrying 1,959 persons (including crew). The vessel, destined for Liverpool, had departed from New York six days earlier. It sank eighteen minutes after being attacked, taking the lives of almost 1,200 people on board, including 128 Americans. The incident—viewed by Americans as the wanton destruction of a non-military vessel and the unnecessary killing of a multitude of noncombatants—provoked outrage and strong anti-German sentiment across the United States. The attack also resulted in an international uproar led by the United States government against Germany's submarine warfare campaign. While the *Lusitania* had been transporting some contraband goods (war materiel), the large number of victims prompted President Wilson to overlook the ship's cargo in his protest over the attack. Americans were stirred to retaliate against Germany, but the destruction of the *Lusitania* did not stimulate the United States to intervene in the war. Germany curtailed its unrestricted submarine warfare nonetheless.[16]

Throughout 1915 and 1916 the ground war settled into a largely immobilized siege along the 450-plus miles of trenches that gashed Belgium and France. Tens of thousands of Allied and German troops faced off against each other, each side occasionally launching out-of-trench assaults with limited success. Neither was able to break through the other's lines.

Americans went to the polls to elect a president on Tuesday, November 7, 1916. Woodrow Wilson, the incumbent Democrat, was pitted against Supreme Court Justice Charles E. Hughes, the Republican. Wilson's campaign platform was founded on his promise to keep the United States

Trenches and structures on fire in France. *Credit:* State Library of South Australia, image number PRG 280/1/34/177.

out of the ongoing European hostilities. The two candidates' bid for the nation's top executive position was strongly contested; Wilson won by a narrow margin. Overall North Carolina voted in the majority (58.1 percent) for Wilson. In contrast to the national and state results, Bertie County overwhelmingly supported Wilson. Of the 1,577 county citizens who voted, 1,461, an astounding 92.6 percent, cast their ballots for the president.[17] Obviously, Bertie County citizens were well pleased with the president's war-evasion policies and stance.

By early 1917 the war was going badly for the Allies overall. Then, on February 1, Germany announced that it was resuming its unrestricted submarine warfare. That blatant announcement again aroused and angered the American nation. On the third of February President Woodrow Wilson alerted Congress of the "sudden and unexpected action of the Imperial German Government ... [to] undertake immediate submarine operations against all commerce, whether of belligerents or of neutrals." The Germans were targeting any vessels that "should seek to approach Great Britain and Ireland, the Atlantic coasts of Europe, or the harbors of the eastern Mediterranean." According to the president, Germany was to conduct the operations "without regard to the established restrictions of international practice, [and] without regard to any consideration of humanity . . . which might interfere with their object[ives]."[18]

President Wilson addressed a joint session of Congress on February 26 and alerted the lawmakers that since resuming unrestricted submarine warfare the Germans had sunk two American vessels. The *Housatonic* (February 3) was carrying foodstuffs to London and the *Lyman M. Law* (February 12) was transporting box staves to Palermo, Italy. The Sixty-fourth Session of Congress, a "lame duck" session, was set to expire on March 3. Wilson, mindful of the United States' volatile situation in dealing with Germany, told the lawmakers, "I feel that I ought . . . to obtain from you full and immediate assurance of the authority which I may need at any moment to exercise." He desired to have "the authority and the power of the Congress" behind him in whatever action he might need to implement during Congress's recess and concluded, "No one doubts what it is our duty to do. We must defend our commerce and the lives of our people in the midst of the present trying circumstances, with discretion but with clear and steadfast purpose."[19]

On March 4, 1917, President Wilson was inaugurated for a second term. In his inaugural address he conveyed that ominous and foreboding events were drawing the American nation closer to conflict: "[O]ther matters have more and more forced themselves upon our attention—matters lying outside our own life as a nation and over which we had no control, but which, despite our wish to keep free of them, have drawn us more and more irresistibly into their own current and influence." He further stated that "some of the injuries done us have become intolerable" as "we wished nothing for ourselves . . . [but] fair dealing, justice, the freedom to live and to be at ease against organized wrong. . . . We stand firm in armed neutrality." He concluded: "The shadows that now lie dark upon our path will soon be dispelled."[20] The president was forthrightly notifying American citizens that their country might soon be at war.

During the ten days from March 12 through the twenty-first, German submarines attacked and sank five more American merchant vessels. Another vessel was torpedoed and sent to the floor of the Atlantic on April 1.[21] America had endured enough, as across the country thousands of its citizens clamored for war with Germany.

President Woodrow Wilson. *Credit:* Library of Congress

Bertie County residents kept abreast of the worsening situation between the United States and Germany in articles and accounts published in state and local newspapers. Nathaniel Asbell, a forty-four-year-old farmer of the Greens Crossroads community, like other county citizens, routinely received a newspaper. In reading war articles he perceived that the United States' entrance into the conflict seemed imminent. Asbell conveyed to his family that "he was afraid . . . there was going to be war." According to one of his daughters, each week he would read more and "each time he spoke of it [the deteriorating situation between the United States and Germany], he seemed a little more disturbed."[22]

On April 2, the Sixty-fifth Congress convened in the nation's capital and President Wilson immediately called a joint session of the body. In addressing the legislators he requested that they approve a declaration of war against Germany. Four days later the Senate and House passed a joint resolution that declared war on Germany. The Senate voted 82 to 6 for war, and the House of Representatives, 373 to 50. North Carolina's two senators and nine of its ten representatives voted for the resolution. However, Rep.

Claude Kitchin of Scotland Neck (Halifax County), the House Majority Leader, voted against the measure. Kitchin addressed his colleagues in the House, explaining that his "conscience and judgment, after mature thought and fervent prayer for rightful guidance, . . . have marked out clearly the path of my duty . . . I have come to the undoubting conclusion that I should vote against this resolution." Later in the day the president delivered a public proclamation to the American people announcing that the country was in a state of war with the "Imperial German Government."[23] Despite American desires and efforts to remain militarily disengaged from the conflict, the United States had now entered a most destructive and deadly war on a trans-ocean continent.

1. *New York Tribune*, June 29, 1914; Samuel R. Williamson, Jr., "The Origins of the War," in Hew Strachan, ed., *The Oxford Illustrated History of the First World War* (Oxford and New York: Oxford University Press, 1998), 9 (hereafter cited as Strachan, *Oxford History of First World War*); "Assassination of Archduke Ferdinand, 1914," "Eyewitness to History," www. eyewitnesstohistory.com.

The assassination of Ferdinand did not generate much coverage across North Carolina. Papers across the state in early July printed rather short, inconspicuous accounts of the affair in Sarajevo. See *Hickory Democrat*, July 2, 1914; *Courier* (Asheboro), July 2, 1914; *Roanoke News* (Weldon), July 2, 1914; *Mebane Leader* (July 2, 1914; *Roanoke Beacon* (Plymouth), July 3, 1914; and *Enterprise* (Williamston), July 3, 1914.

The *Windsor Ledger*, based in Windsor, the Bertie County seat, was published weekly during the 1910s, but a meager few issues of the print have survived for the World War I period. Only the March 21, 1918, issue has been preserved on microfilm by the North Carolina State Archives for the 1917-1918 timeframe. *Windsor Ledger*, January 7-December 23, 1915; 1916–1920 (microfilm), State Archives.

2. Williamson, "The Origins of the War," in Strachan, ed., *Oxford History of First World War*, 9, 22; Michael S. Neiberg, *Fighting the Great War: A Global History* (Cambridge and London: Harvard University Press, 2005), xiii (hereafter cited as Neiberg, *Great War*); H. P. Willmott, *World War I* (New York: Dorling Kindersley Publishing, 2003), 26 (hereafter cited as Willmott, *World War I*); Hew Strachan, *The First World War* (New York: Penguin Group, 2003), 22, 47–48.

3. Williamson, "The Origins of the War" in Strachan, ed., *Oxford History of First World War*, 9–25. See also Sarah McCulloh Lemmon and Nancy Smith Midgette, *North Carolina and the Two World Wars*, (Raleigh: Office of Archives and History, North Carolina Department of Cultural Resources, 2013) (hereafter cited as *North Carolina and the Two World Wars*).

4. David F. Trask, *The War With Spain in 1898* (Lincoln and London: University of Nebraska Press, 1981), xii, 1–3, 24–25, 57–58, 435, 466; "Spanish-American War," *World Book Encyclopedia*, 2000 edition.

5. The major combatants for the Allies were France, Russia, Great Britain, Italy (as of May 22, 1915), the United States (April 6, 1917), and Japan. The Central Powers major combatants were Germany, Austria-Hungary, Bulgaria, and the Ottoman Empire.

6. Thomas G. Patterson, J. Gary Clifford, Shane J. Maddock, Deborah Kisatsky, and Kenneth J. Hagan, *American Foreign Relations: A History, Volume 2 Since 1895* (Boston: Cengage Learning, 2009), 76-77; Woodrow Wilson, *Message to Congress*, 63rd Cong., 2d Sess., Senate Doc. No. 566 (Washington, 1914), 3–4.

7. Enumerations of Bertie County households in the 1910 Federal census disclose that farming was the predominant livelihood within the county. For example, within the Colerain No. 1 District, 555 persons were noted as farmers or farm laborers, whereas 130 individuals listed their occupations as laborers (non-farm), the second most cited occupation in the district. Similarly, within the Roxobel District 656 people were noted as farmers or farm laborers and 66 were laborers. Within that district 33 men were enumerated as employees of lumber/ logging enterprises, whereas 22 persons worked for railroad entities. Occupation patterns were similar within the county's other districts. Thirteenth Census of the United States, 1910 (microfilm): Bertie County, North Carolina, Records of the Bureau of the Census, Record Group 29, National Archives, Washington, D.C. Per capita wealth of Bertie County residents was derived from F. H. Fries, comp., *History of War Savings Campaign of 1918 in North Carolina* (Winston-Salem, N.C.: N.p., n.d.), 47. The cited source is found in Liberty Loan Campaigns, Box 7, World War I Papers, Military Collection, State Archives. The county-wide estimated land value in 1917 was obtained from *Annual Report of the Auditor of North Carolina for the Fiscal Year Ending November 30, 1917* (Raleigh: Edwards & Broughton, 1918), part II, 16.

8. As discussed within this publication, military operations and warfare along the Western Front were characterized by trenches, but trench warfare never developed on the Eastern Front, primarily due to the extreme length of the battle lines and the lesser density of troops assigned to those lines. Strachan, *First World War*, 140. For descriptions of the characteristics of warfare along the cited fronts, see "Trench Systems on the Western Front" and "The Eastern and Balkans Fronts" in Willmott, *World War I*, 110-113, 114–121, respectively.

9. Willmott, *World War I*, 52, 55–57.

10. Willmott, *World War I*, 57–59.

11. Neiberg, *Great War*, 32–33.

12. Willmott, *World War I*, 172–173; Strachan, First World War, 201-202, 214, 222.

13. Willmott, *World War I*, 179, 184; Strachan, *First World War*, 222; Paul G. Halpern, "The War at Sea" in Strachan, ed., *Oxford History of First World War*, 114 (hereafter cited as Halpern, "War at Sea").

14. Navy Department, Historical Section, comp., *American Ship Casualties of the World War, including Naval Vessels, Merchant Ships, Sailing Vessels and Fishing Craft* (Washington: Government Printing Office, 1923), 8, 17 (hereafter cited as *American Ship Casualties*).

15. Halpern, "War at Sea," 114.

16. Willmott, *World War I*, 179; B. J. C. McKercher, "Economic Warfare" in Strachan, ed., *Oxford History of First World War*, 126–128.

17. R. D. W. Connor, comp. & ed., *North Carolina Manual*, 1919 (Raleigh: Edwards & Broughton, 1918), 445; Bertie County Elections, Record of, 1878–1932 (microfilm), State Archives.

18. Neiberg, *Great War*, 139: Arthur S. Link, et al., eds., *The Papers of Woodrow Wilson*, 69 vols. (Princeton, New Jersey: Princeton University Press, 1966-1994), 41: 108–112 (hereafter cited as Wilson Papers).

19. *Wilson Papers*, 41: 283–287.

20. *Wilson Papers*, 41: 332–335.

21. The vessels and dates on which they were sunk were the *Algonquian*, March 12; the *Vigilancia*, March 16; the *Memphis*, March 17; the *Illinois*, March 18; the *Healdton*, March 21; and the *Aztec*, April 1. *American Ship Casualties*, 8.

22. Nova Asbell Leicester, "Tales Told to Me by My Mother When I Was a Child," (unpublished research report, ca. 1977).

23. Wilson Papers, 41: 519–527; Claude Kitchin quoted in *North Carolina and the Two World Wars*, 18-19.

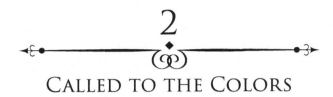

# 2

# CALLED TO THE COLORS

I n early April 1917 the U.S. Army was quite small in terms of manpower and had not been involved in combat, except for some skirmishes along the United States-Mexico border, in the nearly two decades since the Spanish-American War. The nation's total ground force numbered approximately 331,700, of whom fewer than 210,000 were on active duty in the regular army and federalized National Guard organizations. About 122,000 were members of National Guard units in state service and various other reserve categories. Obviously, the nation with its existing forces did not have the military capability to wage war on the scale demanded by the European conflict. The National Defense Act of 1916 (enacted June 3, 1916) had authorized the expansion of the army, but the short period between the passage of the law and the declaration of war against Germany did not permit meaningful and impactful changes. Furthermore, nearly one-half of the country's National Guard personnel, including two North Carolina units, the 2nd and 3rd Infantry Regiments, were on duty supporting operations against Mexico in early 1917.[1]

Legislators and military leaders in the nation's capital determined that the requisite manpower for the armed forces to fight in Europe could not be raised solely through volunteerism. Therefore, Congress passed "An Act to Authorize the President to Increase Temporarily the Military Establishment of the United States," commonly known as the Selective

Service Act. The statute, approved May 18, 1917, authorized the president to immediately raise, organize, and equip all increases in the size of the regular army provided by the National Defense Act of 1916. In short the law provided that the nation would raise through conscription a national army of sufficient size to fight across the Atlantic. All males, ages twenty-one through thirty, were subject to the military draft. Those individuals were required to register for Selective Service (i.e., the draft) at their respective polling precincts across the country.[2]

Brig. Gen. Enoch H. Crowder, the Judge Advocate General of the United States Army, was appointed Provost Marshal General and charged with implementing the requirements of the Selective Service Act. Pursuant to the act's provisions the Provost Marshal General's Office in Washington, D.C. administered the national Selective Service system. The system was based on supervised decentralization, whereby Crowder's office formulated policy and transmitted it to the governors of the forty-eight states, the District of Columbia and three territories (Alaska, Hawaii and Puerto Rico). The states, the District of Columbia, and the territories managed the operations related to drafting men for military service in accordance with regulations promulgated by the Provost Marshal General's Office. The governors of the states and territories were the primary executives responsible for the overall supervision of all matters arising from the execution of the program at the state/territory level. The governors were also delegated the responsibility of organizing both medical advisory and legal advisory boards and appointing the members of such boards. States, including North Carolina, that had an adjutant general to administer military matters utilized that officer to carry out the functions mandated by the Selective Service Act. The president appointed district boards in the federal judicial districts. North Carolina's two district boards—eastern and western—were headquartered in Goldsboro and Statesville.[3]

Before the end of the day on May 18 General Crowder sent a telegram to Gov. Thomas Walter Bickett of North Carolina informing him that the Selective Service law had been approved. Crowder communicated that "all male persons between the ages of twenty-one and thirty both inclusive, except certain persons in the Military and Naval Services of the United States," were required to register for Selective Service on Tuesday, June 5, 1917, a mere eighteen days after the passage of the statute. Registration was to occur in the voting precincts in which the individuals had "their permanent homes" rather than the locales where they may have been residing.[4]

On May 19 Governor Bickett transmitted letters to each county sheriff, clerk of court, and county physician conveying that President Wilson had issued a proclamation calling for the registration on June 5 of all male citizens whose ages were stipulated in the draft law. The governor, by virtue of the power vested in him by the Selective Service Act and based on guidance from the Provost Marshal General's Office, appointed Sheriff John W. Cooper, Clerk of Court William L. Lyon, and Dr. John L. Pritchard as members of the Board of Registration for Bertie County. Cooper was designated as chairman. Bickett next directed the three-member board to appoint one registrar within each voting precinct of the county. Volunteer registrars were encouraged. All registrars were to be appointed by May 24 and were to be provided printed instructions as to their duties (such instructions having been sent to Sheriff Cooper).[5] Cooper, Lyon, and Pritchard immediately set about preparing Bertie County for the forthcoming day of Selective Service registration. The county was comprised of eleven voting precincts: Colerain (two precincts), Indian Woods, Merry Hill, Mitchell's (two precincts), Roxobel, Snakebite, White's, Windsor, and Woodville.[6]

Execution of the Selective Service program was essentially divided into two stages: registration, then selection and determination of exemptions. Guidance from the Provost Marshal General's Office specifically required that the county Boards of Registration be comprised of the sheriff, clerk of court, and county physician. The requirement complied with section 6 of the Selective Service Act, which provided that local boards consist of three or more members, none of whom were connected to the military establishment, to be chosen from the local authorities or other citizens residing in the jurisdiction (such as Bertie County).

Across North Carolina county sheriffs and clerks of court were elected positions. Therefore, appointment of such officials to the county Boards of Registration (subsequently designated as exemption boards), in Governor Bickett's view, represented a serious conflict of interest. On May 28 Bickett communicated to General Crowder that he was profoundly convinced that it would be extremely unfortunate to appoint sheriffs and county clerks to local boards. In North Carolina such officials were elected by voters and therefore were deeply interested in politics. In the governor's view the conscientious discharge of their duty on exemption boards could likely result in their defeat at the next election. Furthermore, the failure of local authorities to conscientiously discharge their duties on exemption boards—influenced by potential political considerations—would result in wholly unfair exemptions. Bickett urged the Provost Marshal to issue a general order that sheriffs and county clerks not be required to serve on local exemption boards in locales where other good citizens were available. In the governor's opinion such an order was vital to impartial administration of the law."[7]

Crowder did not concur with Bickett's view. On the twenty-ninth he telegrammed the governor that the function of local boards was to determine exemptions in a ministerial rather than discretionary manner. In the majority of cases only self-executing exemptions would be subject to the board's jurisdiction. Crowder noted that there would be practically no opportunity for any board to be affected by political consideration. He apprised Bickett that in his view it would be unnecessary for local boards to depart in any "very great measure" from personnel to be constituted from among local officials. He asked the governor to convey back to him his (Bickett's) views after consideration of the points made in the telegram.[8]

Before the day's end Bickett responded to Crowder that in view of the advice in the subject telegram, he would proceed to name the county boards of registration as local exemption boards. He further urged Crowder to ensure that the regulations governing local exemption boards be issued so as to make the boards' duties entirely ministerial. Bickett strongly desired that North Carolina's local officials not be placed in compromising situations regarding any discretion relating to Selective Service exemptions, thereby resulting in confusion and injustice.[9]

Apparently, Governor Bickett's strong views on the composition of local exemption boards and the envisioned potential conflicts associated with elected officials serving on such boards swayed General Crowder to allow other people to be appointed. During the morning of June 5, Crowder telegrammed Bickett that regulations would soon be communicated that he thought would convince Bickett that the federal government's system for determining exemptions would allow for little latitude for political influence. However, Crowder conceded authority to Bickett to appoint other citizens resident in the area over which a board had jurisdiction."[10]

Governor Bickett may have been alerted that a change in General Crowder's strong position on the membership of local exemption boards was forthcoming since, on June 2 he notified specified county officials across the state that local exemption boards would be composed of three citizens recommended by the Governor and appointed by the President. One would be the physician then on the registration board. Desiring that no other county official be a member of the local exemption board, Bickett requested that each designated county point-of-contact wire him the names and addresses of two intelligent, patriotic men who were "in real sympathy with the Government in the prosecution of this war," and who would perform their assigned duties without fear or favoritism. He implored that there be "no politics" in the appointments: "Loyalty to the Nation was to be the singular consideration."[11]

North Carolina's boards of registration ceased to exist in early June 1917 when boards of exemption, most commonly referred to as "local boards," took shape. Sheriff John W. Cooper and Clerk of Court William L. Lyon were relieved from serving on the Bertie County board. In their places Bickett appointed prominent citizens Aaron S. Rascoe of Windsor, a merchant and former representative in the General Assembly, and Clingman W. Mitchell of Aulander, also a merchant and former representative and state senator. Rascoe was designated chairman. Dr. John L. Pritchard continued as the appointed medical member of the board, while Andrew Jackson Dunning, Jr. of Aulander served as board secretary and Arthur Cleveland Mitchell of Windsor as clerk. Rascoe, however, did not fulfill the chairmanship (likely declining the appointment) as Moses Braxton Gillam, an influential Windsor lawyer and banker, was appointed head of the board. Before the end of June Governor Bickett submitted his nominations for the members of the state's local boards, including Bertie's board, to President Wilson, who approved them.[12]

In the early morning hours of June 5, 1917, twenty-two leading citizens of Bertie County stood ready as registrars in the eleven precincts to sign up men for selective service. The registrars were: Moses R. Barnes, Holley M. Bell, John C. Bell, Albert V. Cobb, Julian C. Drake, Andrew J. Dunning Jr., Hosea L. Early, Whitmel F. Early, David A. Fore, Leon H. Freeman, Charles E. Hobbs, Alexander Lassiter, Carl R. Livermon, Arthur C. Mitchell, Charles B. Morris, George T. Parker, Philip T. Perry, John Pritchard, Thomas A. Smithwick, Elmer D. Spruill, Richard A. Urquhart, and Alpheus D. White.

On that first day scores of Bertie County men travelled to polling locations and registered for the draft. Dozens of other county residents who were employed and residing at locales outside the county had registered at those locations, mostly in Virginia, but noted that their registrations were effective in Bertie County, their "permanent" homes of record. The implementing regulations stipulated that people absent from their homes were to go to the clerk of court for the jurisdiction where they were located and register. Such absentee registrations were to be completed and mailed to the individuals' home local boards in sufficient time to reach the boards by June 5.[13]

A total of 1,728 Bertie County men, white and African American, registered on or about June 5. The vast majority registered on the fifth at voting locations within the county. Seven men registered after June 5, and forty-six individuals' registrations were inadvertently not dated, but presumably the vast majority, if not all, of the forms were completed and submitted on the required registration date.[14]

According to information divulged in the registrations, twenty-seven of the draft-age men previously had served in military capacities. A dozen had served in the North Carolina Naval Reserves, and five had served in the state's militia and/or National Guard. Three men each had served in the Coast Artillery Corps and the United States Navy, while only two had served in the army. Two others had served in the Virginia National Guard.[15]

Governor Bickett proudly notified General Crowder on June 6 that the previous day's registration activities within North Carolina had proceeded uneventfully: "Am gratified to report full registration in North Carolina. Not one trace of opposition or disturbance at any precinct in the State." Across the state 200,032 men registered for the draft (including absentees who registered in non-state locales and had their registration cards mailed to their local boards).[16] Thousands of young men's peaceful lives and daily routines across North Carolina's environs, including Bertie County, were soon to become transformed into the arduous training of soldiers and the unforeseeable futures of combatants.

Local boards assigned serial numbers to the registrants. A unique serial number was sequentially assigned to each registrant, beginning with the number one and continuing until the last registrant had been assigned a number. No standard order of registration cards was created in assigning the numbers. For example, local boards did not arrange cards alphabetically and then assign the serial numbers. Unique serial numbers were required in order to ascertain each registrant's military service

Governor Thomas W. Bickett, the "war governor," led North Carolina during the World War I period. Maj. Gen. Enoch H. Crowder, the Army's provost marshal general, implemented and administered the provisions of the Selective Service Act, a statute which resulted in the drafting of thousands of American men into military service during the war, including hundreds from Bertie County. *Credit:* Photograph no. 53.15.1572, Audio Visual and Iconographics Collection, Division of Archives and History Photograph Collection, North Carolina State Archives.

liability based on a forthcoming lottery to be held in the nation's capital. A separate and distinct list of assigned serial numbers was generated for each local board. Thus, the Bertie County board assigned numbers to all the registrants from a consolidated list comprised of the registrants for each of the county's registration locations.[17]

In Washington, D. C. on Friday, July 20, a bevy of federal leaders and officials initiated "selective conscription" with a national lottery to affix the order of military liability for the 9.9 million young Americans who had registered a month and a half earlier. The lottery was held in a public hearing room of the Senate office building and was supervised by key War Department officials. The selection process lasted more than sixteen hours, during which 10,500 capsules were drawn. Members of the Senate and House military committees served as witnesses for the selection process. The lottery gave every registered individual a place in the liability for service list based on the specific serial number assigned by his respective board of registration. The selection of an individual's serial number in the lottery determined his placement and order for potential military service. Federal officials estimated that the first 3,000 numbers drawn would furnish sufficient men to fulfill the "first quota" (687,000) of draftees for the army.[18]

The order of the numbers drawn in the lottery determined the sequence in which men with the corresponding serial numbers would be liable to serve in the nation's military. Individuals selected for potential service would be summoned by local exemption boards for physical examinations and ascertainment of exemptions from service. The lottery drawing was the final activity wherein the federal government impacted mustering soldiers through universal selection. Thereafter, responsibility for calling men to be examined and choosing those to serve rested with the states through the local exemption boards. Only after a drafted man had "joined the colors" would the federal government resume responsibility.

In the days immediately following the draft lottery, newspapers across the country carried headlines and front-page articles regarding the activities, including the list of drawn lottery numbers. Men who had registered in June and who had access to newspaper accounts with the list of draft numbers could quickly ascertain how imminently they might be called to their local boards for physical examinations and exemption determinations. The lottery also stirred numerous men across the nation to volunteer for military service in the army, navy, and national guard. By July 28 more than 165,600 individuals, of whom 1,190 were North Carolinians, had enlisted in the United States Army since April 1, 1917.[19] Thirty-five Bertie County residents were among the North Carolina volunteers for army duty during the roughly four-month period. Additionally, one county resident enlisted in the United States Marine Corps and four signed on with the United States Navy.[20]

Late in the day on Monday, July 23, General Crowder's staff sent copies of the "draft master list" of serial numbers to each of the local exemption boards in the country. The lists were first sent to the state, territory, and District of Columbia offices, which in turn were to transmit two copies of

Major General Enoch H. Crowder. *Credit:* Library of Congress

the list to each local board. Each local board was required to post a copy of the list in a prominent location in its headquarters. Within a few days local exemption boards began posting names of registrants who were ordered to appear before the board for physical examinations.[21]

Under the Selective Service system the Provost Marshal General's Office determined how many men were to be called into service from each state and territory and the dates they were to be entrained to designated training camps. The office then notified the adjutant general of each state (or other appropriate official in cases where adjutant generals were not utilized), who was responsible for having the men called into service by the local boards. The adjutant general ascertained how many men were to be inducted by each local board and the date(s) the men were to be inducted and transported to training camps. The adjutant general then forwarded to the local boards the numbers of men and date(s) for induction. The local boards notified the men to be inducted of the date(s) and time(s) they were to report to the local board's headquarters.

General Crowder established that 687,000 men were required in the first quota to be called into army service. The national quota was allocated to the states and territories based on their individual populations in proportion to the overall national population. North Carolina's quota (based on its estimated population of 2.1 million, or 2.3 percent of the national population) was 15,974 men.[22]

Once the adjutant general's office in Raleigh notified a local board of the serial numbers of the men to be called for potential selection for military service, those whose serial numbers had been selected were called by the local board for physical examinations. Such examinations were conducted by the physician on the board (Dr. John L. Pritchard for Bertie County). Any man whom the physician determined physically unfit for general military service was provided a certificate of discharge from Selective Service by reason of "physical disqualification." Each individual determined to be physically qualified for general military service was allowed to submit a claim for exemption or discharge from Selective Service. Various exemptions were authorized per the Selective Service Act and the implementing regulations. Valid exemptions included (but were not limited to) (1) providing the sole family income for dependent children under the age of sixteen in a family where the registrant's spouse was deceased and (2) providing the sole family income for dependents siblings under age sixteen in a family where both of the registrant's parents were deceased. The local board then held a hearing regarding the validity of the individual's claim for exemption. If the board determined that the claim was valid, it exempted the man from military service under the provisions of the Selective Service Act and issued him a certificate of exemption. In contrast, if the board determined that a person's claim for exemption was invalid, it disallowed the claim and certified the person for military service. He was then inducted into the army. Any man whom the board physician determined to be physically qualified for military service and who did not submit a claim for exemption was likewise certified for military service by the board and inducted. A registrant was permitted to appeal his local board's exemption determination to the applicable district board (North Carolina's Eastern District Board, Goldsboro, for Bertie County registrants).[23]

Across the nation opposition to the draft arose, which led to organized riots, principally in larger cities. Certain European groups in the United States—particularly German and Italian Americans, as well as Irish Americans—opposed the war. Opposition to the conflict was greater among African Americans, who felt that they had not been afforded the same freedoms as white Americans. Numbers of men attempted to avoid military service by not registering for Selective Service, applying for exemptions for which they were not qualified, and deserting from the military. Within Bertie County apparently there were no public exhibitions of opposition to the war and the draft, but dissent surfaced among a number of men who knowingly failed to register for Selective Service or who sought special exemptions. Men who failed to register for the draft were considered delinquents, most commonly called "slackers." During May, June, and September 1918 ten "slackers" and one deserter were arrested and jailed by Sheriff John W. Cooper. Eventually, more than 120 county men were charged with being delinquents or deserters. Additionally, three men, Zebulon Thomas Miller, Van Perry Wadsworth (or Wardsworth), and John Finch Early, applied for agricultural exemptions but were denied by the Bertie County local board. All three individuals appealed the local board's decisions to the Eastern District Board in Goldsboro, which also denied their claims. Finally, the men appealed to the office of the President of the United States, which also upheld the denials. The three men were conscripted into the army. Another method of evading military service arose among men who registered for the draft in Bertie County but subsequently relocated from their homes and did not provide new addresses to officials of the local board. These men essentially evaded conscription if they did not re-register with the local boards that had purview of the conscription system in the areas of their new residences.[24]

In July President Wilson authorized the War Department to call into service the 687,000 men previously determined by General Crowder to constitute the "first draft." Some of the drafted men would fill existing regular army and National Guard units to "war strength," while the other draftees would constitute the first 500,000 members of the new national army. A substantial number of new army regiments were manned, organized, and trained. North Carolina's proportionate gross quota was 23,486 men. Credits were allowed for persons who had enlisted in the armed forces since April 1, 1917. Across North Carolina 7,512 had so enlisted, yielding a net quota of 15,974 individuals to be entered into military service from the Tar Heel State.[25]

On August 13, 1917, Provost Marshal General Crowder issued orders directing that the entire contingent of inductees for the "first draft" be summoned within the near future in four separate calls. All of the men were to be undergoing training at various camps in early October. Crowder's schedule for the calls was:

- the first thirty percent of the quota in each district begin "entrainment for cantonments" on September 5;
- the next thirty percent – September 15;
- the next thirty percent – September 30;
- the remaining ten percent – as soon after September 30 as possible.[26]

Orders to report and the names of the men who were selected for induction into the army were posted at the local board's headquarters and copies were mailed to the men. The selectees were directed to report to the local board at its headquarters not less than twelve hours or more than twenty-four hours before the time of their departure. The local board was explicitly responsible for making lodging arrangements and furnishing meal tickets to the men while they awaited their departures. An inductee was "called to the colors" at his local board's office (Windsor for the Bertie County board) and drafted into the army. He was at that time a member of the military even though he had not reported to an official army station. Next, he was placed aboard a train and transported to the army camp to which he was to report for training. The United States Railway Administration was responsible for transporting the men from their local boards to their assigned military camps.[27] (Draftees who resided in close proximity to the military camps to which they were to report were provided alternative forms of transportation.)

On Tuesday, September 4, 1917, "solemn ceremonies" were conducted in Windsor to patriotically recognize Bertie County's first men to be drafted for army service. Luther Thomas Harden, a twenty-two-year-old farmer who resided in the Sans Souci area, had the distinction of officially being the first county resident inducted. His registration serial number was 458, the sixth number selected in the lottery. He was inducted into the army as a private at Windsor on Wednesday, September 5, 1917, along with eight other Bertie men – Clifton Stallings, Clyde B. Harrell, Robert J. Mitchell, Allen T. Powell, James B. Forehand, Johnnie Johnson, Joseph R. Tarkenton,

Luther Thomas Harden's draft registration. *Credit:* Library of Congress

Form 164-A.                                                                                          Inside List Sheet.

| | | | | | | ENTRIES AT MOBILIZATION CAMP. | | | |
| ENTRIES BY LOCAL BOARD. | | | | | | | | | |
| 1 | 2 | 3 | 4 | 5 | 6 | 7 | 8 | 9 | 10 |
| Order No. | Name. | Red ink No. | Date ordered to report. | Date and hour person reported. See Mobilization Reg., sec. 9. | Date actually forwarded to mobilization camp. See sec. 12, Mobilization Reg. | Date actually reported at mobilization camp. | Failed to report at mobilization camp. Enter X. | Date rejected at mobilization camp. | Date of final acceptance at mobilization camp. |
| | | | | | 1917 | | | | |
| 3 | Luther Thomas Harden | 3 | 458 | 9/4/ | 9/5/ | 9/5/ | 9/5 | | | 10/25 |
| 81 | Clifton Stallings | 3 | 1495 | " | " | " | 9/5 | | | 11/16 |
| 38 | Clyde B. Harrell | 3 | 692 | " | " | " | 9/5 | | | 10/25 |
| 65 | Robert J. Mitchell | 2 | 487 | " | " | " | 9/5 | | | 10/25 |
| 17 | Allen T. Powell | 3 | 874 | " | " | " | 9/5 | | | 10/25 |
| 20 | James B. Forehand | 3 | 679 | " | " | " | 9/5 | | | 10/25 |
| 55 | Johnie Johnson | 3 | 199 | " | " | " | 9/5 | | | 10/25 |
| 96 | Joseph R. Tarkenton | 3 | 368 | " | " | " | 9/5 | | | 11/16 |
| 23 | Edward S. Pugh | 3 | 292 | " | . " | " | 9/6 | | | 10/25 |

No. of men received      9
No. rejected             0
No. accepted             9

Local Board for the County of Bertie,
State of North Carolina,
Windsor, N. C.

321 Inf.

Totals (enter total of entries only in columns for which space is provided)      9   0   0   9

Insert extra pages where necessary.

3

Bertie County's first men selected for service in the army were inducted at Windsor on September 5, 1917. The nine individuals were transported by train to Camp Jackson, Columbia, South Carolina where they were accepted for duty by military authorities. The men were assigned to the 321st Infantry Regiment, 161st Infantry Brigade, 81st Division (per notation on the lower left of the image). *Credit:* War Department, Office of the Provost Marshal General, Selective Service System, 1917–July 15, 1919, Lists of Men Ordered to Report to Local Board for Military Duty, 1917-1918. North Carolina (Bertie County), Records of the Selective Service System (World War 1), Record Group 163, National Archives.

and Edward Stewart Pugh. All nine inductees boarded a Wellington and Powellsville train at the Windsor depot along the Cashie River about eight o'clock in the morning on the fifth. A "large crowd" of people from across Bertie County had taken time from their early morning schedules to assemble at the Windsor train depot to give their patriots a "big sendoff." The men were transported to Camp Jackson in Columbia, South Carolina, where they arrived about midnight.[28]

Soon calls from the War Department for more draftees were routinely transmitted to Adjutant General Lawrence W. Young in Raleigh for North Carolina to furnish men to fill its designated quotas. Across Bertie County "there was a lot of excitement" as individuals were called forth to Windsor by the local board for physical examinations and exemption determinations. Most of the young men of draft age had only grade school educations and had never traveled outside of the county. During their lives the majority of the future soldiers had known only the routine of their "own little world." As the draft board "called the boys a few at a time, they made ready to leave and go to training camps. There was quite a stir."[29]

The next group of county men to be drafted, nineteen in number, departed Windsor on Friday, September 28. They also were transported to Camp Jackson. Throughout 1917 young men gathered at the train station along the banks of the Cashie River, boarded train cars, and were transported to Camp Jackson. By December 26 sixty-four men had been called into military service through the selective draft.[30]

By end of the year Crowder's office had issued calls to the states and territories to fill approximately seventy-five percent of the first draft quota. Of the 687,000 men who were to be inducted across the country, 515,212 had been mobilized to their designated training camps by the end of the year. North Carolina's local boards had inducted 9,992 men, leaving a remaining quota of 5,982 individuals to be drafted across the state.[31]

Concurrently, as young North Carolinians were being drafted into the army, companies of the Home Guard (reserve militia) were organized. The Home Guard was designated principally to maintain security and law and order within the counties in the absence of the state's National Guard, which had been federalized. By late September 1917 Governor Bickett and Adjutant General Young had decided to invoke North Carolina's existing law authorizing the governor to call state citizens to active service in the militia during an "emergency period." The officials presented their plan to the North Carolina Council of Defense during a session in Raleigh in September. (Governor Bickett appointed the state council, a subordinate organization to the Council of National Defense, in May 1917.)

The officials determined to utilize the county councils of defense in the formation of the local military units. Across the state 5,000 men were to be "called into service for home guard purposes." On September 27 Daniel H. Hill Jr., Chairman of the North Carolina Council of Defense, notified the chairmen of the counties' councils of defense that the state was ready "to organize its home defense forces ... as quickly as possible." The officials designated Bertie County to organize a company comprised of fifty "select men." The members of the county unit were selected and mustered into service by John Hilary Matthews, Chairman, Bertie County Council of Defense and Representative in the General Assembly. Fortunately, the services of the Bertie County unit were not needed to quell any disturbances.[32]

The Provost Marshal General's mechanism for the first draft, having been implemented quickly after the enactment of the Selective Service Act, had fulfilled its purpose. The instituted processes, though, required streamlining to improve efficiency, especially those processes related to determining exemptions to military service. Therefore, the War Department, on November 8, 1917, announced new regulations to guide the implementation and administration of the Selective Service system. The regulations, often called "Regulations Number 2," did not impact the first draft ("first quota") since they had no retroactive provisions. The new regulations greatly improved and made more efficient the overall selective process by utilizing a questionnaire to be completed by each registrant. Information derived from the document was used by the registrant's local board to place him in one of five classes. According to the revised regulations, the overall selective service "scheme" was "designed, by the creation of several classes, arranged in the order of their availability for military service, to defer the induction into the Army of registrants upon whom other persons are mainly dependent for support until persons without actual dependents have been called."[33]

Pursuant to the revised regulations, five classes of registrants were defined from which future conscriptions would be selected. Class I—individuals eligible and liable for military service—included unmarried registrants with no dependents and married registrants with independent spouses and/or one or more dependent children over sixteen with sufficient family income to support themselves. Members of each class below Class I were available only if the pool of all available and potential candidates in the class above it was exhausted. Class II—temporarily deferred, but available for military service—principally included married registrants with dependent spouses and children under age sixteen. Class III—exempted, but available for military service—was comprised of local officials, registrants who provided sole family incomes for dependent parents and/or siblings under age sixteen, and registrants employed in agriculture and industry deemed essential to the nation's war effort. Class IV—exempted due to extreme hardship—primarily included persons who provided sole family incomes to support children and/or siblings under age 16. Lastly, Class V—ineligible for military service—covered clergy, federal and state officials, medically or morally unfit persons, and enemy aliens. [34]

Registrants whose primary occupations were industrial, including certain agricultural livelihoods, were allowed deferments from military service if their occupations were deemed essential to the nation's war efforts. District boards were entrusted with the duty of selecting those individuals whose "engagements in industry, including agriculture, were such as to require their continued service in civilian life rather than in the Army."[35]

Three Bertie County registrants, John Finch Early, Zebulon Thomas Miller, and Van Perry Wadsworth, in the early fall of 1917 sought deferments from Selective Service based on their claims that they were involved in essential agricultural endeavors. Early farmed thirty-five acres, Miller cultivated fifteen acres, and Wadsworth tended a "a five[-]horse farm." The Bertie County Local Board denied the three claims. The board's denials were affirmed by the North Carolina Eastern District Board. All three men subsequently appealed the district board's decision to the office of the President. Their appeals were denied and all three men were inducted into the army—Miller on September 28, 1917, and Early and Wadsworth six days later.[36]

In March 1918 the Bertie County Local Board received two calls from the North Carolina adjutant general for men to be sent to training camps. In the March 21 issue of the *Windsor Ledger*, Rosa K. Winston alerted readers that "comfort bags" were needed for the inductees who were soon to depart Windsor. She advised readers, "We should not let a soldier, white or colored, leave our county without carrying with him this useful reminder of the friends at home." The drafted individuals left the county aboard the Wellington and Powellsville train on March 27 (twelve men) and 29 (ten men).[37]

During the next month the War Department's calls for more drafted soldiers continued. On April 2 fifty-three African American residents of Bertie were inducted and transported to Camp Grant in Rockford, Illinois. The *Roanoke Beacon* (Plymouth) reported on April 19, 1918, that the state's office of the adjutant general was mailing orders to the local boards throughout the state for quotas of men to be trained during the five-day period beginning on April 26. Two calls were made to induct African Americans, some to be transported to Camp Grant and others to Camp Jackson. Another call was made for white draftees to be entrained for Camp Jackson. On Friday, April 26, twenty-five African Americans boarded the train in Windsor to commence their trip to Camp Grant, while the same day eight whites entrained for Camp Jackson. Two days later another contingent of twenty-two African American draftees departed for Camp Grant. And on the next day, the twenty-ninth, seventeen black inductees left for Camp Jackson.[38]

By April 1918 General Crowder's office had disseminated to the states and territories calls for mobilization of the entire quota of the first draft. The war in Europe was raging and the Allies desperately needed American ground forces to bolster their defenses along the Western Front. A major German drive launched during the previous month prompted the Allies to call upon America for the "supreme effort"—introduction of tens of thousands of troops into the conflict. By the end of April, nearly thirteen months since the United States declared war on Germany, only nine United States Army divisions had been sent to France.[39] Tens of thousands of men from across the country were still to be inducted. The rate of inductions, necessarily, would have to be increased by the Provost Marshal General's Office.

The impact of the increased draft calls was directly experienced by Bertie County men. During May 1918 a total of ninety-five individuals boarded Wellington and Powellsville train cars at the Windsor depot for transportation to Camp Screven in Georgia (four men), Camp Grant (two), and Camp Jackson (eighty-nine). Eighty-eight of those ordered to Camp Jackson departed Windsor on the same day, Tuesday, the twenty-eight.[40]

On June 5, 1918, the second nationwide registration of young men for Selective Service was carried out across the nation. All men who had reached the age of twenty-one during the year since the first registration were required to register. Across North Carolina 16,218 men registered, of whom 151 were Bertie County residents.[41]

General Crowder and his staff assembled in the nation's capital on June 27, 1918, to randomly select numbers for calling into military service the twenty-one-year-old registrants of June 5, 1918. Due to the substantially smaller universe of men in the second registration versus that of a year earlier, Crowder and his team drew 1,200 numbers. This number was sufficient to cover all the registrants of the largest local board in the country.[42]

By early summer 1918 the strength of the United States Army was approaching more than two million. Still, the War Department "called to the colors" tens of thousands of men from the states. So many of the registrants of June 5 were expected to soon be drafted that some officials anticipated that the requisitions upon the states and territories would "exhaust" the available men in Class I. With substantially more manpower required for military service, the War Department held a supplemental registration on August 24, 1918, of men who had turned twenty-one years old since the registration held on June 5, 1918. Andrew J. Dunning Jr. registered the Bertie County men at the local board's headquarters in Windsor on August 24, 1918. Forty-one men served as registers at the county's voting precincts on September 12, 1918.

Congress amended the Selective Service Act in August 1918 to require a third registration, which was held on September 12, for men ages eighteen through forty-five. On the twelfth 2,366 Bertie County men registered. A total of 2,558 county men signed up during the June 5, August 24 and September 12, 1918, registration sessions. In total 4,286 Bertie County men, ages eighteen through forty-five, signed up for the draft during 1917 and 1918.[43]

As scores of men were being added to Bertie County's registration rolls during the three-month period from June through August, the North Carolina adjutant general transmitted seventeen calls to the county's local board that resulted in 246 individuals being inducted. Additionally, the board inducted four men on June 19 who were classified as Selective Service "delinquents" for having failed to complete and return their questionnaires to the board. In accordance with Selective Service regulations, such persons were liable for immediate induction into the army. During the three-month period the men were sent to army training locations, namely Camp Greene, North Carolina; Camps Jackson and Wadsworth, South Carolina; Camp

Taylor, Kentucky; Florida Agriculture and Mechanical College, Tallahassee; Camps Hancock, Screven, Lytle, and Greenleaf, Georgia; Camp Dix, New Jersey; and Camp Lee, Virginia.

General Crowder announced shortly after the September 12 registration that registrants aged nineteen, twenty, and between thirty-two and thirty-six (inclusive) were to be the "first called to the colors." Local boards were to immediately provide questionnaires to the registrants of the specified ages, and the boards were "ordered to proceed with their speedy classification" so that some of them could be called into military service in October.[44]

On September 30, 1918, General Crowder and other key federal officials held the third random drawing of numbers for the selective draft. Due to the enormous number of registrants on September 12, Crowder and the others drew 17,000 numbers.[45]

During September the Bertie County Local Board filled the quotas of three calls for only eight men—two African Americans were sent to Camp Lee, Virginia on the fourth; two whites were transported to Camp Humphries, Virginia, on the fifth; and four whites were sent to Camp Jackson on the eleventh. By the end of September 1918, the United States government had transported thirty-nine combat divisions to France. Positive battlefield impacts directly related to the nation's warriors were being realized. The tide of war was shifting more favorably to the Allied forces. The Bertie County Local Board was busied classifying the registrants of September 12 into the five registration classifications per Provost Marshal General Crowder's orders. The task was tedious. Much of the work conducted by the local board was, and had been, "irksome and disagreeable," as poignantly characterized by Daniel H. Hill Jr., Chairman of the North Carolina Council of Defense. However, no further calls for men to be entrained for army cantonments would be forthcoming to the Bertie County board. Fighting ceased in Europe at 11 o'clock in the morning on November 11.[46]

Of the 4,286 Bertie County men who registered for Selective Service during the war, 620 registrants were called by the local board and 573 individuals were inducted for military service (army). Thirty-one of the inductees were rejected by military authorities at various training camps, resulting in 542 draftees accepted for service. Furthermore, almost 800 men received deferments from active duty due to dependency and agriculturally- and

Moses Braxton Gillam, a Windsor lawyer and banker, served as chairman of the Bertie County Local Board. Under Gillam's direction the board registered almost 4,300 men and inducted more than 570 individuals. *Credit:* Braxton Gillam

industrially-critical employment. Another 145 individuals were disqualified for military service due to physical impairments and limitations.[47]

The Bertie County Local Board, chaired by Moses B. Gillam, completed its administrative work in March 1919. In accordance with directions from Benedict Crowell, Assistant Secretary of War, that all boards associated with the Selective Service system be discontinued, the members of the Bertie County board were "honorably relieved from their duties" effective March 31. The board's operating expenses during its twenty-two-month existence were $5,490, the majority (almost ninety-two percent) of which was for board members' pay ($3,016) and employees' pay ($2,032). In closing down its operations the board recouped $154 from the sale of office equipment

and supplies.[48] The members and employees' time to serve was over—no
additional Bertie County men would be called to Windsor to be examined
and drafted to serve in the nation's wartime military.'

1. Sarah McCulloh Lemmon and Nancy Smith Midgette, *North Carolina and the Two World Wars*
(Raleigh: Office of Archives and History, 2013), 64 (hereafter cited as *North Carolina and the Two
World Wars*). The 2nd and 3rd Infantry Regiments, North Carolina National Guard, returned
from deployment along the Mexico-United States border in March 1917 and were reactivated
by the federal government in September 1917. Both units were merged with Tennessee
National Guard personnel at Camp Sevier, near Taylors, South Carolina, and formed into new
regiments which were designated as the 119th and 120th Infantry Regiments (United States
Army). The newly formed regiments were moved overseas in May 1918. Richard A. Rinaldi,
comp., *The United States in World War I, Orders of Battle, Ground Units, 1917-1919* (Tiger Lily
Publications, 2005), 84.

2. An Act to Authorize the President to Increase Temporarily the Military Establishment of
the United States, *United States Statutes at Large* 40 (1917-1919): 76–83 (hereafter cited as the
Selective Service Act).

3. *Second Report of the Provost Marshal General to the Secretary of War on the Operations of the Selective
Service System to December 20, 1918* (Washington: Government Printing Office, 1919), 359
(hereafter cited as *Provost Marshal General's Second Report*); *Selective Service Regulations Prescribed
by the President Under the Authority Vested in Him by the Terms of the Selective Service Law* (*Act of
Congress Approved May 18, 1917*) (Washington: Government Printing Office, 1917) (hereafter
cited as Selective Service Regulations); *Pamphlet Describing M1509, World War I Selective Service
System Draft Registration Cards*, 1, National Archives. Enoch H. Crowder was promoted to
major general in October 1917. The Selective Service system was comprised of the Provost
Marshal General's Office, fifty-two state and territory offices, 155 district boards, 1,319
medical advisory boards, and 4,648 local boards. The Bertie County Board of Registration,
subsequently the Bertie County Board of Exemption (i.e., "Bertie County Local Board"),
administered the county's Selective Service activities from temporary offices in Windsor, the
county seat.

4. Prov. Marshal Gen. Enoch Crowder to Gov. Thomas W. Bickett (telegram), May 18, 1917,
Thomas W. Bickett, Governors Papers, State Archives of North Carolina, Raleigh (hereafter
cited as Bickett Governors Papers).

5. Bickett to Sheriffs, County Clerks and County Physicians, May 19, 1917, Bickett Governors
Papers. The cited correspondence did not specifically identity the Bertie County officials by
name. The author determined their identities based on various other records, including:
*Annual Report of the Auditor of the State of North Carolina for the Fiscal Year Ending November 30,
1917* (Raleigh: Edwards & Broughton Printing Co., 1919), 16, 302 (John W. Cooper, sheriff);
Federal census of Bertie County, 1920, enumeration district number 9, family number 33,
Cooper, John W., sheriff, and family number 113, Lyon, William L., superior court clerk,
Fourteenth Census of the United States, 1920 (microfilm): Bertie County, North Carolina,
Records of the Bureau of the Census, Record Group 29, National Archives, Washington, D.C.;
*Minute Book, Bertie County Chapter American Red Cross, Minutes Executive*, 51–53, Bertie County
Register of Deeds Office; Bickett to Crowder (telegram), June 12, 1917, Bickett Governors
Papers.

6. The county's voting precincts were confirmed by the November 1916 general elections. Bertie County Elections, Record of, 1878–1932 (microfilm), State Archives.

7. Bickett to Crowder (telegram), May 28, 1917, Bickett Governors Papers.

8. Crowder to Bickett (telegram), May 29, 1917, Bickett Governors Papers.

9. Bickett to Crowder (telegram), May 29, 1917, Bickett Governors Papers.

10. Crowder to Bickett (telegram), June 5, 1917, Bickett Governors Papers.

11. Bickett to various officials of the counties, June 2, 1917, Bickett Governors Papers.

12. Local Boards of Exemption recommended by T. W. Bickett, Governor for the State of North Carolina, undated (but on or about June 12, 1917), Bickett Governors Papers; *Enterprise* (Williamston), June 29, 1917; Selective Service registration card for William A. G. Morris, World War I Selective Service System Draft Registration Cards (microfilm), Bertie County registrations—rolls NC5 and NC6, Record Group 163, National Archives, Washington, D.C (hereafter cited as Bertie County Selective Service registrations). Gillam signed the card as "M. B. Gillam Cha. [Chairman] For Local Board of Bertie County, N.C."

13. For example, John Leslie Bazemore of Lewiston, an oiler, registered in Prince George County, Virginia; Luther Pope Bazemore, a street car conductor and Albah Abram Burden, a clerk—both of Aulander—registered in Richmond; Thaddeus Brinkley Sitterson of Windsor, a clerk, registered in Norfolk; William Mooring Sutton Jr. of Windsor, a railroad employee, registered in Walker County, Georgia; and G. C. Williford of Aulander, a salesman, registered in Philadelphia, Pennsylvania. Bertie County Selective Service registrations.

14. *Roanoke Beacon* (Plymouth), June 15, 1917; Bertie County Selective Service registrations. Statistics were computed by the author.

15. Bertie County Selective Service registrations. The following individuals indicated in their June 5, 1917, Selective Service registrations that they had previously served in various military units: North Carolina National Guard – Ita Thomas Ayscue, Dorsey M. Evans, Teorle Glenwood Harrell, Grover C. Lee, Stanley B. Sessoms; North Carolina Naval Reserve – David Barry, Joseph S. Byrd, Roy Davis, Joseph Edward Gregory, Jay G. Harrell, Archie P. Hobbs, William Carlton Hoggard, William Dorsey Hoggard, John Webb Nichols, John Thomas Perry, Claude Leonard Pierce, Harry L. Smith; Coast Artillery Corps – Joseph A. Butler, Spurgeon Holloman, Claude Outlaw; United States Navy – Thomas Washington Byrd, Benjamin F. Hoggard, Blackwell Truitt; United States Army – Hubert Elmer Harris, Willard Lee Mitchell; Virginia National Guard – Hugh B. Holloman, Henry D. Thomas.

16. Bickett to Crowder (telegram), June 6, 1917, Bickett Governors Papers; Roanoke Beacon (Plymouth), June 15, 1917; *North Carolina and the Two World Wars*, 24.

17. *Provost Marshal General's General Second Report*, 39.

18. Washington Post, July 21, 1917; *Provost Marshal General's Second Report*, 5, 41–42.

19. New York Times, July 21–25, 1917.

20. Statistics computed by the author based on information he compiled in Appendix 1.

21. New York Times, July 25, 1917; *News and Observer* (Raleigh), July 25, 1917.

22. New York Times, July 24, 1917; *Provost Marshal General's Second Report*, 463.

23. *Provost Marshal General's Second Report*, 45–46; *Selective Service Act*, section 4.

24. "Secrets of World War I," History Channel (2006); List of Delinquents and Deserters for Military Duty: Form 4003, Selective Service System, Provost Marshal General's Office Records of Local Boards, 1917–1919 (Bertie County, NC), Record Group 163, National Archives, Atlanta, GA; *Jail Record*, Bertie County Register of Deeds Office; Appeals to the President and Correspondence from the Provost Marshal's Office, Selective Service System (WWI), 1917-1918, Mississippi, North Carolina, Bertie County, NC, Record Group 163, National Archives, Atlanta.

25. *Roanoke Beacon* (Plymouth) and *Enterprise* (Williamston), July 27, 1917. The "national army" was comprised of Selective Service inductees and differentiated from the "regular army" which was predominantly constituted by volunteers. The distinctions between the two classes of soldiers were discontinued on August 7, 1918. See *The Official Record of the United States' Part in the Great War* (Washington: Government Printing Office, 1920), 13 (hereafter cited as *Official Record*).

26. *Literary Digest* 55 (July 1917–December 1917) (New York: Funk and Wagnalls Company), 95; *Enterprise* (Williamston), August 17, 1917.

27. D. H. Hill to Chairman County Council of Defense [J. H. Matthews, Bertie County], July 31, 1917, County Councils, form letters to, 1917, North Carolina Council of Defense, World War I Papers, Military Collection, State Archives (hereafter cited as Council of Defense, World War I Papers); *Provost Marshal General's Second Report*, 239; *Enterprise* (Williamston), August 17, 1917.

28. Luther Thomas Harden draft registration, June 5, 1917, Bertie County Selective Service registrations; *Bertie Ledger-Advance, Bicentennial Edition*, November 28, 1968. Individuals inducted into the army were to serve for the duration of the national emergency. The Wellington and Powellsville Railroad line ran twenty-two miles from Windsor to Ahoskie (Hertford County) where the passengers (such as the Bertie County military inductees) who were travelling to further destinations disembarked and transferred to trains of the Atlantic Coast Line Railroad for continuation of their trips. George W. Hilton, *American Narrow Gauge Railroads* (Stanford, California: Stanford University Press, 1990), 461.

29. Nova Asbell Leicester, "Tales Told to Me by My Mother When I Was a Child" (unpublished research report, ca. 1977).

30. War Department, Office of the Provost Marshal General, Selective Service System, 1917–July 15, 1919, Lists of Men Ordered to Report to Local Board for Military Duty, 1917–1918, North Carolina (Bertie County), Records of the Selective Service System (World War 1), Record Group 163, National Archives (hereafter cited as Lists of Men Ordered to Report – Bertie County). The dates and numbers of Bertie County men drafted in 1917 subsequent to September 28 were: October 4, eleven; October 22, twelve; November 16, four; November 28, one; December 6, one, December 18, five; December 25, one; and December 26, one. Statistics were developed by the author based on his analysis of pertinent Lists of Men Ordered to Report – Bertie County.

31. *Provost Marshal General's Second Report*, 463.

32. D H. Hill to Chairmen, County Council[s] of Defense, September 27, 1917, County Councils, form letters to, 1917, Council of Defense, World War I Papers. Enterprise (Williamston), September 28, October 5, 1917; *North Carolina and the Two World Wars*, 71; William J. Breen, "The North Carolina Council of Defense During World War I, 1917–1918,"

*North Carolina Historical Review*, 50 (January 1973): 1-2. See Chapter 3 for a discussion of the establishment and functions of the national, state and county councils of defense. The author discovered no records documenting the identities of the Bertie County company.

33. *Selective Service Regulations*, 33-34.

34. *Selective Service Regulations*, 36–46.

35. *Selective Service Act*, section 4; *Selective Service Regulations*, 42–45; *Provost Marshal General's Second Report*, 135.

36. Appeals to the President and Correspondence from the Provost Marshal General's Office, Selective Service System (WWI), 1917–1918, Mississippi, North Carolina (Bertie County), Record Group 163, National Archives, Atlanta; Army service cards (John Finch Early, Zebulon Thomas Miller, Van Perry Wadsworth), Adjutant General – World War I Service Cards (microfilm), Adjutant General, Military Collection, State Archives; Lists of Men Ordered to Report – Bertie County.

37. *Windsor Ledger*, March 21, 1918; Lists of Men Ordered to Report – Bertie County. The Bertie County Local Board received no calls for men to be inducted during January and February 1918. The call for March 27 induction was the first the board had received since the call for December 26, 1917.

38. *Roanoke Beacon* (Plymouth), April 19, 1918; Lists of Men Ordered to Report – Bertie County. Statistics compiled by the author.

39. Official Record, 12, 111.

40. Bertie County Selective Service registrations.

41. *Annual Report of the Adjutant General of the State of North Carolina, 1917–1918* (Raleigh: Edwards & Broughton Printing Co., 1920), 249 (hereafter cited as *Adjutant General Annual Report); Alamance Gleaner* (Graham), July 11, 1918. Holley M. Bell and Andrew J. Dunning Jr. registered the Bertie County men at the Bertie County Local Board's headquarters in Windsor.

42. *Provost Marshal General's Second Report*, 42.

43. *Adjutant General Annual Report*, 249; Bertie County Selective Service registrations.

44. *Roanoke Beacon* (Plymouth), September 13, 1918.

45. *Provost Marshal General's Second Report*, 42.

46. Lists of Men Ordered to Report – Bertie County; *Official Record*, 111; *Raleigh Times*, November 11, 1918; Chairman [D.H. Hill] to Chairman of each county Council of Defense, November 9, 1917, County Councils, form letters to, 1917, Council of Defense, World War I Papers.

47. *Final Report of the Provost Marshal General to the Secretary of War on the Operations of the Selective Service System to July 15, 1919* (Washington: Government Printing Office, 1920), 95 (hereafter cited as *Provost Marshal General's Final Report); Annual Report of the Adjutant General of the State of North Carolina, 1917–1918* (Raleigh: Edwards & Broughton Printing Co., 1920), 249. The author notes that the numbers of Bertie County men inducted and rejected cited in the Provost Marshal General's report do not agree with the numbers of men as listed in Appendix 1. The report did not have supporting details or schedules for the presented statistics. Since the

author necessarily had to identify Bertie County soldiers from a number of disparate sources, some of which contained incomplete service information, he was unable to reconcile the numbers of men in the appendix with the Provost Marshal General's statistics. See Note 1 for Appendix 1 regarding the sources used by the author and their inherent limitations.

48. *Provost Marshal General's Final Report*, 208; *Adjutant General Annual Report*, 287.

# 3

# SERVICE AND SACRIFICE ON
# THE HOME FRONT

Raising, organizing, and training military forces were the predominant and most documented tasks that faced the United States as it prepared to go to war. Yet, other activities, such as fundraising, food production, and conservation of resources, were also critical components of the overall preparation. Fighting forces could not be raised, trained, and transported, and war could not be waged, without substantial funding and numerous other resources.

In order to coordinate resources and industry, including agricultural production, the federal government established the Council of National Defense in August 1916. The Army Appropriations Act of that year provided funding for the emergency agency, the membership of which consisted of the Secretaries of War, Navy, Interior, Agriculture, Commerce, and Labor. In addition to coordinating resources and industries, the council stimulated civilian morale and coordinated the work of state and local councils of defense and women's committees. Each state was encouraged to establish its own council. On May 24, 1917, Governor Bickett organized North Carolina's State Council of Defense. Per Bickett's direction each county established its own local council, which reported to the state council. One of the objectives of the state and county councils was to "help the people at home in every way" they could. The governor appointed John Hilary

Matthews, a prominent Windsor lawyer and state house member, as chairman of the Bertie County Council of Defense.[1]

In early July Matthews nominated six members for the Bertie County council to Governor Bickett, who formally appointed them. They were William L. Lyon, Windsor; J. H. Etheridge, Merry Hill; Dr. L. A. Nowell, Colerain; Charles H. Jenkins, Aulander; Dr. Jacob M. Jacobs, Roxobel; and Dr. Wayland Mitchell, Lewiston. Etheridge declined membership on the council, and in his stead Matthews nominated, and the governor approved, H. J. Ward of Merry Hill.[2]

Also in July, the North Carolina Council of Defense authorized special legal committees, known as Soldiers' Business Committees, to assist drafted soldiers in organizing their business affairs prior to departing for military training camps. A Soldiers' Business Committee was organized in each county and was subordinate to the county council of defense. The county chairman selected the members of the committee. The members of the Bertie County committee selected by John Hilary Matthews are apparently not documented, except for Solomon B. Adams, a farmer and businessman of Merry Hill, who accepted his appointment on July 16, 1917.[3]

Raising revenues in sufficient amounts to implement the nation's war effort was a major challenge for the federal government. North Carolina Representative Claude Kitchin of Scotland Neck, chairman of the Ways and Means Committee, piloted the war revenue bill through the House of Representatives—legislation which designated income taxes as the federal government's primary source of funding during the war. Kitchin viewed the war as a European power struggle and opposed United States involvement. He voted against declaring war on Germany but subsequently supported the war effort overall, although he opposed certain war policies, including raising money through the sale of Liberty Bonds. The Kitchin-supported War Revenue Act of 1917 did significantly increase federal income tax rates, but sufficient funds could not be generated for the nation's war machine through income taxes alone.

On April 24, 1917, President Wilson signed a bill that instituted the first Liberty Loan drive, authorizing Treasury Secretary William G. McAdoo to sell $3 billion of debt to the American public. Under the program the federal government sold Liberty Bonds to raise money to support the war effort. Governor Bickett strongly encouraged North Carolinians to support the troops by purchasing bonds. President Wilson designated

The federal government disseminated various posters and other printed materials to encourage the nation's citizens to buy liberty loan bonds (i.e., "war bonds"). This poster marketed the Third Liberty Loan campaign initiated in April 1918. *Credit:* Library of Congress.

Wednesday, October 24, 1917, as "Liberty Bond Day," while McAdoo encouraged governors to proclaim that day a legal holiday. On October 19 Bickett, in concert with the secretary's desire, proclaimed the twenty-fourth a legal holiday in North Carolina and "earnestly" urged the state's citizens to "devote their energies on that day to the sale of Liberty Bonds."[4]

During the whole of the United States' involvement in the war, the federal government conducted four Liberty Loan campaigns, which were launched in April and October of 1917, and in April and September of 1918. A total of $17 billion in bonds were sought during the campaigns. The fourth campaign was conducted during the three-week period of September 28-October 19, 1918, during which the Department of the Treasury sought $6 billion. North Carolina's designated share of this amount was $39.9 million. The total amount of funds generated from Bertie County residents during the Liberty Loan campaigns cannot be determined from extant records. The county's citizens did purchase almost

Five-dollar war savings certificate stamps could be purchased at a discount ($4.12 in January 1918) or acquired by individuals by redeeming war savings stamps. *Credit:* www. google.com

$74,000 in bonds during the second campaign and $156,000 during the fourth fund drive. During the fourth campaign county women subscribed for $91,700 through the Bertie County committee of the North Carolina Division of the National Woman's Liberty Loan Committee. Governor Bickett fully supported each campaign and actively encouraged the purchase of Liberty Bonds by North Carolina's citizens, whose financial contributions as a result of the campaigns were $110.2 million.[5]

In addition to war bonds, beginning in late 1917, the Department of the Treasury sold war savings stamps to the public. Sales of the stamps were aimed at "average citizens." Each stamp was sold for twenty-five cents, allowing individuals to collect a sufficient number of the low-price stamps over time to acquire a $5 war savings certificate stamp. During the war the federal government sold about $930 million worth of the stamps, of which North Carolinians purchased $37 million. C. W. Mitchell and John Hilary Matthews served as co-chairmen of the Bertie County War Savings Stamp Committee.[6]

Although not all Bertie County residents were financially able to acquire significant amounts of war bonds and savings stamps/certificates, some were of sufficient wealth to invest substantial amounts in the war-supportive financial instruments. For example, Dr. Clifford A. Whitehead, an affluent dentist in Woodville, in early 1918 sold a "valuable property" in Edgecombe County, his former residence, for "many thousand dollars." In a patriotic act the doctor invested the entire proceeds from the real estate sale in Liberty Bonds.[7]

Besides financial contributions Bertie County residents provided physical items for the county's military service inductees. The people organized knitting classes in which socks, sweaters, and other garments were made for the men being drafted into the army. People donated as much time as was needed in rolling bandages or packing "go-away kits." Anything that could be helpful was done with great pride.[8]

Furthermore, send-off services were held at churches during which prayers were offered for the men's wellbeing and safe return: "Tears were shed. The boys were hugged and sent off with prayers for all." When the day came for the men to leave for training camp, a "great throng of people" would be present at the train station to wish them the best and wave good-bye. On many occasions Rosa K. Winston, wife of North Carolina Superior Court Judge Francis D. Winston, "personally kissed each boy good-bye."[9]

After the men had departed and arrived at various camps, family members waited anxiously to hear from their loved ones. When a card or letter arrived, residents in the community were interested in hearing how the service member was faring. Such information about the county's military men was considered "real news" and was proudly shared with others. Prayers for the boys were rendered at each church service, but especially on Wednesday and Sunday nights, generally the times when churches held weekly prayer meetings. At the Greens Cross Baptist Church there was "no lack of a crowd, for the little church would be filled with mothers, fathers, kinfolks and sweethearts" during the services. County residents donned khaki clothing—hats, shirts, pants, dresses and skirts—as a patriotic gesture since that color was worn by the service personnel. Nova Asbell, ten years old in 1917, recalled years later that she "had a hat made just like the soldiers." And numerous other citizens had similar hats made; everyone proudly displayed their patriotism.[10]

Some county residents began to go to Norfolk to work in plants that manufactured ammunition. Others worked in the Norfolk shipyard, built crates and did anything they could to help win the war: "Everybody wanted to help and most everybody did in some way." The "little world" of Bertie

County began to expand. In the words of Nova Asbell, "No more were we a little corner of the world, shut off from everyone else. Things began to change. There were a lot of people before now that had been born, lived and died ... in Bertie County who never went out of it."[11]

As the United States experienced the upheaval of the Great War, an influenza outbreak coursed through North Carolina, causing the deaths of more than 13,600 state residents. The disease broke out in military camps, and communities situated near the cantonments suffered tremendous losses. Bertie County was heavily impacted by the pandemic, which came at the height of the nation's involvement in the war, the fall of 1918. Some soldiers came home to the county and introduced the influenza virus to inhabitants. According to one account, the flu "spread ... across the county. Nearly every neighborhood reported cases, so in a matter of weeks, it grew to be an epidemic. Every family ... was being struck by it." All the members of some families were simultaneously sickened by the virus, leading compassionate neighbors to help the families by tending to the sick and furnishing and cooking food. Those who visited and assisted sickened families, in a number of instances, themselves contracted the flu. Foy A. Sawyer of Windsor noted on October 8 that "we are having an alarming siege of the Spanish influenza in town." Her husband, Dr. Charles J. Sawyer, was forced to "turn away" calls for medical attention since he was unable to accommodate so many sickened patients. Twelve days later Mrs. Sawyer wrote, "So many, many homes in Bertie county are in mourning [due to deaths from influenza], and two-thirds of our population are suffering from the malady."[12]

Bertie County residents served and sacrificed individually. Similarly, the county government had to forego an undetermined amount of tax revenue. The Board of Commissioners met on March 4, 1918, and made a patriotic decision in honor of the county's military personnel. The board declared that all of the young men serving in the armed forces were relieved from the payment of poll taxes during the period of war.[13] There is no estimate of the taxes that were not collected, but the commissioners decided that the county would forego the revenue from its active duty military members.

About the time that the United States declared war on Germany, the federal government reported that the nation was "facing a serious food famine." A few days following the declaration, President Wilson appealed to the American people and urged them to increase food supplies "as a patriotic duty." Obviously, inordinate quantifies of food and provisions were needed for the military forces, an amount that increased daily. One ready avenue to increasing food production was to cultivate vacant farmland. On April 11 Governor Bickett established a State Food Conservation Commission with a primary function to oversee the cultivation of productive vacant lands. The commission had subordinate organizations set up within the counties. In August the state and county food conservation organizations were folded into the North Carolina Food Administration, a state agent of the United States Food Administration.[14]

In every county a sub-commission was appointed so that a farm-to-farm canvass could be made. Bickett observed that on almost every farm there were "idle patches of ground" that could be planted with sweet potatoes, peas, beans, and Irish potatoes, greatly increasing the productivity of the land. The governor stated, "We have … a plain and pressing duty which gives to all alike the opportunity for a great and patriotic service." On April 21 Governor Bickett wrote to the chairmen of each county's board of commissioners and urged them to locate all vacant farms in their county and to make arrangements to secure such farms for nominal rent and cultivate those using county prisoners who could be spared from laboring on county roads. If convicts could not be used, the county chairman was authorized to utilize "additional labor employed by the county." The responsibilities delineated by Bickett fell to Daniel R. Britton of Colerain, chairman of the Bertie County Board of Commissioners.[15]

On August 10, 1917, President Wilson signed into law the Food and Fuel Control Act. On the day the law became effective, he issued an executive order which officially established the United States Food Administration. The primary functions of the administration were to control production, distribution, and conservation of food. The agency was also responsible for preventing monopolies and hoarding of foods, and maintaining governmental control of food, although it had little enforcement powers, relying instead on voluntary cooperation of entities and people.[16]

Bertie County's economy was dominated by agriculture. Daniel H. Hill Jr., Chairman of the North Carolina Council of Defense, appealed to the chairmen of the counties' Councils of Defense to have every acre cultivated for which labor to tend it was available, in order to generate "a liberal yield." The number of vacant farms and associated acreage in Bertie County at that time is not ascertainable from available records. The citizens of the county responded splendidly to the governor's and Hill's appeals to increase food production. John Hilary Matthews was appointed as the Bertie County Food Administrator and oversaw efforts to increase food production. Fifty-four committees were established throughout the county to coordinate production of foodstuffs. Four hundred boys and girls formed clubs dedicated to raising crops (corn, wheat, oats), as well as livestock (primarily pigs) and poultry (chickens). During the 1917 growing season county residents produced 88,730 containers (glass and tin) of fruits and vegetables and 11,983 gallons of brined produce. Additionally, they produced 11,100 pounds of dehydrated fruits and vegetables. Overall, for the year state residents produced 5.7 million containers and 279 tons of dried produce and 288,568 gallons of brined products. The state's total production of all the cited products increased 1,800 percent (18 times) from the 1916 production.[17] While North Carolina was not one of the most heavily populated or more prosperous states, its citizens, including those of Bertie County, rallied to Governor Bickett's appeals and contributed significantly to increasing the state's and nation's food supply at a time when it was desperately needed.

The March 21, 1918, issue of the *Windsor Ledger* included an article, "Thrift Gardens and Victory Acres," which called for county residents to plant gardens, the produce from which could be sold and the resulting proceeds invested in war savings stamps: "Every farmer and farmer's son is called upon to plant a 'Victory Acre' to help with the war. The proceeds from the acre are to be invested in War-Savings Stamps. Those who cannot plant an acre are called upon to plant a garden or part of an acre. . . Men, women and children in town are asked to plant 'Thrift Gardens.'" The article specifically implored girls within the county to plant garden plots.[18]

Rosa Winston, an influential officer of the Bertie County Red Cross Chapter and Chair of the Woman's Committee, Bertie County Council of Defense, was recognized by her fellow citizens for being "so very patriotic." She exemplified the commitment of county residents in contributing to the war effort by having the front lawn of "Windsor Castle," her and Judge Winston's residence, plowed and planted to "help out" in winning the war.[19]

The residents of Bertie County were, to a significant extent, self-sufficient in providing food for their families. Numerous families lived on the vegetables, livestock, and poultry they raised on their family farms and in back-of-the-house gardens. While certain commodities were rationed,

Credit: Library of Congress.

mainly sugar and wheat products, those families that lived primarily on the items that they raised did not experience impacts as severe as the non-farming families. Some county residents planted their own wheat, harvested it with hand scythes, and "rode the grain out [of the fields] with horses." They next transported the grain to neighborhood mills where it was ground into flour.[20]

Conservation of all classes of items (food, metals, sugar, gasoline, etc.) became a high priority. Meatless meals were prepared so that more beef, pork, and poultry could be sent to the troops in Europe. By March 1918 the federal government called for drastic reductions in the consumption of wheat. The Food Administration notified citizens that consumption of the commodity must be reduced thirty to fifty percent in order to feed Allied troops and prevent a flour famine within the United States.[21]

Patriotism and support for the troops demanded that individuals do everything within their means to conserve food. Wastefulness was considered unpatriotic—and residents did not overuse or waste "anything that the soldiers needed." Nathaniel Asbell's family "had plenty of cornmeal made at home . . . [and] egg bread with milk." The Asbells raised dairy

Rosa K. Winston, wife of Judge Francis D. Winston, tirelessly strived to implement war-supporting measures in Bertie County. She often came to the Windsor train station to personally encourage departing military inductees and provide them needed items for their journeys. She had the front lawn of her stately Windsor home converted to a garden with food-producing crops. She served as chair of the Women's Committee of the Bertie County Council of Defense and as secretary of the county's chapter of the American Red Cross. She was widely recognized by her fellow citizens for being so unselfishly patriotic. *Credit: Minute Book, Bertie County Chapter American Red Cross (unlabeled), 1917–1918* — First World War, Bertie County Register of Deeds Office.

cows that supplied "plenty of homemade butter," along with "grits and fried ham for breakfast [which] was not bad" for a morning's meal during tough times. Nathaniel enjoyed coffee sweetened with sugar, but due to that commodity's scarcity, he resorted to sweetening his morning beverage with honey or molasses, which "did not fit his taste." He did not complain because he and his family "were to make some sacrifice for the boys."[22]

Another campaign launched by President Wilson in June 1917 sought to raise funds for the American Red Cross. Wilson proclaimed the week of June 18 through 25 "Red Cross Week," whose goal was to raise $100 million across the nation for the organization. On June 12 Governor Bickett issued a proclamation announcing the fundraising campaign and beseeching the citizens to make "real self-sacrificing gifts" to the Red Cross.[23]

The presidential and gubernatorial appeals to aid the American Red Cross spurred Bertie County citizens to action. On August 22, 1917, county residents met at Bazemore's Opera House in Windsor and "permanently" organized a chapter of the organization. According to the minutes of the gathering, a "large number of representative people from all parts of the County were present." John Hilary Matthews called the meeting to order and was elected as the chapter's chairman. Clingman W. Mitchell was elected vice chairman, Rosa Winston secretary, and William L. Lyon treasurer.[24] (Mrs. Winston subsequently became chairwoman of the chapter.)

The citizens of Bertie County by late summer 1917 were fully engaged in doing their part to support the national war effort. Much of the administration and oversight for the citizens' actions were attributable to John Hilary Matthews. Obviously, Governor Bickett held a great deal of confidence in Matthews to mobilize the residents, marshal the county's available resources (human, financial, land, etc.) and achieve the greatest efficiencies and productivity from those resources. Bertie County citizens exhibited their love and devotion to their country and graciously responded to calls for sacrifice and service.

On September 10 Matthews conveyed to Daniel H. Hill Jr. that during the previous week a "public patriotic meeting" was held in Windsor "in which the entire county engaged." According to Matthews, the "meeting was very successful and great enthusiasm prevailed. ... Our people are very patriotic and are willing to perform their full duty as patriotic citizens."[25] By the conclusion of the war, Bertie County citizens had pledged $475,520, almost ninety-four percent of the county's established war savings quota. The percentage was substantially greater than that achieved across the state as a whole. During the war North Carolina's total war savings allotment was $48,661,380. As of October 1, 1918, state residents had pledged 76.2 percent of that amount.[26]

The mammoth war-supporting activities and programs instituted by the federal government and implemented across the county impacted the lives of every individual. Throughout 1917 and 1918 Bertie County residents, under the purview and direction of the Bertie County Council of Defense, contributed to the effort. Citizens sacrificed at the personal level so that the troops might have needed resources to fully sustain themselves, whether engaged in combat in France or supporting combatants at home and in Europe. The citizens, individually and collectively, had done their parts in serving humanity at a very critical time in the nation's history. In the words of John Hilary Matthews, "the people" of Bertie County were "very loyal in their support to every measure in which they [were] called upon by the government."[27]

1. John L. Cheney, Jr., ed., *North Carolina Government, 1585–1974: A Narrative and Statistical Abstract* (Raleigh: North Carolina Department of the Secretary of the State, 1975), 1057; Records of the Council of National Defense, Finding Aid, Record Group 62, National Archives; Santford Martin, comp., R. B. House, ed., *Public Letters and Papers of Thomas Walter Bickett, Governor of North Carolina, 1917–1921* (Raleigh: Edwards & Broughton Printing Company, 1923), 328; R. D. W. Connor, comp. & ed., *North Carolina Manual, 1919* (Raleigh: Edwards & Broughton Printing Company, 1918), 445; D. H. Hill to the Chairman of the County Council of Defense, July 21, 1918, North Carolina Council of Defense, County Councils, form letters to, 1918, n.d. [no date], World War I Papers, Military Collection. State Archives of North Carolina (hereafter cited as Council of Defense, World War I Papers). John Hilary Matthews accepted the appointment as Chairman of the Bertie County Council of Defense on June 14, 1917. Matthews was a partner with Judge Francis D. Winston in a Windsor law firm. J. H. Matthews to D. H. Hill, June 14, 1917, County Councils – Bertie, Council of Defense, World War I Papers.

2. J. H. Matthews to W. S. Wilson [Secretary, North Carolina Council of Defense], July 5, 1917, Secretary [Wilson] to Matthews, July 6, 1917, J. H. Etheridge to Wilson, August 4, 1917, Matthews to Wilson, August 8, 1917, Wilson to H. J. Ward, August 15, 1917, County Councils – Bertie, Council of Defense, World War I Papers.

3. William J. Breen, "The North Carolina Council of Defense During World War I, 1917–1918," *North Carolina Historical Review*, 50 (January 1973), 11 [hereafter cited as Breen, "North Carolina Council of Defense"]; S. B. Adams to D. H. Hill, July 16, 1917, County Councils – Bertie, Council of Defense, World War I Papers.

4. Sarah McCulloh Lemmon and Nancy Smith Midgette, *North Carolina and the Two World Wars* (Raleigh: Office of Archives and History, 2013), 4, 15, 18-19, 26 (hereafter cited as *North Carolina and the Two World Wars*); An Act to Authorize an Issue of Bonds to Meet Expenditures for the National Security and Defense …, *United States Statutes at Large* 40 (1917-1919): 35–37; Santford Martin, comp., and R. B. House, ed., *Public Letters and Papers of Thomas Walter Bickett, Governor of North Carolina, 1917–1921* (Raleigh: Edwards & Broughton Printing Company, 1923), 88 (hereafter cited as Martin, *Bickett Public Letters and Papers*).

5. Martin, *Bickett Public Letters and Papers*, 88, 92–93, 99; *North Carolina and the Two World Wars*, 62; Anne Cipriano Venzon, ed., *The United States in the First World War: An Encyclopedia* (New York and London: Garland Publishing, 1995), 341–342; [Second] Liberty Loan Sales by North Carolina Counties, December 15, 1917, Statement of County Totals [Central Liberty Loan Committee for North Carolina], November 5, 1918, and Total Amount Subscribed Through National Woman's Liberty Loan Committee, North Carolina Division, [undated], Liberty Loan Campaigns, General Records, World War I Papers, Military Collection, State Archives (hereafter cited as Liberty Loan Campaigns, World War I Papers).

6. North Carolina and the Two World Wars, 62; Finding Aid, Liberty Loan Campaigns, World War I Papers; R. D. W. Connor, comp. & ed., *North Carolina Manual, 1919* (Raleigh: Edwards & Broughton Printing Company, 1918), 445 (hereafter cited as *North Carolina Manual, 1919*); F. H. Fries, State Director, comp., *History of War Savings Campaign of 1918 in North Carolina* (Winston Salem: publication facts missing), 9 (hereafter cited as Fries, *North Carolina War Savings Campaign*). The cited source is found in Box 7, Liberty Loan Campaigns, World War I Papers.

7. *Windsor Ledger*, March 21, 1918.

8. Nova Asbell Leicester, "Tales Told to Me by My Mother When I Was a Child" (unpublished research report, ca. 1977), hereafter cited as Leicester, "Tales."

9. Leicester, "Tales."

10. Leicester, "Tales."

11. Leicester, "Tales."

12. The number of deaths across North Carolina from the influenza outbreak likely exceeded 13,600, since "many deaths" were not recorded and the causes of deaths as disclosed on an undermined number of death certificates may have been erroneously indicated as non-influenza. Leicester, "Tales"; Foy A. Sawyer to My dear Mrs. Latham, October 8, 1918 and October 20, 1918, Liberty Loan Campaigns, World War I Papers; http://ncpedia.org/history/health/influenza; http://www.flu.gov/pandemic/history/1918;

13. Bertie County, County Commissioners Minutes, 1896–1918, (microfilm), State Archives (hereafter cited as Bertie County Commissioners Minutes).

14. Finding Aid for Food Administration Papers, World War I Papers, Military Collection, State Archives.

15. Martin, *Bickett Public Letters and Papers*, 271–272; Bickett to Chairman of Board of County Commissioners, April 21, 1917, Thomas W. Bickett, Governors Papers, State Archives of North Carolina, Raleigh (hereafter cited as Bickett Governors Papers).
　　Various minute entries for 1917 reveal that Daniel R. Britton served as chairman of the Bertie County Board of Commissioners. Members of the board were Thomas W. Griffin, J. T. Stokes, W. L. Baker, and Abner W. Early. Bertie County Commissioners Minutes.

16. Food and Fuel Control Act, *United States Statutes at Large* 40 (1917–1919): 276–287; American Presidency Project, Presidential Executive Orders (Woodrow Wilson, E.O. 2679–A), University of California, Santa Barbara, www.presidency.ucsb.edu (hereafter cited as Presidential Executive Orders, UCSB); Records of the United States Food Administration, Finding Aid, Record Group 4, National Archives.
　　President Wilson established the Federal Fuel Administration on August 23, 1917, by Executive Order Number 2690. Presidential Executive Orders, UCSB.

17. D. H. Hill to County Committees, June 21, 1917, Council of Defense, County Councils, form letters to, 1917, World War I Papers, Military Collection; County Organization, Food Administration, Bertie County, N.C., County War Records, World War I Papers, Military Collection; "Information Relative to Club Work in North Carolina [December 1917]" by the Cooperative Extension Work in Agriculture and Home Economics, Bickett Governors Papers; *North Carolina Manual, 1919*, 445.

18. *Windsor Ledger*, March 21, 1918.

19. Leicester, "Tales."

20. Leicester, "Tales."

21. Windsor Ledger, March 21, 1918.

22. Leicester, "Tales."

23. S. W. McGill, Divisional Director [American Red Cross] to Bickett (telegram), June 7, 1917, Bickett Governors Papers; Martin, *Bickett Public Letters and Papers*, 84.

During World War I American Red Cross employees and volunteers provided medical and recreational services for military personnel at home and abroad. Approximately 18,000 Red Cross nurses provided medical care for American military personnel during the war, and about 4,800 Red Cross ambulance drivers provided first aid on the front lines. During the war 1,296 Red Cross nurses and 127 Red Cross ambulance drivers died in humanitarian service. www. redcross.org.

24. Minute Book, Bertie County Chapter American Red Cross, Minutes Executive, 1–2, Bertie County Register of Deeds Office, Windsor.

25. J. H. Matthews to D. H. Hill, September 10, 1917, County Councils – Bertie, Council of Defense, World War I Papers, Military Collection.

26. Fries, *North Carolina War Savings Campaign*, 40, 42; *Enterprise* (Williamston), November 15, 1918.

27. Breen, "North Carolina Council of Defense," 1; J. H. Matthews to D. H. Hill, January 1, 1917 [1918], County Councils – Bertie, Council of Defense, World War I Papers.

# 4

## SERVICE IN THE ARMED FORCES

When Pres. Woodrow Wilson delivered the war declaration against Germany on April 6, 1917, at least twenty-two Bertie County residents were serving in the nation's armed forces, thirteen men in the Army and nine individuals, including one woman (Mary J. Jordan), in the Navy. Five months passed from the delivery of the declaration until the first Bertie County Selective Service inductees departed Windsor for Camp Jackson, Columbia, South Carolina. By the end of 1917 more than sixty men had been drafted by the local board in Windsor. While no county men were drafted during January and February 1918, twenty-two were inducted in March, which marked the beginning of a seven-month period during which more than 500 sons of the county, white and African American, were called into service and transported to army training camps.[1]

Other Bertie County men volunteered and enlisted in the National Guard and the army. A few individuals enlisted in North Carolina's Guard, while others traveled to southeastern Virginia where they enlisted in units of that state's Guard. County men enlisted in army units at various locations, including a number of other southern states. Additionally, between late April and the end of June 1917, eleven county men journeyed to Fort Thomas, Kentucky (near Cincinnati, Ohio), where they enlisted. Fort Thomas was a recruit depot where civilians who enlisted were processed and quickly transitioned to their designated training camps. Before the end of 1917,

Jonathan S. Tayloe (left) and John Alexander Thomas (right), both of Windsor, enlisted in National Guard units during late spring and early summer, 1917. Tayloe, age 27, enlisted as a private in the North Carolina National Guard at Goldsboro on June 6, 1917. As a member of Company I, 119th Infantry Regiment, 60th Infantry Brigade, 30th Division, Private Tayloe was killed in action in France on August 9, 1918. Thomas journeyed to Franklin, Virginia where, at age 19, he enlisted as a private in that state's National Guard on July 3, 1917. Private Thomas subsequently served in France as a member of Headquarters Company, 111th Field Artillery Regiment, 54th Field Artillery Brigade, 30th Division. He was honorably discharged at Camp Lee, Petersburg, Virginia on June 2, 1919. *Credit:* State Archives of North Carolina, Raleigh. Image of John Alexander Thomas is from the the "Author's collection."

seventeen Bertie County army volunteers were processed at the post. It is unknown why the county men travelled more than 625 miles from Bertie County to join the military, when other recruiting facilities were located significantly closer. As of September 30, 1918, fifty-nine Bertie County residents had volunteered to serve in the army after the United States declared war on Germany.

Concurrently with inductions and enlistments of county men into the army, thirty-one Bertie County residents, twenty-eight men and three women, traveled to various Navy recruiting stations, bases and ships. The majority of these volunteers journeyed to Norfolk, Virginia, approxi-

The Carolina Wildcat insignia displayed above is a reproduction of the shoulder patches worn by Headquarters units of the 81st Infantry Division during World War I. *Credit:* North Carolina Museum of History.

mately 100 miles from Bertie County. A few enlisted at nearby recruiting stations in Plymouth and Edenton, while several signed up in Baltimore and Richmond.[2]

Once the army draftees and enlistees arrived at their designated training camps, most often they were assigned to depot brigades until they were transferred to permanent units. Depot brigades were originally organized as components of tactical divisions but were soon detached and placed under the control of camp commanders as independent units. The depot brigades received and organized draftees and recruits, providing them with uniforms, equipment, and initial military training. Thereafter, the men were transferred to their units of record for more involved training related to their principal duties (such as infantry, artillery, machine gun, medical, transportation, service, and labor). In most cases the men remained in the depot brigades for rather short but varying durations before they were placed in their assigned units.[3]

The Bertie County inductees who were transported to Camp Jackson were predominantly assigned to units of the 81st Division. The War Department on August 5, 1917, ordered the division to be formed and comprised of draftees. Military authorities organized the division at Camp Jackson during the fall of 1917. The unit became commonly known as the "Wildcat Division" in recognition of both the irascible creature that inhabited Southern woodlands and Wildcat Creek, a stream flowing close to the unit's home base. A silhouette of a wildcat was adopted as an identifying shoulder patch for the division's members. The division was the first in the history of the United States Army to authorize a patch as an identifying symbol of a military unit.[4]

The men were assigned and trained primarily as infantrymen, machine gunners, and artillerists. In October 1917 a number of men were transferred from the division to the 119th Infantry Regiment, 60th Infantry Brigade, 30th Division. On the sixteenth of the month, a dozen Bertie County soldiers—William Howard Bazemore, Clyde B. Harrell, Roland Harrell, Joseph Wright Hoggard, Osie Clarence Jernigan, Jesse Jones, Robert Edward Lee, Zebulon Thomas Miller, William Joseph Perry, Ernest Linwood Quincey, Van Perry Wadsworth, and Leslie Walston—were transferred from Company E, 321st Infantry Regiment, 161st Infantry Brigade to the 119th Infantry Regiment. Military authorities transferred the men along with others from the 81st Division to help fill the ranks of the 30th Division, which was being organized at Camp Sevier, near Taylors, South Carolina.

County men sent to military training camps, the vast majority of whom had previously never been away from their homes, suffered from homesickness, an intense longing to be reunited with families, friends, and familiar surroundings. Coupled with the anxiety of potentially being sent to a combat zone, soldiers had thoughts that naturally turned to their pre-military lives. Twenty-eight–year-old Pvt. Joseph Levy Byrd of Windsor conveyed his longings in a letter dated July 3, 1918, to his father, James Robert Byrd. Pvt. Byrd had been inducted five weeks earlier (May 28, 1918) and sent to Camp Jackson along with eighty-seven other Bertie County men. He wrote that he would like to see his father's in-the-field cotton crop, but there was "no chance" that he would. Rumors were circulating among the men of Byrd's regiment (316th Field Artillery) that they were to be shipped to France in August. He informed his father that if he was to go overseas, "I am going to try to come home before I go. If I can[']t come I want you to come to see me. . . . I would like to see . . . home. I would like to see you all. A boy never knows how [to] appre[ci]ate home until he gets in the army. . . . I would not mind the army but I don't want to go to France."[5]

TABLE 1   81st Division – Number of Bertie County Men Assigned to Constituent Units, August 1, 1918

| Brigade Unit | | Number of Bertie County Men |
| --- | --- | --- |
| 161st Infantry | 321st Infantry Regiment | 16 |
| | 322nd Infantry Regiment | 13 |
| | 317th Machine Gun Battalion | 1 |
| 162nd Infantry | 323rd Infantry Regiment | 2 |
| | 324th Infantry Regiment | 2 |
| | 318th Machine Gun Battalion | 2 |
| 156th Field Artillery | 316th Field Artillery Regiment | 44 |
| None (unassigned to a brigade) | 306th Ammunition Train | 3 |
| | 306th Engineers Regiment | 3 |
| | 316th Machine Gun Battalion | 1 |

As of August 1, 1918, eighty-seven Bertie County soldiers were members of constituent units of the 81st Division, including men who were initially assigned to the division and others who had been transferred to it. More than half of the county men were serving in the 316th Field Artillery Regiment. The division was sent overseas in July and August 1918.

Although the majority of the Bertie County draftees sent to Camp Jackson were assigned to units of the 81st Division, a significant number of county men were placed in units of the 30th Division. As of May 1, 1918, twenty-seven of the county's soldiers were assigned to constituent units of the division. Seventeen were members of the 119th and 120th Infantry

William Miles Phelps    Joseph Levy Byrd    David Rix Harrell

William Haywood Farless    James Norman Phelps    Edmund J. Pruden

More than forty Bertie County men served in the 316th Field Artillery Regiment, 156th Artillery Brigade, 81st Division. The individuals pictured above – William Miles Phelps, Joseph Levy Byrd, David Rix Harrell, William Haywood Farless, James Norman Phelps, and Edmund J. Pruden – were inducted as privates at Windsor on May 28, 1918, and transported to Camp Jackson, Columbia, South Carolina. All were assigned to the 316th Field Artillery Regiment. The regiment was sent overseas on August 5, 1918. *Credits:* William Miles Phelps, Joseph Levy Byrd, and David Rix Harrell provided by Dennis Phelps. The photos of Joseph Levy Byrd and Harrell are from the *Windsor Ledger*. William Haywood Farless, James Norman Phelps, and Edmund J. Pruden provided by Angie White.

Regiments, 60th Infantry Brigade. Military authorities had organized the division primarily with National Guard personnel from North Carolina, South Carolina, and Tennessee during August and September 1917. The unit was nicknamed the "Old Hickory Division" in honor of United States army general and seventh president, Andrew Jackson, who had connections to all three states. The division was sent overseas in May and June 1918.[6]

Soldiers of the 316th Field Artillery Regiment, including a number of Bertie County men, boarding a train at a depot near Liverpool en route for Southampton and France, August 14, 1918. *Credit:* Imperial War Museums, England, © IWM(Q69062)

Members of a signal detail of Battery D, 316th Field Artillery Regiment. Pvt. Edmund J. Pruden of Aulander, Bertie County is in the center of the back row. *Credit:* Angie White

TABLE 2  Number of Bertie County Men Assigned to Quartermaster Corps
and Transportation Corps Units at Camp Grant, Illinois, 1917-1918

| Corps/Units | Number of Men |
|---|---|
| *Quartermaster Corps* | |
| Labor Battalions | 11 |
| Service Battalions | 13 |
| 301st Stevedore Regiment | 8 |
| *Transportation Corps* | |
| Stevedore Battalions | 3 |
| Transportation Companies | 8 |

More than three dozen of the county's African American inductees who were sent to Camp Grant were assigned to the 92nd Division, an all-black division formed at various stateside locations during the fall of 1917. All of the Bertie County men were assigned to units of the 183rd Infantry Brigade: 365th Infantry Regiment (nineteen men), 366th Infantry Regiment (five men), and the 350th Machine Gun Battalion (fourteen men).[7]

The 92nd Division did not assemble or train as a singular entity in the United States prior to being moved overseas in June and July 1918. It was known as the "Buffalo Division" in recognition of the sobriquet accorded black cavalrymen who served during the frontier wars with the Great Plains Indians in the 1880s. By the twentieth century the term "buffalo" was broadly applied to African American soldiers in the United States Army.[8]

More than forty men sent to Camp Grant were assigned to noncombat units in the Quartermaster Corps and Transportation Corps. The units—labor battalions, service battalions, stevedore battalions and a regiment, and transportation companies—performed critical support functions for combat troops. Table 2 summarizes the number of Bertie County men assigned to these noncombat units.

One hundred sons of Bertie County, nearly all of whom were African Americans, were assigned training at Camp Greene in Charlotte. More than half were assigned to labor battalions (39 men) and service battalions (13 men). Another sixteen county men were assigned to pioneer infantry regiments. A pioneer soldier performed engineering and construction tasks—building roads, digging trenches, and other construction projects.

Brothers, James Alexander Speight (left) and Lloyd Wood Speight (right), both enlisted and served in the military during the war. James enlisted as a private in the United States Marine Corps at Norfolk on June 23, 1917. He was wounded in combat in France on July 19, 1918, and was returned to the United States where he served until discharged on June 25, 1919. Lloyd enlisted as a private in the Army at Fort Thomas, KY on August 1, 1917, and served in the Medical Department. He died at home in Bertie County on December 29, 1918, a victim of the influenza epidemic that swept the nation in 1918. *Credit:* Francis Speight and Sarah Blakeslee Speight Papers (04196), Southern Historical Collection, University of North Carolina

The United States Army formed pioneer infantry regiments for the war. The regiments were cross-trained in combat engineering and infantry tactics and included such specialists as mechanics, carpenters, farriers, and masons. The pioneer infantrymen were intended to work under the direction of engineers to build roads, bridges, gun emplacements, and camps. The men received standard infantry training so that they could defend themselves if attacked.[9]

The United States combat troops sent to Europe in June 1917, the first so deployed, were the initial members of the American Expeditionary Forces under the command of Gen. John J. Pershing. When the nation entered the war, American leaders did not anticipate, nor did France and England suggest, that the forces to be shipped overseas would approximate

TABLE 3 Numbers of Bertie County Men Transported to Europe, May 1918 through November 1918

| Month | Number of Bertie County Men |
|---|---|
| May | 48 |
| June | 46 |
| July | 74 |
| August | 81 |
| September | 59 |
| October | 26 |
| November | 10 |

the numbers eventually committed to the conflict. In March 1918, though, German ground forces launched a formidable drive into France, prompting the Allies to call upon America for a "supreme effort."[10]

By spring 1918 the United States was transporting tens of thousands of troops to Europe each month. In March almost 85,000 men sailed overseas. The number increased to approximately 119,000 in April and nearly a quarter of a million in May. During the months from June through September, more than one million soldiers crossed the Atlantic Ocean to become members of the American Expeditionary Forces.[11]

The troops departed from ten ports, six in the United States (Portland, Boston, New York, Philadelphia, Baltimore, and Newport News) and four in Canada. The United States did not have the capacity, either in the Navy or on commercial liners, to transport the huge numbers of men to Europe. Therefore, it relied upon the Allies, primarily Great Britain, to furnish the ships upon which the men embarked. Approximately forty-five percent of the men sailed on American-registered vessels, while forty-nine percent went aboard British ships and the remainder (about six percent) on French, Italian, and Russian ships. Almost 2.1 million Americans reached France during the war.[12]

The largest numbers of Bertie County soldiers served in three divisions—the 30th, the 81st, and the 92nd. By August 1918 all three divisions had been sent to Europe, many of the units' constituent members having been transported in extremely overcrowded merchant ships. One county resident later commented on the less-than-stellar vessels that carried the

Aerial view of Camp Greene. *Credit:* Robinson-Spangler Carolina Room, Charlotte Mecklenburg Library

soldiers across the Atlantic Ocean: "The boys were . . . shipped to France in cattle ships, freight boats or anything that would carry them."[13]

More than 365 Bertie County military personnel were sent overseas. Only twenty-two county men were transported to France during 1917 and the first four months of 1918. Beginning in May 1918, dozens of the county's soldiers were included in the influx of American troops who boarded crowded troop transports at American and Canadian seaports and sailed to Europe. The numbers of Bertie County men sent overseas by month from May through November 1918 are presented in Table 3.

Elements of the 30th Division began departing the United States on May 7. The 119th Infantry Regiment assembled at Camp Merritt, New Jersey on May 8. Two days later members of the regiment, organized into three battalions, began departing the camp for the ports of Hoboken, Philadelphia, and Boston. The three battalions all departed their assigned ports in transport ships on May 11. The 120th Infantry Regiment also assembled at Camp Merritt and departed Boston in two overcrowded ships over a week-long period in May. By the middle of June, all divisional personnel had arrived in France. Immediately upon arrival, the 55th

Field Artillery Brigade (including the 113th Field Artillery Regiment, of which three Bertie County men were members) was detached from the division and sent into training at a separate location. During June the division received extensive training from British military supervisors, and in early July it was assigned to the British Second Army in Belgium, where it received additional combat training. During the first nine days of August three Bertie County members of the 119th Infantry Regiment were killed in the area immediately southeast of Ypres, Flemish Province, Belgium: Pvt. Roland Harrell on the second, Pvt. Leslie Walston on the fourth, and Pvt. Jonathan S. Tayloe on the ninth. On August 16 the division was sent to the front and placed in canal sector trenches between Ypres and Voormezeele. The British Ypres-Lys offensive began three days later.[14]

The division was involved in its first intense battle action in late August and early September. On August 31 combat patrols of the 60th Infantry Brigade (119th and 120th Infantry Regiments) engaged German forces, forcing the patrols to return to their lines. On September 1 both regiments moved forward and in two days of fighting captured a lock on the Ypres Canal and the village of Voormezeele. The regiments suffered 37 men killed and 128 wounded, none of whom were Bertie County soldiers. On September 3 the division was withdrawn and sent to the St. Pol area for rest.[15]

Following the respite and additional training for its role in the Somme offensive, the division – along with other American army divisions – was by September 25 in position opposite the Hindenburg Line's St. Quentin complex. The 59th Infantry Brigade (117th and 118th Infantry Regiments) was placed in the front, the 118th Regiment in the frontline trench and the 117th Regiment in support to its rear. The 60th Infantry Brigade was held in reserve. During the evening of the twenty-sixth, the American divisions each sent a regiment forward to capture the German outpost line, a critical component of the planned assault against the overall Hindenburg Line. The 118th Infantry Regiment successfully captured its portion of the outpost line, but the 27th Division failed to achieve its objective due to concerted German resistance.[16]

The British military readied for a massive assault against the German lines by launching a two-day artillery bombardment on the enemy positions. During the bombardment the 30th Division prepared to attack, as engineers, under the cover of nighttime darkness, ventured forth to cut paths through barbed wire so that the attacking infantrymen could maneuver

Joseph Wright Hoggard. *Credit:* W. M. Haulsee, F. G. Howe and A. C. Doyle, comps., *Soldiers of the Great War*, 3 vols. (Washington: Soldiers Record Publishing Association, 1920), 2:382 [public domain].

forward. During the night of September 27, the 119th and 120th Infantry Regiments moved into position on the front line, replacing the 118th Infantry Regiment. Shortly before 6 A.M. on the twenty-ninth, the men of the 119th and 120th Infantry Regiments climbed out of their trenches, "went over the top" and attacked the German forces. The 117th Infantry Regiment followed, along with thirty tanks. Despite the several days of preparation, the advancing American line became entangled in barbed wire and disoriented due to heavy smoke and the chaos of violent combat.

High casualties resulted, yet in spite of the confusion and losses, soldiers of the 30th Division fought through the Hindenburg Line before 8 A.M. Before mid-morning the 120th Infantry entered Bellicourt and continued on to Nauroy, its principal objective, which was captured before noon. Contrarily, the 119th Infantry crossed the Hindenburg Line but soon was forced to halt and fight, having lost support and coverage on its left flank from the 27th Division, which had encountered stubborn enemy resistance. The unprotected left flank of the 119th Infantry left its members vulnerable to enfilading fire. During the day's action Cpl. Joseph Wright Hoggard (119th Infantry Regiment) of Bertie County was killed. Three other Bertie County soldiers of the 119th Infantry Regiment, Pfc. William Simon Bell, Cpl. William King Parker, and Pfc. Reuben DeJohnette Bishop, were wounded. The next afternoon the Americans were withdrawn from the battle, as Australian troops, as planned, had taken up offensive positions confronting the Germans on the line. The attack carried out by the 30th Division was deemed an overwhelming success.[17]

Members of the 92nd Division. Approximately 260 Bertie County African Americans served in the army during the war, more than three dozen of whom were members of the all-black 92nd Division. The division was engaged along the western front in the last battle of the war. (The author was unable to locate any images of Bertie County soldiers who were members of the division.). *Credit:* www.oldmagazinearticles.com / WW1-African-Americans, 92nd Infantry Division in World War One.

The division was allowed only two days of rest before it was ordered back to the front lines. Once re-engaged, the unit fought continuously for five days, advancing more than six miles, often outpacing British troops. German forces stopped the division's advance at Vaux-Andigny on October 11. On the front line that night the 27th Division replaced the 30th Division, which had lost more than 1,100 men during the five days of ferocious combat. Again it was sent rearward to rest and reorganize, but again, only for a few days. During the evening of October 15, the division was sent back to almost the same location near Vaux-Andigny where it had been pulled away only days previously. Following a British bombardment of the village on the sixteenth, the 59th Infantry Brigade attacked and captured the town on the seventeenth. The 60th Infantry Brigade then carried forward the assault that night and continued until ordered to terminate its advance on the nineteenth. Military authorities then withdrew the 30th Division from the combat and sent it to the rear. It would not again be called upon to battle enemy forces. For the remainder of October until the ceasefire of November 11, the division was being reorganized at a rear location.[18]

The all-black 92nd Division began sailing from the United States on June 10, 1918. By mid-July all components of the division had arrived in France, where they were transported by rail to an Allied training area near Bourbonne-les-Bains. On August 22 the 367th Infantry Regiment, commonly known as the "Buffalo Regiment," participated in an Allied offensive into Lorraine, while the overall division was tasked with securing the area about St. Die. Elements of the division participated in skirmishes and small firefights with German soldiers, but the men mainly repaired local roads. By September 20 the majority of the division's constituent units had been transferred to the Argonne Forest northwest of Clermont. Allied commanders, in planning the Meuse-Argonne offensive, decided to include the "Buffalo Regiment" in the main assaulting forces. On October 10 the regiment, along with three other American regiments, was transferred to the Marbache sector, south of Metz. Allied military strategists for some time had planned a major assault on a formidable German fort at Metz. On November 9—with Armistice talks well advanced—the Allies attacked the fortress. The 92nd Division, which had been included in the overall Allied attack force, filled the center of the assaulting line. The Allies inflicted heavy losses on the Germans, who battled with great ferocity. Late in the day of the tenth, intense fighting ceased. At eleven o'clock in the morning of the next day, bugles sounded to signal a ceasefire. At that moment the members of the 367th Infantry Regiment were the nearest Allied troops to Metz.[19]

During the 92nd Division's service in France, none of its Bertie County members were killed in combat. Two county men were wounded, Pvt. John B. Small (September 4 and November 11, 1918) and Pvt. William Melton (October 1, 1918). Both served in the 366th Infantry Regiment.

The 81st Division, in which more Bertie County men served than any other division, was ordered from South Carolina to Camp Upton on Long Island in New York in July 1918 in preparation to transfer overseas. The first units sailed from New York on July 31 and by the end of August all

African American soldiers advancing in France. *Credit:* Thomas Herbert Russell, *America's War for Humanity: Pictorial History of the World War for Liberty* (—: *L. H. Walter, 1919*) [public domain]. Also, digitally available at New York Public Library—no known copyright restrictions; "From the New York Public Library."

divisional personnel had arrived in France. The division was sent to the Tonnerre Training Area where the 156th Field Artillery Brigade (316th, 317th, and 318th Field Artillery Regiments, and 306th Trench Mortar Battery) was immediately detached and transferred to another area for training. Following a month of combat training, in mid-September military commanders ordered the division to the front in the St. Die sector. There it arrived on the nineteenth and was assigned to the XXXIII Corps and subsequently to the X Corps of the French Seventh Army. While assigned to the sector, the division fought off German trench raids and endured artillery bombardments. On October 19 the division was withdrawn from the line and sent to the rear to await transfer to the American First Army, which was then engaged in the fighting of the Meuse-Argonne offensive.[20]

The division moved to the Sommedieve sector south of Verdun in early November to join French troops in reserve. On November 6 the division's four infantry regiments (321st, 322nd, 323rd, and 324th) joined the front line east of Verdun, relieving units of the 35th Division. At the time Allied forces were slowly beating back the German forces. Allied commanders decided to throw all available Allied divisions against the enemy to drive the Germans back farther. As part of the all-out thrust, the 81st Division was ordered to attack east of Verdun on November 8. The front to be covered by the division was so long that all four infantry regiments were placed on the front line with no reserve elements held for support. Moreover, the middle portion of the line was densely wooded and heavily defended by German troops, leading division commanders to bypass the terrain and attack on either side. The 161st Infantry Brigade (321st and 322nd Infantry Regiments, and 317th Machine Gun Battalion) was to move to the north and the 162nd Infantry Brigade (323rd and 324th Infantry Regiments and 318th Machine Gun Battalion) to the south. Both brigades were supported by machine gun and engineers units.[21]

During the morning of November 9, both brigades lurched toward the German lines and ran into heavy machine gun and artillery fire. By midday elements of the division had advanced to Moranville, which was captured before nightfall. Other elements forced the Germans to move back, which exposed Noir-Haies and Claires-Chenes; both villages were captured during the afternoon. However, by late afternoon, the 324th Infantry Regiment withdrew from much of the ground that it had captured in order to move to safer locations. One company of the regiment was not informed of the withdrawal and thus was isolated. German forces counterattacked and decimated the company.

The next day various infantry units of the division attacked enemy positions. Cpl. Herman E. Tarkenton of Bertie County, 322nd Infantry Regiment, was wounded on November 10. That night the 321st Infantry Regiment moved into position on the battle line as plans were made for the regiment to make an early morning attack. Rumors circulated that a ceasefire was pending, but no official communications were received regarding a cessation of combat. At daybreak on the eleventh, the 321st Infantry went "over the top" and attacked German positions north of the forest. At 10:30 A.M. the 323rd Infantry Regiment attacked to the south of the woods. Shortly thereafter the 321st Regiment reached barbed wire entanglements along the main German line. It fought through the wire and some men entered the German trenches.

James P. Saunders (left) and Reddick N. Freeman (right). James P. Saunders was inducted as a private at Windsor on April 26, 1918, and transported to Camp Jackson, Columbia, South Carolina. He was assigned to the 324th Infantry Regiment, 162nd Infantry Brigade, 81st Division and served in companies D and M. He was sent overseas on August 5, 1918, and returned to the United States on June 18, 1919. Private Saunders was honorably discharged on June 25, 1919. Reddick N. Freeman was inducted as a private at Windsor on May 28, 1918, and transported to Camp Jackson, Columbia, South Carolina. He served in the 5th Company, 305th Motor Supply Train, Quartermaster Corps at Camp Jackson. Freeman served overseas from August 5, 1918, until June 24, 1919, and was honorably discharged on July 9, 1919.

At eleven o'clock the firing suddenly stopped. The armistice took effect at that hour. The 81st Division's fighting had concluded. Sgt. Lodowick White of Bertie County, 321st Infantry Regiment, was wounded during the morning's action. The 316th Field Artillery Regiment, which was detached from the division upon its arrival in France, did not rejoin the division while it operated on the front lines. Consequently, more than forty Bertie County men assigned to the regiment were not called into combat; the regiment's ranks remained "practically intact."[22]

The majority of Bertie County's African Americans in the army served in support or non-combat units. Most of the units were in the Quartermaster

Corps and the Transportation Corps. It is estimated that during the war about thirty-three percent (or a ratio of 2:1 combat versus support) of the army's total manpower was assigned to non-combat units.[23]

When the United States entered the Great War, its Army had extremely limited experience with expeditionary warfare and no experience in the type of combat being waged in France. Accordingly, the Army planned and raised from scratch the types of support units needed overseas. In 1912 Congress had authorized the Army to establish a Quartermaster Corps to be derived from the then existing Quartermaster Department and several other commands. The core mission of the Quartermaster Corps was the management and delivery of subsistence and supplies. Specially trained units were deemed the most reliable means of providing vital logistical support and services.[24]

Within the Quartermaster Corps Bertie County's soldiers served predominantly in labor and service battalions. Labor battalions provided manual labor to complete a wide range of functions, including working on roads, maintaining camps, clearing areas of foliage, and even sweeping battlefields and lines of advancement to recover and salvage equipment and weapons. Service battalions provided logistical support to combat units. Although no county men were killed or wounded in action while serving in labor or service battalions, eight men did die of disease while members of such units. All eight were African Americans.

Additionally, Bertie County soldiers served in units of the Transportation Corps, which was responsible for the movement of troops, equipment, and supplies. Nearly all the county men served either in stevedore units or transportation companies. Soldiers in stevedore regiments and battalions were primarily engaged in loading and unloading war materiel onto or off freighters and cargo ships. Members of transportation companies helped move men and materiel from embarkation points to operational locations. All of the Bertie County men who served in stevedore and transportation companies were African American. None was killed, wounded, or died of disease.

The majority of the Bertie County military service personnel served in the Army, but forty men and women of the county voluntarily served in the United States Navy during the war (including those individuals who were serving when war was declared). Two served as officers, Joseph P. Norfleet (lieutenant commander) and Cola Castelloe (assistant surgeon).

All the other naval personnel served in the enlisted ranks in a wide variety of roles, including nurses, hospital apprentices, pharmacist's mates, seamen, firemen, yeomen, mess attendants, cooks, ship's fitters, and enginemen. They served at seven naval hospitals, three naval bases and aboard more than forty-five naval vessels, including thirteen battleships, four destroyers, two destroyer tenders, three cruisers, one submarine, three freighter/cargo ships, six troop transports, and three hospital ships. The Bertie County sailors universally served singly, not in groups, aboard their assigned ships. No Bertie County naval personnel were killed, wounded, or otherwise died while serving during the war.

The summer of 1918 passed and autumn set in as the residents of Bertie County carried on with their daily lives, ever mindful of the horrors of war being experienced by those county sons fighting along the Western Front in France. Eventually, by late October and early November, rumors or "a little news" circulated among the people that the war might "soon be over." Skeptical optimism began to surface in conversations and discussions among the residents. Then, throughout the county on Monday, November 11, jubilant clamors flared. The citizens wherever they happened to be—in the yards and fields, in their houses, on the roads and streets, and at their work locations—"all at once" heard whistles blowing, church bells ringing, automobile horns blowing, sawmills blaring their whistles, and neighbors "hollering." Grand news had arrived—the war was over! "This November day would not ever be forgotten."[25]

Fighting in the Great War abruptly ceased at eleven o'clock in the morning on November 11. The Allies had signed an armistice with Germany that terminated combat in western Europe. Bertie County's young men who had been "called to the colors" soon would be returning to their beloved "little world" to reunite with anxiously waiting families and friends. Newspapers carried front-page headlines joyously announcing that combat had ended in Europe.

Four Bertie County men, all members of the 119th Infantry Regiment, were killed in action, while twenty-two county men died of disease and illness. Upon the families of these men fell the heaviest burden and sacrifice of the war. Table 4 identifies the county service personnel who lost their lives while serving the country.

In addition to the Bertie County men who died, twenty-five county men (twenty-four soldiers and one Marine) were wounded in combat, some severely and others slightly. An additional thirty-five men incurred service-connected disabilities of varying severities with which they were encumbered when discharged from military service.

The Armistice of November 11 was consummated much sooner than American military officials had anticipated, transpiring as army officers were focused on generating a military sufficiently large to fight at least another year. The Army's high command was not prepared to begin immediately dismantling the 4-million-man Army that had been raised in about a year and a half. Army leaders considered a number of demobilization programs before settling on a plan that called for releasing the members of various units when the military rationale for their existence no longer continued. The plan provided that most troops serving stateside be released from active duty by the end of February 1919. Subsequently, military personnel serving overseas would be transported back to the states and mustered out in the following order: casuals, surplus and special service troops, troops in England, Air Service personnel, troops in Italy, combat divisions, and, finally, supply troops.[26]

Accordingly, Bertie County's military members began arriving home, singly and severally, before the end of 1918, having been discharged upon the demobilization of the armed forces. One hundred of the county's military personnel were honorably discharged in December; another 127, from January through March. More than 325 military members from the county were discharged during the six months from April through September. Across the county citizens gave thanks and praises that the service personnel were out of harm's way. As the veterans returned to Bertie and disembarked from the train at the Windsor station, they were joyfully greeted by area citizens.

The county's military personnel who had served in France were undoubtedly excited about being back on United States soil and returning to their homes. Many of the soldiers' impressions of France were likely summarized by PFC William Miles Phelps in an undated letter he penned from St. Blin, France, to the Windsor Ledger. Phelps was impressed by that nation's overall "stone and brick" architecture of public buildings and churches, which were most often lavishly decorated with paintings and sculptures. He also observed that the French post roads were exceptional, "graded and hard surfaced ... to bear the greatest weights." In contrast, he considered the French railway system "a joke," characterized by miserable

TABLE 4  Bertie County Military Personnel Who Were Killed in Action or Died in Service

| Name | Unit | Location | Cause | Date |
|------|------|----------|-------|------|
| Bazemore, Tommie* | 323rd Labor Battalion | Camp Grant, IL | cerebro-spinal meningitis | June 3, 1918 |
| Bell, Jim* | 155th Depot Brigade | Camp Dix, NJ | pneumonia | Sept. 27, 1918 |
| Bond, Armstead* | 347th Labor Battalion | France | lobar pneumonia | Feb. 11, 1919 |
| Brinkley, Raymond Miles | Machine Gun Training Detachment | Camp Hancock, GA | bronchial pneumonia | Jan. 10, 1919 |
| Clark, Isaac* | 156th Depot Brigade | Camp Jackson, SC | lobar pneumonia | May 23, 1918 |
| Coffield, Willie* | 532nd Engineers Regt. | France | peritonitis, tuberculosis | March 14, 1919 |
| Cotton, William* | 810th Pioneer Infantry Regt. | Camp Greene, NC | Pneumonia | Oct. 17, 1918 |
| Harrell, Roland | 119th Infantry Regt., 30th Division | France | killed in action | Aug. 2, 1918 |
| Harrell, Wesley P. | 316th Field Artillery Regt., 81st Division | France | bronchial pneumonia | Oct. 6, 1918 |
| Hoggard, Joseph Wright | 119th Infantry Regt., 30th Division | France | killed in action | Sept. 29, 1918 |
| Houston, Leopold H.* | Motor Transport Corps | France | pneumonia | Oct. 18, 1918 |
| Hyman, Alexander* | 344th Labor Battalion | aboard transport ship in route to France | pneumonia | Oct. 4, 1918 |

| Name | Unit | Location | Cause of death | Date |
|---|---|---|---|---|
| Johnson, Cornelius* | 344th Labor Battalion | France | pneumonia | Oct. 21, 1918 |
| Jones, Leander* | 323rd Labor Battalion | France | bronchial pneumonia | Feb. 23, 1919. |
| Lee, Norman B. | 316th Field Artillery Regiment. 81st Division | France | bronchial pneumonia | Oct. 5, 1918 |
| Mizell, Willie | 810th Pioneer Infantry Regt. | Camp Greene, NC | lobar pneumonia | Oct. 14, 1918 |
| Riddick, Whit D.* | 348th Labor Battalion | Camp Greene, NC | lobar pneumonia | Oct. 14, 1918 |
| Ruffin, John Hardy* | 321st Labor Battalion | France | tuberculosis | Jan. 9, 1919 |
| Speight, Lloyd Wood | Medical Department | Bertie County | bronchial pneumonia, influenza | Dec. 29, 1918 |
| Speller, Noah Cooper* | 161st Depot Brigade | Camp Grant, IL | pneumonia | April 14, 1918 |
| Tarkenton, Eric Lee | Navy | Hampton Roads, Virginia | pneumonia | Oct. 9, 1918 |
| Tayloe, Jonathan Stanley | 119th Infantry Regt., 30th Division | France | killed in action | Aug. 9, 1918 |
| Walston, Leslie | 119th Infantry Regt., 30th Division | France | killed in action | Aug. 4, 1918 |
| Williams, Frank B.* | 365th Infantry Regt., 92nd Division | France | bronchial pneumonia, influenza | March 17, 1919 |
| Williams, Frank* | 344th Labor Battalion | France | pneumonia | Oct. 5, 1918 |
| Williams, Whittie* | 366th Infantry Regt., 92nd Division | Camp Grant, IL | cerebro-spinal meningitis | July 17, 1918 |

* Asterisks identify African Americans

Richardson tandem biplane hydroplane taking off on Potomac, April, 1916. *Credit:* Library of Congress.

service, slow trains, and poor accommodations. Nearly everyone there observed the Catholic Religion; Phelps, who resided in a Protestant-dominated community, noted that he had met only one non-Catholic family during his time in France. The overall farming populace was extremely impoverished and cultivated their lands with antiquated tools, "the crudest implements imaginable." Fields were predominantly plowed "with the same medieval implements used . . . a hundred years ago . . . drawn by horses, oxen and milch cows." In conclusion Phelps wrote that France was "one hundred years behind the United States." He lamented how he desired to return to America: "I want to settle back into my old place as tho I had never been out of it, and it will be seldom, very seldom . . . that I'll talk of France."[27]

The people of Bertie County planned a festive celebration publicly honoring the veterans. By mid-summer 1919 the majority of the service personnel had arrived home, prompting county officials to orchestrate a grand, seven-day event, Welcome Home Week. In July U.S. Sen. Furnifold M. Simmons (Jones County), on behalf of the citizens of Bertie County, extended an invitation to Sen. Joseph Taylor Robinson (Arkansas) to speak

Navy dirigible, 1900. *Credit:* Library of Congress, Bain News Service, publisher.

at the event in early August. The county commissioners authorized the use of county funds to pay for half the expenses (not to exceed $500) associated with the "Home Coming." Rear Admiral Augustus F. Fechteler, Commandant of the Fifth Naval District, Norfolk, authorized two sub-chasers, a dirigible, and a hydroplane to be detached from the Norfolk Naval Base to participate in the celebration. The commandant also detailed a naval band to play during the "Home Coming," to further enhance the festive atmosphere.[28]

The celebration began at 10 A.M. on Sunday, August 3, when church bells in the county simultaneously rang, and subsequently the churches held services attended by troops. The next day an estimated sixty family reunions with troop members were held across the county. On Tuesday, August 5, thousands of citizens poured into Windsor for a day-long program planned and executed by Rosa Winston, chair of the Bertie County chapter of the American Red Cross. Two Navy aircraft circled in the sky over the town and two naval sub-chasers were moored at the local wharves along the banks of the Cashie River. The vessels were of much interest to the attendees.

Submarine chasers between 1916–1917. *Credit:* National Photo Company Collection, Library of Congress.

Throughout the day the Navy band "was very liberal with magnificent music." Senator Robinson spoke, rendering a "great oration" that "was received with much applause." Cameron A. Morrison, honored guest from Mecklenburg County and governor-to-be of North Carolina, "made a splendid speech." Judge Francis D. Winston, a well-respected local dignitary, also spoke to the gathered crowd. A parade traced through the town and included "many handsome floats," one of which bore a white banner embroidered with golds stars solemnly "denoting Bertie's loss in men to the allied cause." A half-dozen carrier pigeons, gold-starred veterans of the French flying corps that had seen service for several months on the Western Front, were released. Mrs. Winston released the first pigeon, which conveyed a written message to Admiral Fechtler, Norfolk Naval Base, expressing to him the thanks of the people of Bertie County for having provided the various naval assets for the day's festivities. (The bird made the trip from Windsor to Hampton Roads, a distance of nearly one hundred miles, in an hour and five minutes.)[29]

A portion of the crowd present at the post-war celebration in Windsor on August 5, 1919.
*Credit: Credit: Minute Book, Bertie County Chapter American Red Cross (unlabeled), 1917–1918—First World War,* Bertie County Register of Deeds Office.

The citizens enthusiastically approved a set of resolutions in which they "joyously welcome[d] home" the returning military personnel, who had "maintained the highest standards of Bertie County manhood, devotion to duty [and] courage in times of danger and faithfulness." The citizens also publicly recognized the families of the deceased military members, extending to those families their "sincere sympathy." Further, they thanked the Bertie County Chapter of the American Red Cross and the "patriotic men and women of the County" who had served during the war.[30]

The day's festivities concluded that evening at "Windsor Castle," the stately home of Judge and Mrs. Winston, where nearly 2,000 visitors, including 200 soldiers and sailors, were entertained and enjoyed the splendid music of the Navy band. A feature of the evening's activities was a "lawn exhibition of moving pictures showing great war scenes." The *News and Observer* characterized Tuesday, August 5, as the "greatest day in the history of Bertie county."[31]

Two unidentified military service personnel who attended the day's post-war festivities in Windsor. *Credit: Minute Book, Bertie County Chapter American Red Cross (unlabeled), 1917–1918—First World War,* Bertie County Register of Deeds Office.

Nova Asbell Leicester years later described the day's events:

> There was a big homecoming parade. . . . [S]ubmarine chasers were brought up [the] Cashie River. A blimp was brought [in] to fly overhead. A stand was built at the courthouse for the dignitaries. Every plan was made to give the boys a welcome home. A band was summoned. The whole thing went off with a bang. Carts, buggies and a few Model T's lined the road going to town. All in all, it was a great day to be remembered. There was a long parade of soldiers in uniforms . . . and jeeps. Speeches were made . . . flags flew everywhere.[32]

On Wednesday township meetings were held in the ten townships of the county, which "large gatherings of people attended." On Thursday the Confederate Veterans Association met in Windsor and troops attended the meeting as "honored guests." During Friday returning troops visited their friends. The week's activities closed on Saturday in Windsor, where "club rooms" in the Rascoe Building were opened to the troops for their comfort and convenience.[33]

The time for Bertie County's citizens to serve humanity unselfishly and sacrificially had concluded—life could return to prewar normalcy for the county's residents.

1. Statistics regarding Bertie County residents' induction into, and service in, the armed forces were compiled by the author based on information contained in Appendix 1. Other statistics presented within this chapter were similarly compiled by the author, unless otherwise noted.

2. Navy service cards (for Bertie County residents), Adjutant General – World War I Service Cards (microfilm), Adjutant General, Military Collection, State Archives (hereafter cited as World War I Service Cards, with pertinent military service member(s) identified).

3. *Order of Battle of the United States Land Forces in the World War*, 3 vols. (Washington: Government Printing Office, 1931–1949; Washington, Center of Military History, 1988), 3:1277 (hereafter cited as Order of Battle); *Official Record of the United States' Part in the Great War* (Washington: Government Printing Office, 1920), 22 (hereafter cited as Official Record).

4. Anne Cipriano Venzon, ed., *The United States in the First World War: An Encyclopedia* (New York and London: Garland Publishing, 1995), 675 (hereafter cited as Venzon, *First World War Encyclopedia*) .

5. J. L. Byrd to Papa [James Robert Byrd], July 3, 1918, Joseph Levy Byrd letters (courtesy of Carolyn Dail).

6. Richard A. Rinaldi, *The United States Army in World War I, Orders of Battle, Ground Units, 1917–1919* (Tiger Lily Publications, 2005), 38–39 (hereafter cited as Rinaldi, *United States Army Orders of Battle*); Venzon, 641.

7. The 92nd Division was one of two all-black divisions that served in the war against the Central Powers. The other was the 93rd Division, in which five Bertie County men served in France. Mitchell Yockelson, "They Answered the Call: Military Service in the United States Army During World War I, 1917–1919," *Prologue*, vol. 30, no. 3 (Fall 1998), 232 (hereafter cited as Yockelson, "They Answered the Call").

8. Rinaldi, *United States Army Orders of Battle*, 54; Venzon, *First World War Encyclopedia*, 687–688.

9. Yockelson, "They Answered the Call," 232; Doughboy Center, www.worldwar1.com.

10. *Official Record*, 11–12.

11. *Official Record*, 36.

12. *Official Record*, 40–41, 110.

13. Rinaldi, *United States Army Orders of Battle*, 38–39, 48–49, 54; Nova Asbell Leicester, "Tales Told to Me by My Mother When I Was a Child," (unpublished research report, ca. 1977) (hereafter cited as Leicester, "Tales").

14. Venzon, *First World War Encyclopedia*, 641–642; World War 1 Service Cards for Roland Harrell and Jonathan S. Tayloe; *History, 119th Infantry, 6th Brigade, 30th Division, U.S.A., Operations in Belgium and France, 1917–1919* (Wilmington: Wilmington Chamber of Commerce, 1920), 4 (hereafter cited as *History of 119th Infantry*); Maj. John O. Walker and others, *Official History*

*of the 120th Infantry,* "*3rd North Carolina*" *30th Division, from August 5, 1917, to April 17, 1919* (Lynchburg, Virginia: J. P. Bell Co., 1919), 9 (hereafter cited as *Official History of 120th Infantry*).

15. Venzon, *First World War Encyclopedia,* 642; *History of 119th Infantry,* 29–32; *Official History of 120th Infantry,* 16–17.

16. Venzon, *First World War Encyclopedia,* 642; *History of 119th Infantry,* 41.

17. Venzon, *First World War Encyclopedia,* 642–643; History of 119th Infantry, 46–47; *Official History of 120th Infantry,* 26–27.

18. Venzon, *First World War Encyclopedia,* 643; *History of 119th Infantry,* 52–55; *Official History of 120th Infantry,* 29–30.

19. Venzon, *First World War Encyclopedia,* 688–689.

20. Venzon, *First World War Encyclopedia,* 675; Joseph L. Byrd [316th Field Artillery Regiment], "A Little About My Trip to France," (undated), Joseph L. Byrd letters and papers (courtesy of Buck Sitterson and Sue Byrd Sitterson).

21. Venzon, *First World War Encyclopedia,* 676.

22. *Alamance Gleaner,* Graham, NC, June 12, 1919.

23. John J. McGrath, *The Other End of the Spear: The Tooth-to-Tail Ratio(T3R) in Modern Military Operations* (Fort Leavenworth, Kansas: Combat Studies Institute Press, 2007), 11 (hereafter cited as McGrath, *Other End of the Spear*).

24. McGrath, *Other End of the Spear,* 11; *A Brief History of the Quartermaster Corps,* Quartermaster Museum, Fort Lee, Virginia, www.qmmuseum.lee.army.mil.

25. Leicester, "Tales."

26. Venzon, *First World War Encyclopedia,* 197–198.

27. William M. Phelps to "The Ledger" [*Windsor Ledger*], undated (courtesy of Dennis Phelps).

28. *Daily Times* (Wilson), July 19, 1919; *News and Observer* (Raleigh), August 7, 9, 1919; *Review* (High Point), August 14, 1919; Minute Book, Bertie County Chapter American Red Cross (unlabeled), 1917–1918 – First World War, Bertie County Register of Deeds Office, Windsor (hereafter cited as Minute Book, Bertie County Chapter American Red Cross (unlabeled)); Bertie County Commissioners Minutes, 1918-1933 (microfilm), State Archives.

29. *News and Observer* (Raleigh), August 7, 9, 1919.

30. Minute Book, Bertie County Chapter American Red Cross (unlabeled).

31. *News and Observer* (Raleigh), August 7, 9, 1919; *Review* (High Point), August 14, 1919.

32. Leicester, "Tales."

33. *News and Observer* (Raleigh), August 9, 1919.

# Appendix 1

## Roster of Bertie County
## Military Service Personnel
## During World War I

Bertie County's World War I military service personnel were identified and information related to the service thereof was compiled from: Adjutant General – World War I Cards (microfilm), Military Collection, State Archives; Local Board of Bertie County to Adjutant General, Raleigh, (undated), Bertie County Local Board Report of Inducted Men (undated, but likely prepared in early January 1919), Local Draft Boards and Recruiting, Bertie County, Military Collection, World War I Papers, 1903-1933, State Archives; War Department, Office of the Provost Marshal General, Selective Service System, 1917–July 15, 1919, Lists of Men Ordered to Report to Local Board for Military Duty, 1917–1918, North Carolina (Bertie County), Records of the Selective Service System (World War 1), Record Group 163, National Archives; World War I Selective Service System Draft Registration Cards (Bertie County), (microfilm), Record Group 163, National Archives; Applications for Headstones for U. S. Military Veterans, 1925-1941 (microfilm), Records of the Office of the Quartermaster General, Record Group 92, National Archives; "Soldiers and Sailors Discharge Records (9 vols.), Bertie County Register of Deeds Office, Windsor; W. M. Haulsee, F. G. Howe and A. C. Doyle, comps., Soldiers of the Great War, 3 vols., (Washington: Soldiers Record Publishing Association, 1920); American Battle Monuments

Commission, www.abmc.gov; U.S. Navy Casualties Books, 1776–1941, Officers and Enlisted Men, 1917–1918, Navy Department, Washington, D.C.; Record of Soldiers From Bertie County in the World War, 1917–1918, Bertie County Register of Deeds Office; Jail Record, Bertie County Register of Deeds Office.

Supplemental service information on a number of personnel was compiled from a variety of other sources, namely: Fifteenth Census of the United States, 1930 (microfilm): Bertie County, North Carolina, Records of the Bureau of the Census, Record Group 29, National Archives; Sixteenth Census of the United States, 1940 (microfilm): Bertie County, North Carolina, Records of the Bureau of the Census, Record Group 29, National Archives; death certificates of select World War I veterans on file in the Bertie County Register of Deeds Office; military headstones in Bertie County cemeteries; veterans' obituaries (primarily from issues of the *Bertie Ledger-Advance* (Windsor); and two volumes maintained in the Bertie County Register of Deeds office – (1) Minute Book, Bertie County Chapter American Red Cross (unlabeled), 1917–1918 – First World War and (2) Special Report, 1914, Bertie County.

The author's objective was to identify those Bertie County residents who served in the nation's armed forces during the war. Since there apparently has never been published a comprehensive roster of the county's service personnel, the author reviewed all military service cards in Adjutant General – World War I Cards (microfilm), Military Collection, State Archives seeking to identify Bertie County men and women in the United States Army, United States Marine Corps, United States Navy, and United States Coast Guard. The author notes that the subject cards contain abstracts of information from service personnel tours of duty and all pertinent information related to such tours was not always comprehensively entered onto the cards.

The author further notes that he identified some Bertie County residents who served in the military during 1917 and 1918, but for whom he could not locate a military service card in the records of the State Archives. The United States Congress passed an act in July 1919 mandating that a record of service for each soldier, sailor (including Coast Guardsmen), and Marine who served between April 6, 1917, and November 11, 1919, be created and furnished to the adjutant general of the individual states. Clerks in the Department of the Army and the Department of the Navy created those cards beginning in 1919 and continuing into the 1920s. As noted in the roster, a number of Bertie County men were, according to certain records, inducted into the Army, but no service cards seem to exist to document their military service. Apparently, service cards for such persons are not to be found in the relevant North Carolina State Archives records. Possibly, pertinent cards were not provided to the state of North Carolina in 1919 and the 1920s for every state resident who served in the armed forces during the relevant period. For those persons for whom no cards were found, the author noted in their summaries of military service "no record found of military service performed."

An undetermined number of Bertie County natives who were of age for military service during the war originally lived within the county, but by the time they reached adulthood they had departed and relocated to other jurisdictions both within and outside of North Carolina. The individuals established their permanent residencies at the new jurisdictions, where they enlisted or were drafted into the military during 1917 and 1918. They are not included within the roster since they were no longer residents of Bertie County. One such individual was William Gurley Castellow, a brother of the author's grandmother (Annie Bessie Castellow Hoggard), who registered and was drafted in Norfolk, Virginia. William and Annie's brother, Ernest Elwood Castellow, resided in Bertie County, where he registered for Selective Service and was subsequently inducted into Army at Windsor. Relatedly, people who were born outside of Bertie County and who, at the time of the conflict, were residents of the county and subsequently served in the armed forces are included in the roster.

All men who were inducted, in accordance with Selective Service regulations, were deemed members of the military at the location and time of their inductions. Men were inducted into the army as privates. Some individuals were inducted and transported to training camps where they were rejected by military authorities. Therefore, the ranks of men who were inducted at Windsor and transported to training camps, but then rejected for military service, are shown as privates, even though in actuality the rejected persons did not perform any substantive military service.

African Americans are indicated by asterisks (*). Periods of overseas service are dates of departure from and arrival back in the continental United States or Canada.

## UNITED STATES ARMY AMERICAN EXPEDITIONARY FORCES, FRANCE

### 1st ARMY CORPS

### HEADQUARTERS REGIMENT

### Company A

TARKENTON, JOSEPH R., private: Previously served in Company A, Military Police, 81st Division. Transferred to this company on January 21, 1918. Sent overseas on March 30, 1918. Transferred to 208th Military Police Company on September 25, 1918.

### 3rd ARMY CORPS

SITTERSON, THADDEUS BERKLEY, sergeant: Previously attended the Central Officers Training School, Camp Gordon, Augusta, Georgia. Transferred to headquarters of this corps on November 11, 1918, while serving overseas. Returned from overseas on September 10, 1919, and honorably discharged at Camp Lee, Petersburg, Virginia on September 17, 1919.

### 4th ARMY CORPS

### ARTILLERY PARK

PERRY, WILLIAM LEWIS, private: Previously served in Company A, 57th Pioneer Infantry Regiment. Transferred to this unit on August 27, 1918, in which he served as a horseman. Served overseas from September 3, 1918, until June 28, 1919. Honorably discharged at Camp Lee, Petersburg, Virginia on July 18, 1919.

PHELPS, NORMAN HENSON, private: Previously served in Company A, 57th Pioneer Infantry Regiment. Transferred to Headquarters Company of this unit on August 27, 1918. Served overseas from September 3, 1918, until July 2, 1919. Honorably discharged on July 17, 1919.

### ARMY SERVICE CORPS

BURKETT, JAMES ANDREW, private: Previously served in Company F, 55th Pioneer Infantry Regiment. Transferred to the 56th Guard Company of this corps on November 1, 1918. Served overseas from September 1, 1918, until March 26, 1919. Honorably discharged on December 22, 1919, with a service-connected disability rated as 20 percent.

DAVENPORT, JOHN WALTER, captain: Registered for Selective Service on September 12, 1918, at age 32; occupation – lawyer. Appointed captain in this corps on November 21, 1918 (after the cessation of combat in Europe). Served at Camp Upton, Long Island, New York, and honorably discharged on December 14, 1918.

EARLY, SCARBOROUGH, private: Previously served in the 156th Depot Brigade, Camp Jackson, Columbia, South Carolina. Transferred to the Provost Guard Company, Camp Sevier, near Taylors, South Carolina on November 14, 1918. Honorably discharged at Camp Sevier on March 21, 1919, having performed no overseas service.

MORRIS, ROLAND L., sergeant: Enlisted as a private at Fort Slocum, Long Island, New York on August 12, 1915, at age 28. Assigned to 1st Company, United States Guards, Fort Leavenworth, Kansas. Promoted to cook on September 4, 1915, and reduced to private on August 13, 1917. Promoted to private first class on December 12, 1917, to corporal on April 4, 1918, and to sergeant on September 14, 1918. Honorably discharged on December 20, 1919, in order to re-enlist. No overseas service performed.

MIZELL, DAVID ROBERT, private: Previously served in Company F, 55th Pioneer Infantry Regiment. Transferred as a cook to the 59th Guard Company of this corps on an undisclosed date, while serving overseas. Promoted to sergeant on April 28, 1919, and reduced to private on May 21, 1919. Returned from overseas on July 11, 1919, and honorably discharged at Camp Lee, Petersburg, Virginia on July 20, 1919.

MOUNTAIN, JAMES T.*, first sergeant: Previously served as a private in the Main Training Depot, Machine Gun Training Center, Camp Hancock, near Augusta, Georgia. Transferred to the 26th Company, Depot Service of this corps on November 7, 1918, while serving overseas. Promoted to sergeant on an undisclosed date and to supply sergeant on November 9, 1918. Promoted to first sergeant on March 15, 1919. Returned from overseas on July 10, 1919, and honorably discharged on July 19, 1919.

WHITE, ASA W., private first class: Previously served in the 308th Motor Supply Train, Quartermaster Corps. Transferred to Company C, Mechanical Unit of this corps on March 11, 1919, while serving overseas. Promoted to private first class on April 17, 1919. Returned from overseas on July 12, 1919, and honorably discharged at Camp Lee, Petersburg, Virginia, on July 18, 1919.

# DIVISIONS

## 1st DIVISION

## 1st AMMUNITION TRAIN (FIELD ARTILLERY)

### Company B

SLADE, CECIL E., corporal: Previously served in Truck Company F of this ammunition train. Transferred as a corporal to this company on an undisclosed date, while serving overseas. Reduced to private on January 4, 1918, and promoted to private first class on March 20, 1918. Promoted to corporal on August 1, 1919, and returned from overseas on September 15, 1919. Transferred to Company I, 13th Infantry Regiment, 16th Infantry Brigade, 8th Division on September 18, 1919.

### Truck Company F

SLADE, CECIL E., corporal: Previously served in the 4th Company, Coast Artillery Corps, Fort Howard, Baltimore County, Maryland. Transferred to this company on July 26, 1917. Sent overseas on August 7, 1917. Transferred to Company B, of this ammunition train on an undisclosed date.

## 1st INFANTRY BRIGADE

## 16th INFANTRY REGIMENT

### Company M

COOK, ARTHUR, private first class: Previously served in the Medical Department, Base Hospital, at Fort Sill, Lawton, Oklahoma. Transferred to this company on July 4,

1918. Served overseas from July 14, 1918, until December 16, 1918. Transferred to the Medical Department of the 90th Infantry, 40th Infantry Brigade, 20th Division on January 24, 1919.

## 2nd INFANTRY BRIGADE

## 28th INFANTRY REGIMENT

### Company K

DUNNING, GARFIELD, private: Previously served in Company G, 163rd Infantry Regiment, 82nd Infantry Brigade, 41st Division. Transferred to this company on May 24, 1918. Severely wounded in action in the Toul Sector of France on August 21, 1918, resulting in the loss of his left arm. Returned from overseas on November 3, 1918. Honorably discharged on April 10, 1919, with a service-connected disability resulting from wound received in combat. Disability rated as 70 percent.

## 1st FIELD ARTILLERY BRIGADE

## 6th FIELD ARTILLERY REGIMENT

### Battery A

BUTTERTON, WALTER R., mechanic: Enlisted as a private at Fort Slocum, Davids Island, New York on October 19, 1915, at age 21. Assigned to this battery. Promoted to mechanic on May 21, 1917. Served overseas from May 26, 1918, until August 23, 1919. Honorably discharged on September 17, 1920, on abolishment of Regular Army Reserves.

## 3rd DIVISION

## 5th INFANTRY BRIGADE

## 4th INFANTRY REGIMENT

### Company M

LANGDALE, EDWARD JESSE, private: Previously served in the 330th Infantry Regiment, 165th Infantry Brigade, 83rd Division. Transferred to this company on November 6, 1918, while serving overseas. Returned from overseas on August 22, 1919, and honorably discharged at Camp Lee, Petersburg, Virginia on September 3, 1919.

## 6th INFANTRY BRIGADE

## 30th INFANTRY REGIMENT

### Company A

JENKINS, HENRY, C., mechanic: Previously served in Company H, 120th Infantry Regiment, 60th Infantry Brigade, 30th Division. Transferred as a corporal to this company on January 23, 1918. Reduced to private on March 20, 1918, and sent overseas on April 7, 1918. Promoted to mechanic on May 4, 1918. Returned from overseas on August 20, 1919, and honorably discharged on September 3, 1919.

## 4th DIVISION

### 7th INFANTRY BRIGADE

### 47th INFANTRY REGIMENT

#### Company A

LEE, GROVER C., private: Previously served for one year as a private in the North Carolina State Militia (specific regiment not disclosed). Registered for Selective Service on June 5, 1917, at age 24; occupation – farmer. Inducted as a private at Windsor on March 27, 1918, and transported to Camp Jackson, Columbia, South Carolina. Initially assigned to the 156th Depot Brigade and transferred to this company on April 29, 1918. Served overseas from July 6, 1918, until December 16, 1918. Honorably discharged on January 8, 1919.

#### Company B

SWAIN, CHARLIE CULLEN, private: Registered for Selective Service on June 5, 1917, at age 24; occupation – farmer. Inducted as a private at Windsor on March 29, 1918, and transported to Camp Jackson, Columbia, South Carolina. Initially assigned to the 156th Depot Brigade and transferred to this company on April 28, 1918. Served overseas from May 10, 1918, until July 26, 1919. Honorably discharged on August 1, 1919.

## 5th DIVISION

### 9th INFANTRY BRIGADE

### 6th INFANTRY REGIMENT

#### HEADQUARTERS COMPANY

WHITE, JAMES BINGHAM, private first class: Previously served in Company E, 321st Infantry Regiment, 161st Infantry Brigade, 81st Division. Transferred as a private to this company on February 16, 1918. Promoted to corporal on February 23, 1918. Sent overseas on April 9, 1918. Slightly wounded on August 18, 1918. Reduced to private first class on December 5, 1918. Returned from overseas on July 22, 1919, and honorably discharged on July 29, 1919.

#### Company D

JOHNSON, JOHNNIE, private: Previously served in Company F, 321st Infantry Regiment, 161st Infantry Brigade, 81st Division. Transferred to this company on February 6, 1918. Sent overseas on April 19, 1918. Severely wounded on September 13, 1918, and again on October 15, 1918. Returned from overseas on May 21, 1919, and honorably discharged on June 17, 1919.

#### Company I

BAZEMORE, TURNER FRANKLIN, supply sergeant: Previously served in Company F, 336th Infantry Regiment, 168th Infantry Brigade, 84th Division. Transferred as a sergeant to this company on February 16, 1918. Reduced in rank to private on February 17, 1918; promoted to corporal on April 2, 1918, to sergeant on August 4, 1918, and appointed supply sergeant on August 11, 1918. Sent overseas on April 9, 1918. Severely wounded in both knees and the left hand at Argonne Forest, France on October 14, 1918. Returned from overseas on March 13, 1919. Honorably discharged at Fort McPherson, Atlanta, Georgia, on February 3, 1920, due to service-connected disability rated as one hundred percent. "Disabled for life" as a result of his wounds.

# 61st INFANTRY REGIMENT

## MISCELLANEOUS (NO COMPANY IDENTIFIED)

POWELL, JUNIUS BISHOP, second lieutenant: Previously served in the enlisted ranks of the 7th Company, Coast Artillery Corps, Cape Fear, Fort Caswell. Honorably discharged on November 2, 1917, and appointed second lieutenant on February 25, 1918. Assigned to this regiment. Served overseas from April 30, 1918, until October 16, 1918. Honorably discharged on October 18, 1919, with a disability rated as 25 percent.

# 10th INFANTRY BRIGADE

# 11th INFANTRY REGIMENT

## MACHINE GUN COMPANY

NORFLEET, WILLIAM SMITH, mechanic: Previously served in Company C, 318th Machine Gun Battalion, 162nd Infantry Brigade, 81st Division. Transferred as a private to this company on February 6, 1918. Promoted to mechanic on April 5, 1918. Sent overseas on April 24, 1918. Wounded on an undisclosed date in early November 1918; severity of wound "undetermined." Returned from overseas on July 19, 1919, and honorably discharged at Camp Lee, Petersburg, Virginia on July 25, 1919.

# 5th FIELD ARTILLERY BRIGADE

# 19th FIELD ARTILLERY REGIMENT

## Battery B

THOMAS, ISAIAH W., private: Enlisted as a private at Fort Thomas, Kentucky on June 5, 1917, at age 21. Assigned to this battery. Transferred to 5th Trench Mortar Battalion (corps troops) on December 20, 1917.

# 6th DIVISION

# 12th INFANTRY BRIGADE

# 54th INFANTRY REGIMENT

## MEDICAL DEPARTMENT

JONES, JOHN P., private: Previously served in Company A of this regiment. Transferred to this department of the regiment on December 26, 1917. Transferred to United States General Hospital Number 14 (location not disclosed) on January 23, 1918.

## Company A

JONES, JOHN P., private: Enlisted as a private at Fort Thomas, Kentucky on May 14, 1917, at age 23. Assigned to this company. Transferred to the Medical Department of this regiment on December 26, 1917.

## Company E

HARRELL, DALLIS WINSTON, corporal: Registered for Selective Service on June 5, 1917, at age 23; occupation — farmer. Inducted as a private at Windsor on May 10,

1918, and transported to Camp Screven, Georgia. Assigned to this company. Sent overseas on July 6, 1918, and promoted to corporal on August 1, 1918. Returned from overseas on December 20, 1918, and honorably discharged on January 21, 1919.

## Company F

DUKES, HUGH FOND, corporal: Registered for Selective Service on June 5, 1917, at age 27; occupation – salesman. Inducted as a private at Windsor on May 10, 1918, and transported to Camp Screven, Georgia. Assigned to this company and served overseas from July 6, 1918, until June 10, 1919. Honorably discharged on June 24, 1919.

ROANE, PERRY TYLER, private: Registered for Selective Service on June 5, 1917, at age 25; occupation – clerk. Inducted as a private at Windsor on May 10, 1918, and transported to Camp Screven, Georgia. Assigned to this company. Transferred to Company C, 162nd Infantry Regiment, 75th Infantry Brigade, 38th Division on July 3, 1918.

## Company M

THOMAS, CLYDE P., private first class: Enlisted as a private at Fort Thomas, Kentucky on May 14, 1917, at age 21. Assigned to this company. Promoted to private first class on October 13, 1917. Transferred to Company A, 6th Military Police on April 24, 1918.

# 7th DIVISION

# 13th INFANTRY BRIGADE

# 55th INFANTRY REGIMENT

## Company G

LANGDALE, EDWARD JESSE, private: Registered for Selective Service on June 5, 1917, at age 23; occupation – farmer. Inducted as a private at Windsor on August 5, 1918, and transported to Camp Wadsworth, Spartanburg, South Carolina. Assigned to this company. Sent overseas on September 15, 1918. Transferred to the 330th Infantry Regiment, 165th Infantry Brigade, 83rd Division on November 2, 1918.

# 56th INFANTRY REGIMENT

## Company K

PARKER, JOHN DEMPSEY, cook: Registered for Selective Service on June 5, 1917, at age 24; occupation – farm laborer. Enlisted as a private at Fort Thomas, Kentucky on May 31, 1917, at age 21. Assigned to this company. Promoted to cook on June 15, 1918. Served overseas from August 3, 1918, until June 27, 1919. Honorably discharged on July 10, 1919.

## 7th FIELD ARTILLERY BRIGADE

## 8th FIELD ARTILLERY REGIMENT

### Battery C

BAKER, WALTER R., private first class: Previously served in Battery C, 80th Field Artillery Regiment of this brigade. Transferred as a private to this battery at Camp Wheeler, near Macon, Georgia on August 15, 1918. Sent overseas on August 15, 1918. Promoted to private first class on May 10, 1919. Returned from overseas on June 20, 1919, and honorably discharged on July 1, 1919.

## 79th FIELD ARTILLERY REGIMENT

### Battery E

MYERS, GEORGE W., private: Enlisted as a private at Camp Screven, Georgia on March 26, 1916. Assigned to this battery. Served overseas from August 18, 1918, until June 20, 1919. Honorably discharged on July 1, 1919.

## 80th FIELD ARTILLERY REGIMENT

### Battery C

BAKER, WALTER R., private: Previously served in Battery D, 316th Field Artillery Regiment, 156th Field Artillery Brigade, 81st Division. Transferred to this battery at Fort Oglethorpe, Chickamauga Park, Georgia on August 13, 1918. Transferred to Battery C, 8th Field Artillery Regiment on August 15, 1918.

## 8th DIVISION

## 16th INFANTRY BRIGADE

## 13th INFANTRY REGIMENT

### Company I

SLADE, CECIL E., corporal: Previously served in Company B, 1st Ammunition Train, 1st Division. Transferred to this company on September 18, 1919. Honorably discharged on March 5, 1920, with a service-connected disability rated as 10 percent.

## 9th DIVISION

## 17TH INFANTRY BRIGADE

## 45TH INFANTRY REGIMENT

### SUPPLY COMPANY

ACREE, WILLIAM THOMAS, supply sergeant: Previously served in Company K of this regiment. Transferred as a private first class to this company on March 2, 1918, and designated wagoner. Promoted to sergeant on March 4, 1918, and designated supply sergeant on March 21, 1918. Honorably discharged at Camp Sheridan, near Montgomery, Alabama on May 28, 1919, having performed no overseas service.

### Company K

ACREE, WILLIAM THOMAS, private first class: Enlisted as a private at Fort Thomas, Kentucky on May 31, 1917, at age 21. Assigned to this company. Promoted to private first class on August 17, 1917. Transferred to Supply Company of this regiment on March 2, 1918.

## 14th DIVISION

## 214th ENGINEERS REGIMENT

### Company D

COX, WILLIAM LEE, private: Registered for Selective Service on June 5, 1918, at age 21. Inducted as a private at Windsor on July 29, 1918, transported to Camp Forest, Lytle, Georgia. Assigned to this company and transferred to the 116th Engineers Regiment, 41st Division on September 14, 1918.

## 16th DIVISION

## 31st INFANTRY BRIGADE

## 47th MACHINE GUN BATTALION

### Company B

ASBELL, LUTHER LEE, private: Registered for Selective Service on June 5, 1917, at age 22; occupation – farmer. Inducted as a private at Windsor on July 22, 1918, and transported to Camp Hancock, near Augusta, Georgia. Assigned to the 3rd Company, Recruit Receiving Depot, Machine Gun Training Center. Transferred to the 51st Company, 5th Group, Main Training Depot at Camp Hancock on August 23, 1918. Transferred to this company and honorably discharged at Camp Wadsworth, Spartanburg, South Carolina on February 5, 1919, having performed no overseas service. Date of transfer to Camp Wadsworth not disclosed in extant records.

BAZEMORE, WILLIAM RAYMOND, private: Registered for Selective Service on June 5, 1917, at age 23; occupation - farmer. Name appears on a list of Bertie County men in-

ducted on May 28, 1918, who were transported to Camp Jackson, Columbia, South Carolina; however, the entry for Bazemore was lined through. Inducted as a private at Windsor on July 22, 1918, and transported to Camp Hancock, near Augusta, Georgia. Assigned to the 51st Company, 5th Group, Machine Gun Training Division, Machine Gun Training Corps. Transferred to this company on October 31, 1918. Honorably discharged on February 5, 1919, having performed no overseas service.

## 32nd INFANTRY BRIGADE

## 48th MACHINE GUN BATTALION

### Company B

MIZELL, AARON LEWIS, private: Registered for Selective Service on June 5, 1917, at age 30; occupation – farmer. Inducted as a private at Windsor on July 22, 1918, and transported to Camp Hancock, near Augusta, Georgia. Assigned to the Machine Gun Training Center until transferred to this company on October 31, 1918. Honorably discharged on February 13, 1919, having performed no overseas service.

## 18th DIVISION

## 218th ENGINEERS REGIMENT

RAYNER, THOMAS AUGUSTUS, first lieutenant: Registered for Selective Service on June 5, 1917, at age 27; occupation – farmer. Enlisted on May 14, 1918, and appointed first lieutenant on May 31, 1918. Served in this regiment. Also served in the 118th Engineers Regiment, and the 19th Division during undisclosed dates. Honorably discharged on January 29, 1919.

## 20th DIVISION

## 39th INFANTRY BRIGADE

## 89th INFANTRY REGIMENT

### Company E

DEBERRY, JOSEPH ROBERT, private: Registered for Selective Service on June 5, 1918, at age 21; occupation – laborer, public roads. Inducted as a private at Windsor on August 25, 1918, and transported to Camp Jackson, Columbia, South Carolina. Initially assigned to the 156th Depot Brigade and transferred to this company at Camp Sevier, near Taylors, South Carolina on November 3, 1918. Honorably discharged at Camp Sevier on March 16, 1919, having performed no overseas service.

## 40th INFANTRY BRIGADE

## 90th INFANTRY REGIMENT

## MEDICAL DETACHMENT

COOK, ARTHUR, private first class: Previously served in Company M, 16th Infantry Regiment, 1st Infantry Brigade, 1st Division. Transferred to this unit on January 24, 1919. Furloughed to the Regular Army Reserves on February 25, 1919, and honorably discharged on June 4, 1920, upon abolishment of the Regular Army Reserves.

### SUPPLY COMPANY

HALL, ELBERT J., private: Registered for Selective Service on June 5, 1917, at age 22; occupation – farmer. Inducted as a private at Windsor on May 28, 1918, and transported to Camp Jackson, Columbia, South Carolina. Initially assigned to the 156th Depot Brigade and transferred to this company at Camp Sevier, near Taylors, South Carolina on October 12, 1918. Honorably discharged on November 21, 1918, with a service-connected disability rated as 6½ percent.

## 27th DIVISION

## 53rd INFANTRY BRIGADE

## 106th INFANTRY REGIMENT

### Company L

PIERCE, SAMUEL WHITE., private: Previously served in the 55th Pioneer Infantry Regiment. Transferred to this company on December 9, 1918, while serving overseas. Returned from overseas on March 6, 1919, and assigned to the 155th Depot Brigade, Camp Lee, Petersburg, Virginia. Honorably discharged at Camp Lee on April 4, 1919.

## 54th INFANTRY BRIGADE

## 107th INFANTRY REGIMENT

### Company A

MORRIS, LEROY, private: Previously served in Company A, 57th Pioneer Infantry Regiment. Transferred to this company on August 27, 1918. Served overseas from September 15, 1918, until March 9, 1919. Honorably discharged at Camp Lee, Petersburg, Virginia on April 2, 1919.

### Company B

PHELPS, WILLIAM GRADY, private: Previously served in Company A, 57th Pioneer Infantry Regiment. Transferred to this company on August 27, 1918. Served overseas from September 15, 1918, until March 9, 1919. Honorably discharged on April 2, 1919.

## Company I

SMITHWICK, JOSEPH EDWARD, private: Previously served in Company F, 55th Pioneer Infantry Regiment. Transferred to this company on November 11, 1918, while serving overseas. Returned from overseas on March 9, 1919, and honorably discharged on April 2, 1919.

THURSTON, FRED WARD, private: Previously served in Company A, 57th Pioneer Infantry Regiment. Transferred to this company on December 7, 1918, while serving overseas. Returned from overseas on March 9, 1919, and honorably discharged on April 2, 1919.

## 29th DIVISION

## 104th SANITARY TRAIN

## 115TH AMBULANCE COMPANY

MITCHELL, HENRY BISMARK, private first class: Registered for Selective Service on June 5, 1917, at age 22; occupation – tinner (tinsmith). Enlisted at Norfolk, Virginia on August 22, 1917, as a private in the Virginia National Guard. Assigned or transferred to this company on an undisclosed date. Promoted to private first class on November 27, 1917. Served overseas from July 5, 1917, until May 22, 1919. Honorably discharged on June 2, 1919.

## 57th INFANTRY BRIGADE

## 114th INFANTRY REGIMENT

## SANITARY DETACHMENT

CLEATON, JOHN THOMAS, private: Previously served in Company B, 112th Machine Gun Battalion, 58th Infantry Brigade of this division. Transferred to this detachment on December 10, 1917. Transferred to the Sanitary Detachment, 116th Infantry Regiment, 58th Infantry Brigade of this division on April 17, 1918.

## 58th INFANTRY BRIGADE

## 115th INFANTRY REGIMENT

## MACHINE GUN COMPANY

MINTON, PATRICK WINSTON, private: Previously served in Company M, 4th Infantry Regiment, Virginia National Guard. Transferred to this company on November 8, 1917. Transferred to the 309th Auxiliary Remount Depot, Quartermaster Corps on November 25, 1917.

## 116th INFANTRY REGIMENT

## Company B

HAIGHT, THOMAS EDWIN, supply sergeant: Previously served in Company C, 118th Infantry Regiment, 59th Infantry Brigade, 30th Division. Transferred to this company on December 26, 1918, while serving overseas. Returned from overseas on May 1, 1919, and honorably discharged at Camp Lee, Petersburg, Virginia on an undisclosed date, but likely in May 1919.

## Company E

BELL, FRANK, private: Previously served in Company F, 4th Infantry Regiment, Virginia National Guard. Transferred to this company on October 4, 1917. Transferred to Company C, 1st Pioneer Infantry Regiment on April 6, 1918.

DAVIDSON, CLAUDE D., private: Previously served in Company F, 4th Infantry Regiment, Virginia National Guard. Transferred to this company on an undisclosed date. Honorably discharged at Camp Lee, Petersburg, Virginia on May 12, 1919, having performed no overseas service.

## SANITARY DETACHMENT

CLEATON, JOHN THOMAS, private: Previously served in the Sanitary Detachment, 114th Infantry Regiment, 57th Infantry Brigade of this division. Transferred to this detachment on April 17, 1918. Sent overseas on June 14, 1918. Transferred to Company A, 317th Infantry Regiment, 159th Infantry Regiment, 80th Division on December 5, 1918.

## MISCELLANEOUS (NO COMPANY IDENTIFIED)

NORFLEET, ERIC P., second lieutenant: Previously served in the enlisted ranks of Company H, 120th Infantry Regiment, 60th Infantry Brigade, 30th Division prior to attending Army Officers Candidate School. Appointed second lieutenant on October 1, 1918, and assigned to this regiment while serving overseas. Severely wounded on October 17, 1918. Returned from overseas on May 18, 1919, and honorably discharged on June 12, 1919.

## 54th FIELD ARTILLERY BRIGADE

## 111th FIELD ARTILLERY REGIMENT

## HEADQUARTERS COMPANY

CASPER, ROY ADSON, private: Previously served in Company I, 4th Infantry Regiment, Virginia, National Guard. Transferred to this company on October 10, 1917. Transferred to Battery C of this regiment on October 26, 1917.

HARRINGTON, JAMES O., private: Previously served in Company I, 4th Infantry Regiment, Virginia National Guard. Transferred to this company on October 10, 1917. Transferred to Battery C of this regiment on January 18, 1918.

HUGHES, DAVID AARON, private: Previously served in Company I, 4th Infantry Regiment, Virginia National Guard. Transferred to this company on October 10, 1917. Served overseas from June 28, 1918, until May 25, 1919. Honorably discharged at Camp Lee, Petersburg, Virginia on June 2, 1919.

THOMAS, JOHN ALEXANDER, private: Previously served in Company I, 4th Infantry Regiment, Virginia National Guard. Transferred to this company on October 10, 1917. Served overseas from June 28, 1918, until May 25, 1919. Honorably discharged at Camp Lee, Petersburg, Virginia on June 2, 1919.

WILLIAMS, ABNER WRIGHT, private first class: Previously served in Company I, 4th Infantry Regiment, Virginia National Guard. Transferred as a private to this company on October 10, 1917. Promoted to private first class on July 1, 1918. Served overseas from July 4, 1918, until May 25, 1919. Honorably discharged at Camp Lee, Petersburg, Virginia on June 2, 1919.

## Battery C

CASPER, ROY ADSON, private first class: Previously served in Headquarters Company of this regiment. Transferred as a private to this battery on October 26, 1917. Promoted to private first class on July 1, 1918, and served overseas from July 4, 1918, until May 25, 1919. Honorably discharged at Camp Lee, Petersburg, Virginia on June 2, 1919.

HARRINGTON, JAMES O., private first class: Previously served in Headquarters Company of this regiment. Transferred as a private to this battery on January 18, 1918. Promoted to private first class on July 1, 1918. Served overseas from July 4, 1918, until May 25, 1919. Honorably discharged at Camp Lee, Petersburg, Virginia on June 2, 1919.

## 112th MACHINE GUN BATTALION

## Company B

CLEATON, JOHN THOMAS, private: Previously served in the Machine Gun Company, 4th Infantry Regiment, Virginia National Guard. Transferred to this company on September 27, 1917. Transferred to the Sanitary Detachment, 114th Infantry Regiment, 57th Infantry Brigade of this division on December 10, 1917.

MCDANIEL, THOMAS, private: Previously served in Machine Gun Company, 4th Infantry Regiment, Virginia National Guard, subsequently designated as this company. Promoted to mess sergeant on March 19, 1918, and reduced to private on May 11, 1918. Transferred to the Sanitation Detachment of this company on June 1, 1918. Served overseas from June 15, 1918, until May 22, 1919. Honorably discharged on May 29, 1919.

WILLIAMS, THOMAS L., private: Previously served in Machine Gun Company, 4th Infantry Regiment, Virginia National Guard, subsequently designated as this company. Honorably discharged on January 21, 1919, having performed no overseas service.

## 30th DIVISION

## 105th AMMUNITION TRAIN (FIELD ARTILLERY)

## Company D

WHITE, WILLIE DAVID, private: Registered for Selective Service on June 5, 1917, at age 27; occupation – farmer. Inducted as a private at Windsor on September 28, 1917, and transported to Camp Jackson, Columbia, South Carolina. Assigned to this company. Transferred to the 55th Depot Brigade, Camp Sevier, South Carolina on May 13, 1918.

## 105th ENGINEERS REGIMENT

## Company A

BRACY, ODIE LAWRENCE, private: Previously served in Company B, 331st Infantry, 166th Infantry Brigade, 83rd Division. Transferred to this company on an undisclosed date subsequent to December 5, 1918, while serving overseas. Returned from overseas on April 13, 1919, and was honorably discharged at Camp Jackson, Columbia, South Carolina on April 19, 1919.

## 55th FIELD ARTILLERY BRIGADE

## 113TH FIELD ARTILLERY REGIMENT

### HEADQUARTERS COMPANY

HALE, ARTHUR ELMER, private: Registered for Selective Service on June 5, 1917, at age 21; occupation – farmer. Inducted as a private at Windsor on March 29, 1918, and transported to Camp Jackson, Columbia, South Carolina. Assigned to this company. Served overseas from May 26, 1918, until March 19, 1919. Honorably discharged at Camp Jackson on March 29, 1919.

MIZELL, CHARLES MACK, private: Registered for Selective Service as a Bertie County resident in Berkley, Virginia on June 5, 1917, at age 22; occupation – ship carpenter. Inducted as a private at Windsor on May 28, 1918, and transported to Camp Jackson, Columbia, South Carolina. Assigned to this company. Served overseas from May 1918 until March 1919. Honorably discharged at Camp Jackson on April 4, 1919.

### SUPPLY COMPANY

HARRELL, LONNIE EDWARD, wagoner: Previously served in Battery E, 143rd Field Artillery Regiment, 65th Field Artillery Brigade, 40th Division. Transferred as a private to this company on August 2, 1918, while serving overseas. Promoted to wagoner on August 28, 1918. Returned from overseas on March 19, 1919, and honorably discharged at Camp Jackson, Columbia, South Carolina on March 28, 1919.

### SANITARY DETACHMENT

NORFLEET, FRANK PUGH, private: Registered for Selective Service on June 5, 1917, at age 24; occupation – farm laborer. In-
ducted as a private at Windsor on March 27, 1918, and transported to Camp Jackson, Columbia, South Carolina. Initially assigned to the 156th Depot Brigade and transferred to this detachment on April 23, 1918. Served overseas from May 27, 1918, until March 18, 1919. Honorably discharged at Camp Jackson on March 29, 1919.

### Battery F

COWAND, ALLCY, private: Previously served in Battery A, 2nd Battalion, Field Artillery Replacement Draft, Camp Jackson, Columbia, South Carolina. Transferred to this battery on July 13, 1918, while serving overseas. Returned from overseas on March 18, 1919, and honorably discharged at Camp Jackson on March 28, 1919.

VAN NORTWICK, DAVID, private: Previously served in the Camp Jackson Automatic Replacement Draft (field artillery). Transferred to this battery on August 27, 1918, while serving overseas. Returned from overseas on March 19, 1919. Honorably discharged at Camp Jackson, Columbia, South Carolina on March 28, 1919.

## 59th INFANTRY BRIGADE

## 117th INFANTRY REGIMENT

### SUPPLY COMPANY

WHITE, OSCAR SUTTON, private first class: Registered for Selective Service on June 5, 1917, at age 23; occupation – farmer. Inducted as a private at Windsor on March 27, 1918, and transported to Camp Jackson, Columbia, South Carolina. Assigned to this company. Sent overseas on May 11, 1918. Promoted to private first class on January 7, 1919. Returned from overseas on March 27, 1919, and honorably discharged at Fort Oglethorpe, Chickamauga Park, Georgia on April 17, 1919.

YATES, WILLIAM J., private: Registered for Selective Service on June 5, 1917, at age 22; occupation – farmer. Inducted as a private at Windsor on March 29, 1918, and transported to Camp Jackson, Columbia, South Carolina. Initially assigned to the 156th Depot Brigade and transferred to this company on an undisclosed date, but likely on or about April 25, 1918. Served overseas from May 11, 1918, until March 27, 1919. Honorably discharged at Fort Oglethorpe, Chickamauga Park, Georgia on April 17, 1919.

## Company G

CHERRY, WILLIAM ALGA, private: Registered for Selective Service on June 5, 1917, at age 22; occupation – farmer. Inducted as a private at Windsor on March 27, 1918, and transported to Camp Jackson, Columbia, South Carolina. Initially assigned to the 156th Depot Brigade and transferred to this company on April 25, 1918. Sent overseas on May 11, 1918. Slightly wounded on September 10, 1918. Returned from overseas on April 2, 1919. Honorably discharged at Fort Oglethorpe, Chickamauga Park, Georgia, on April 15, 1919.

## Company K

MORRIS, SOLIE LEE, private: Registered for Selective Service on June 5, 1917, at age 21; occupation – farmer. Inducted as a private at Windsor on March 27, 1918, and transported to Camp Jackson, Columbia, South Carolina. Initially assigned to the 156th Depot Brigade and transferred to this company on April 25, 1918. Sent overseas on May 11, 1918. Severely wounded and "shell shocked" on October 6, 1918. Returned from overseas on April 2, 1919, and honorably discharged at Fort Oglethorpe, Chickamauga Park, Georgia, on April 16, 1919.

## Company L

ROANE, JULIUS VANCE, private: Registered for Selective Service on June 5, 1917, at age 23; occupation – farmer. Inducted as a private at Windsor on March 29, 1918,

and transported to Camp Jackson, Columbia, South Carolina. Initially assigned to the 156th Depot Brigade and transferred to this company on April 24, 1918. Served overseas from May 11, 1918, until April 2, 1919. Honorably discharged at Fort Oglethorpe, Chickamauga Park, Georgia on April 16, 1919.

## 118th INFANTRY REGIMENT

## Company C

HAIGHT, THOMAS EDWIN, supply sergeant: Previously served in Company C, 2nd Infantry Regiment, Virginia National Guard. Transferred as a private to this company on August 17, 1917. Promoted to corporal on January 25, 1918, to sergeant on May 10, 1918, and to supply sergeant on June 7, 1918. Sent overseas on June 15, 1918. Transferred to Company B, 116th Infantry Regiment, 58th Infantry Brigade, 29th Division on December 26, 1918.

## 60th INFANTRY BRIGADE

## 119th INFANTRY REGIMENT

## (ORIGINALLY 2nd INFANTRY REGIMENT, NORTH CAROLINA NATIONAL GUARD)

## Machine Gun Company

PERRY, WILLIAM JOSEPH, private first class: Previously served in Company E, 321st Infantry Regiment, 161st Infantry Brigade, 81st Division. Transferred to this company on an undisclosed date, but likely on or about October 16, 1917. Sent overseas on May 11, 1918. Promoted to private first class on November 1, 1918. Returned from overseas on April 22, 1919, and honorably discharged at Camp Jackson, Columbia, South Carolina on April 7, 1919.

## Company H

JERNIGAN, OSIE CLARENCE, private first class: Previously served in Company E, 321st Infantry Regiment, 161st Infantry Brigade, 81st Division. Transferred as a private to this company on October 16, 1917. Sent overseas on May 12, 1918, and promoted to private first class on June 1, 1918. Returned from overseas on April 2, 1919, and honorably discharged at Camp Jackson, Columbia, South Carolina on April 7, 1919.

## Company I

BRITT, JAMES HENRY, sergeant: Enlisted as a private in the North Carolina National Guard at Edenton on June 28, 1916, at age 21; occupation – farmer. Served in Company I, 2nd Infantry Regiment, North Carolina National Guard, subsequently redesignated as this company. May have served in Company D of this regiment, but no dates of transfer or period of service disclosed in extant records. Promoted to corporal on March 2, 1917, and to sergeant on August 30, 1918. Served overseas from May 12, 1918, until April 2, 1919. Honorably discharged at Camp Jackson, Columbia, South Carolina on April 7, 1919.

HARRELL, ROLAND, private: Previously served in Company E, 321st Infantry Regiment, 161st Infantry Brigade, 81st Division. Transferred to this company on October 16, 1917. Sent overseas on May 21, 1918. Killed in action in France on August 2, 1918.

LEE, ROBERT EDWARD, private: Previously served in Company E, 32st Infantry Regiment, 161st Infantry Brigade, 81st Division. Transferred to this company on October 16, 1917. Sent overseas on May 12, 1918. Severely wounded on October 8, 1918. Returned from overseas January 22, 1919. Honorably discharged on May 13, 1920,

with a service-connected disability rated as 40 percent.

MILLER, ZEBULON THOMAS, private: Previously served in Company E, 321st Infantry Regiment, 161st Infantry Brigade, 81st Division. Transferred to this company on October 16, 1917. Sent overseas on May 12, 1918. Severely wounded on September 5, 1918. Returned from overseas on April 2, 1919, and honorably discharged at Camp Jackson, Columbia, South Carolina on April 7, 1919.

TAYLOE, JONATHAN STANLEY, private: Enlisted at Goldsboro in the North Carolina National Guard on June 6, 1917, at age 27. Assigned to Company I, 2nd Infantry North Carolina National Guard, subsequently redesignated as this company. Sent overseas on May 12, 1918. Killed in action in a "front line trench" on August 9, 1918.

## Company K

BAZEMORE, WILLIAM HOWARD, private: Previously served in Company E, 321st Infantry Regiment, 161st Infantry Brigade, 81st Division. Transferred to this company on an undisclosed date, but likely on October 16, 1917. Honorably discharged on November 1, 1917, by reason of an "erroneous induction."

HOGGARD, JOSEPH WRIGHT, corporal: Previously served in Company E, 321st Infantry Regiment, 161st Infantry Brigade, 81st Division. Transferred as a private to this company on October 16, 1917. Sent overseas on May 12, 1918, and promoted to corporal on July 7, 1918. Killed in action at Bellicourt, France on September 29, 1918.

WALSTON, LESLIE, private: Previously served in Company E, 321st Infantry Regiment, 161st Infantry Brigade, 81st Division. Transferred to this company on October 16, 1917. Sent overseas on May 12, 1918. Killed in action by an exploding shell in a "front line trench" on August 4, 1918.

## Company M

HARRELL, CLYDE B., corporal: Previously served in Company E, 321st Infantry Regiment, 161st Infantry Brigade, 81st Division. Transferred as a private to this company on October 16, 1917. Promoted to corporal on January 21, 1918. Served overseas from May 12, 1918, until April 2, 1919. Honorably discharged at Camp Jackson, Columbia, South Carolina on April 7, 1919.

HUGHES, WHITTIE H., private: Registered for Selective Service on June 5, 1917, at age 21; occupation – laborer at lumber company. Inducted as a private at Windsor on September 28, 1917, and transported to Camp Jackson, Columbia, South Carolina. Assigned to this company. Honorably discharged at Camp Sevier, near Taylors, South Carolina on November 15, 1917, having performed no overseas service. Discharged due to a service-connected disability the degree of which is not disclosed in service record.

JONES, JESSE, private: Previously served in Company E, 321st Infantry Regiment, 161st Infantry Brigade, 81st Division. Transferred to this company on October 16, 1917. Incarcerated at the United States Disciplinary Barracks, Fort Leavenworth, Kansas on April 22, 1918. Dishonorably discharged on June 9, 1919, pursuant to a general court martial.

QUINCY, ERNEST LINWOOD, private: Previously served in Company E, 321st Infantry Regiment, 161st Infantry Brigade, 81st Division. Transferred to this company on October 16, 1917. Sent overseas on May 12, 1918, and promoted to private first class on June 1, 1918. Reduced to private on July 1, 1918. Returned from overseas on April 2, 1919, and honorably discharged at Camp Jackson, Columbia, South Carolina on April 7, 1919.

WADSWORTH (WARDSWORTH), VAN PERRY, private: Previously served in Company E, 321st Infantry Regiment, 161st Infantry Brigade, 81st Division. Transferred to this company on October 16, 1917. Deserted at Camp Sevier, near Taylors, South Carolina on December 23, 1917.

WHITE, JAMES E., private: Registered for Selective Service on June 5, 1917, at age 22; occupation – farmer. Inducted as a private at Windsor on September 28, 1918, and transported to Camp Jackson, Columbia, South Carolina. Initially assigned to the 156th Depot Brigade and transferred to this company on October 15, 1917. Honorably discharged on May 20, 1919, having performed no overseas service.

# 120th INFANTRY REGIMENT

# (ORIGINALLY 3rd INFANTRY REGIMENT, NORTH CAROLINA NATIONAL GUARD)

## Company B

PARKER, WILLIAM KING, corporal: Registered for Selective Service as a Bertie County resident at Norfolk, Virginia on June 2, 1917, at age 24; occupation – salesman. Enlisted as a private in the North Carolina National Guard at Raleigh on May 28, 1917, at age 24. Assigned to Company B, 3rd Infantry Regiment, subsequently redesignated as this company. Promoted to corporal on November 1, 1917. Sent overseas on May 12, 1918. Severely wounded on September 29, 1918. Returned from overseas on January 19, 1919. Honorably discharged on February 6, 1919, with a disability rated as 20 percent.

## Company H

**BELL, WILLIAM SIMON**, private first class: Enlisted as a private at Roxobel on June 5, 1917, at age 21. Transported to Camp Sevier, near Taylors, South Carolina. Served in Company H, 3rd Infantry Regiment, North Carolina National Guard, subsequently redesignated as this company. Promoted to private first class on August 25, 1917, or October 18, 1917, and reduced in rank to private on January 20, 1918. Sent overseas on May 12, 1918. Promoted to private first class on June 1, 1918. Slightly wounded by shrapnel in action on the Hindenburg Line of the Western Front on September 29, 1918. Returned from overseas to Charleston, South Carolina on April 13, 1919. Honorably discharged at Camp Jackson, Columbia, South Carolina on April 18, 1919.

**BISHOP, REUBEN DEJOHNETTE**, corporal: Enlisted as a private at Warrenton on August 21, 1917, at age 18. Served in Company H, 3rd Infantry Regiment, North Carolina National Guard, subsequently redesignated as this company. Promoted to private first class on March 21, 1918. Served overseas (dates not reported) during which he was "severely wounded" in the shoulder on the Hindenburg Line of the Western Front on September 29, 1918. Promoted to corporal on November 1, 1918. Returned from overseas on an undisclosed date and honorably discharged on February 8, 1919.

**BRACY, WILLIE E.**, private: Enlisted as a private at Warrenton on August 8, 1917, at age 23. Served in Company H, 3rd Infantry Regiment, North Carolina National Guard, subsequently redesignated as this company. Sent overseas on May 12, 1918. Wounded, either on October 15, 1918 or October 21, 1918. Returned from overseas on January 31, 1919, and honorably discharged on June 5, 1919.

**JENKINS, HENRY, C.**, corporal: Enlisted in the North Carolina National Guard as a private in Bertie County on May 7, 1917, 1917, at age 22. Served in Company H, 3rd Infantry Regiment, North Carolina National Guard, subsequently redesignated as this company. Promoted to corporal on November 1, 1917. Transferred to Company A, 30th Infantry Regiment, 6th Infantry Brigade, 3rd Division on January 23, 1918.

**NORFLEET, ERIC P.**, second lieutenant: Enlisted as a private at Warrenton on November 29, 1915, at age 18. Served in Company H, 3rd Infantry Regiment, North Carolina National Guard, subsequently redesignated as this company. Promoted to corporal on October 27, 1916, to sergeant on July 26, 1917, and to first sergeant on February 12, 1918. Sent overseas on May 22, 1918. Transferred to Army Officers Candidate School on July 26, 1918. Honorably discharged on September 30, 1918, to accept an officer's commission. Appointed second lieutenant on October 1, 1918, and assigned to the 116th Infantry Regiment, 58th Infantry Brigade, 29th Division.

## 35th DIVISION

## 69th INFANTRY BRIGADE

## 137th INFANTRY REGIMENT

## Company K

**MIZELL, THOMAS FRANKLIN**, private: Previously served in the Field Artillery Replacement Draft, Camp Jackson, South Carolina. Transferred to this company on July 10, 1918. Served overseas from July 23, 1918, until April 23, 1919. Honorably discharged at Camp Funston, near Manhattan, Kansas on May 8, 1919.

## 38th DIVISION

### 75th INFANTRY BRIGADE

### 162nd INFANTRY REGIMENT

#### Company C

ROANE, PERRY TYLER, private: Previously served in Company F, 54th Infantry Regiment, 12th Infantry Brigade, 6th Division. Transferred to this company on July 3, 1918. Served overseas from September 1, 1918, until May 26, 1919. Honorably discharged on June 10, 1919.

## 40th DIVISION

### 80th INFANTRY BRIGADE

### 159th INFANTRY REGIMENT

#### MACHINE GUN COMPANY

LAWRENCE, LUTHER COHEN, private: Registered for Selective Service on June 5, 1917, at age 22; occupation – farmer. Inducted as a private at Windsor on July 22, 1918, and transported to Camp Hancock, near Augusta, Georgia. Assigned to the 53rd Depot Brigade. Sent overseas on November 10, 1918. Transferred to this company on January 13, 1919. Returned from overseas on April 5, 1919, and honorably discharged on April 16, 1919.

#### Company G

RAWLS, CLARENCE, private: Previously served in the Camp Hancock Automatic Replacement Draft (machine gun). Transferred to this company on November 24, 1918,

while serving overseas. Returned from overseas on April 5, 1919, and honorably discharged on April 16, 1919.

## 65th FIELD ARTILLERY BRIGADE

### 143rd FIELD ARTILLERY REGIMENT

#### Battery E

HARRELL, LONNIE EDWARD, private: Registered for Selective Service on June 5, 1917, at age 24; occupation – farmer. Inducted as a private at Windsor on March 29, 1918, and transported to Camp Jackson, Columbia, South Carolina. Initially assigned to the 156th Depot Brigade and transferred to this battery on May 15, 1918. Sent overseas on May 27, 1918. Transferred to Supply Company, 113th Field Artillery Regiment, 55th Field Artillery Brigade, 30th Division on August 2, 1918.

## 41st DIVISION

### 116th ENGINEERS REGIMENT

### MISCELLANEOUS (NO COMPANY IDENTIFIED)

BURDEN, WALTER JACKSON, private: Transferred to this company from the October Automatic Replacement Draft (Engineers) at Washington Barracks, Washington, D.C. on September 30, 1918. Sent overseas on October 20, 1918. Transferred to Company E, 306th Engineers Regiment, 81st Division on December 18, 1918.

COX, WILLIAM LEE, private: Previously served in Company D, 214th Engineers

Regiment, 14th Division. Transferred to this regiment on September 14, 1918. Sent overseas on October 1, 1918, and transferred to Company B, 128th Engineers Regiment on November 20, 1918.

## 82nd INFANTRY BRIGADE

## 163rd INFANTRY REGIMENT

### Company G

DUNNING, GARFIELD, private: Previously served in Company A, 318th Machine Gun Battalion, 162nd Infantry Brigade, 81st Division. Transferred to this company on May 21, 1918, while serving overseas. Transferred to Company K, 28th Infantry Regiment, 2nd Infantry Brigade, 1st Division on May 24, 1918.

## 42nd DIVISION

## 117th ENGINEERS REGIMENT

### Company C

JONES, RUBIN, private: Previously served in Company G, 2nd Infantry Regiment, North Carolina National Guard. Transferred to this company on August 20, 1917. Served overseas from October 17, 1917, until April 28, 1919. Honorably discharged on May 12, 1919.

## 83rd INFANTRY BRIGADE

## 166th INFANTRY REGIMENT

### Company G

BEASLEY, CLARENCE WOOD, private first class: Previously served in Company E, 322th Infantry Regiment, 161st Infantry Brigade, 81st Division. Transferred as a private to this company on August 26, 1918, while serving overseas. Promoted to private first class on November 1, 1918. Returned from overseas on April 2, 1919. Honorably discharged at Camp Merritt, New Jersey on April 12, 1919.

## 84th INFANTRY BRIGADE

## 168th INFANTRY REGIMENT

### Company D

MINTON, JOHN BAYARD, private: Previously served in Company L, 323rd Infantry Regiment, 162nd Infantry Brigade, 81st Division. Transferred to this company on August 24, 1918, while serving overseas. Slightly wounded on October 16, 1918. Returned from overseas on February 22, 1919. Honorably discharged on March 6, 1919, with a physical disability rated as ten percent.

## 78th DIVISION

## 153rd FIELD ARTILLERY BRIGADE

## 307th FIELD ARTILLERY REGIMENT

### Battery B

BEASLEY, JOHN CECIL, private: Previously served in Battery C, 8th Field Artillery Regiment Replacement Draft, Camp Jackson, South Carolina, and transferred to this battery on an undisclosed date. Served overseas from October 28, 1918, until May 14, 1919, and honorably discharged at Camp Dix, near Trenton, New Jersey on May 23, 1919.

## Battery C

EARLY, JOSEPH MERRILL, private: Transferred to this battery from Battery 14, October Automatic Replacement Draft, Field Artillery, Camp Jackson, South Carolina on an undisclosed date, apparently while serving overseas. Returned from overseas on May 14, 1919, and honorably discharged at Camp Dix, near Trenton, New Jersey on May 23, 1919.

## Battery D

BAKER, HIRAM STANLEY, private: Transferred to this battery from Battery C, 8th Field Artillery Regiment Replacement Draft, Camp Jackson, South Carolina on October 15, 1918. Served overseas from October 28, 1918, until May 14, 1919, and honorably discharged at Camp Dix, near Trenton, New Jersey on May 23, 1919.

## 308th FIELD ARTILLERY REGIMENT

## Company B

TODD, WILLIAM AUGUSTA, private: Registered for Selective Service on June 5, 1918, at age 21; occupation – undisclosed. Inducted as a private at Windsor on August 25, 1918, and transported to Camp Jackson, Columbia, South Carolina. Initially assigned to the 156th Depot Brigade and transferred to this battery on October 15, 1918. Served overseas from October 18, 1918, until May 14, 1919. Honorably discharged at Camp Dix, near Trenton, New Jersey on May 27, 1919.

## 309th FIELD ARTILLERY REGIMENT

## HEADQUARTERS COMPANY

PRITCHARD, LLOYD ERNEST, wagoner: Previously served in the October Automatic Replacement Draft, Camp Jackson, Columbia, South Carolina. Transferred as a private to this company on December 9, 1918, while serving overseas. Promoted to wagoner on April 1, 1919. Returned from overseas on May 10, 1919, and honorably discharged at Camp Dix, near Trenton, New Jersey on May 18, 1919.

## Battery C

TODD, FRANK CRAIG, private: Previously served in the Field Artillery Replacement Draft, Camp Jackson, South Carolina. Transferred to this battery on October 15, 1918. Served overseas from October 28, 1918, until May 10, 1919. Honorably discharged at Camp Dix, near Trenton, New Jersey on May 18, 1919.

## 79th DIVISION

## 158th INFANTRY BRIGADE

## 316th INFANTRY REGIMENT

## MISCELLANEOUS (NO COMPANY IDENTIFIED)

HALE, JOHN CLIFTON, second lieutenant: Honorably discharged while serving overseas as a supply sergeant in Company E, 321st Infantry Regiment, 161st Infantry Brigade, 81st Division on October 31, 1918, to accept an officer's commission. Appointed second lieutenant in this regiment on November 1, 1918. Returned from overseas on

June 4, 1919, and honorably discharged on June 13, 1919.

# 80th DIVISION

## 159th INFANTRY BRIGADE

## 317th INFANTRY REGIMENT

### Company A

CLEATON, JOHN THOMAS, private: Previously served in the Sanitary Detachment, 116th Infantry Regiment, 58th Infantry Brigade, 29th Division. Transferred to this company on December 5, 1918, while serving overseas. Returned from overseas on June 1, 1919, and honorably discharged at Camp Lee, Petersburg, Virginia on June 11, 1919.

# 81st DIVISION

## 306th AMMUNITION TRAIN (FIELD ARTILLERY)

### Company B

GREEN, DAVID CROCKETT, private first class: Previously served in Company D of this ammunition train. Transferred as a private to this company on January 19, 1919, while serving overseas. Promoted to private first class on April 1, 1919. Transferred back to Company D on May 21, 1919.

HARMON, JAMES REDDICK, private: Registered for Selective Service on June 5, 1917, at age 30; occupation – farmer. Inducted as a private at Windsor on March 27, 1918, and transported to Camp Jackson, Columbia, South Carolina. Initially assigned to the

156th Depot Brigade and transferred to this company on May 25, 1918. Transferred to the 156th Depot Brigade on June 21, 1918.

### Company C

HOLLOMON, DAVID GEORGE, wagoner: Registered for Selective Service on June 5, 1917, at age 21; occupation – farmer. Inducted as a private at Windsor on April 26, 1918, and transported to Camp Jackson, Columbia, South Carolina. Initially assigned to the 156th Depot Brigade and transferred to this company on May 18, 1918. Promoted to wagoner on July 12, 1918. Served overseas from August 8, 1918, until June 22, 1919. Honorably discharged at Camp Jackson on June 26, 1919.

### Company D

GREEN, DAVID CROCKETT, private first class: Registered for Selective Service on June 4, 1917, at age 27; occupation – section foreman, railroad. Inducted as a private at Windsor on March 29, 1918, and transported to Camp Jackson, Columbia, South Carolina. Assigned to this company. Sent overseas on April 8, 1918. Transferred to Company B of this ammunition train on January 19, 1919. Transferred back to this company as a private first class on May 21, 1919, while still serving overseas. Returned from overseas on June 22, 1919, and honorably discharged at Camp Jackson on June 26, 1919.

WILLIFORD, COLBERT, wagoner: Registered for Selective Service as a Bertie County resident in Norfolk, Virginia on May 31, 1917, at age 23; occupation – salesman. Inducted as a private at Windsor on April 26, 1918, and transported to Camp Jackson, Columbia, South Carolina. Assigned to this company. Promoted to private first class on July 18, 1918. Sent overseas on August 8, 1918. Promoted to wagoner on April 1, 1919. Returned from overseas on June 22, 1919, and honorably discharged at Camp Jackson on June 27, 1919.

# 306th ENGINEERS REGIMENT

## Company A

PIERCE, JOSEPH NORMAN, private first class: Registered for Selective Service on June 5, 1917, at age 22; occupation – farmer. Inducted as a private at Windsor on May 28, 1918, and transported to Camp Jackson, Columbia, South Carolina. Initially assigned to the 156th Depot Brigade and transferred to this company on June 23, 1918. Sent overseas on July 31, 1918. Promoted to private first class on May 1, 1919. Returned from overseas on June 15, 1919, and honorably discharged on June 18, 1919.

ROGERSON, JESSE W., private first class: Registered for Selective Service on June 5, 1917, at age 21; occupation – mechanic. Inducted as a private at Windsor on May 28, 1918, and transported to Camp Jackson, Columbia, South Carolina. Assigned to this company. Sent overseas on July 31, 1918, and promoted to private first class on May 19, 1919. Returned from overseas on June 15, 1919, and honorably discharged on June 23, 1919.

## Company C

MINTON, SELBY RADNOR, private: Registered for Selective Service on June 5, 1917, at age 23; occupation – farmer. Inducted as a private at Windsor on November 16, 1917, and transported to Camp Jackson, Columbia, South Carolina. Assigned to this company. Honorably discharged on January 22, 1918, due to a service-connected disability rated as 50 percent.

## Company E

BURDEN, WALTER JACKSON, private: Previously served in the 116th Engineers Regiment, 41st Division. Transferred to this company on December 18, 1918, while serving overseas. Returned from overseas on April 17, 1919. Honorably discharged on May 17, 1919.

## Company F

THOMAS, FRED WILLIAM, private: Registered for Selective Service on June 5, 1917, at age 30; occupation – mechanic. Inducted as a private at Windsor on May 28, 1918, and transported to Camp Jackson, Columbia, South Carolina. Assigned to this company. Served overseas from July 31, 1918, until June 15, 1919. Honorably discharged on June 20, 1919.

# MISCELLANEOUS (NO COMPANY IDENTIFIED)

WHITE, ERNEST RUSSELL, private: Previously served in Machine Gun Company, 322nd Infantry Regiment, 161st Infantry Brigade, 81st Division. Transferred to this regiment on April 19, 1919, while serving overseas. Transferred back to Machine Gun Company, 322nd Infantry Regiment on May 31, 1919.

# 316th MACHINE GUN BATTALION

## Company B

ALEXANDER, SEATON NORWOOD, private: Registered for Selective Service on June 5, 1917, at age 26; occupation – laborer. Inducted as a private at Windsor on October 22, 1917, and transported to Camp Jackson, Columbia, South Carolina. Assigned to this company in which he served until transferred to the 19th Engineers Regiment on February 21, 1918.

COBB, DAVID LEE, corporal: Registered for Selective Service on June 5, 1917, at age 22; occupation — farm laborer. Inducted as a private at Windsor on October 23, 1917, and transported to Camp Jackson, Columbia, South Carolina. Assigned to this company and transferred to the School for Bakers and Cooks at Camp Jackson on January 17, 1918. Transferred back to this company on March 18, 1918. Promoted to private first class on October 1, 1918, and to corporal on October 25, 1918. Served overseas from July 31, 1918, until June 20, 1919. Honorably discharged at Camp Lee, Petersburg, Virginia on June 28. 1919.

## MILITARY POLICE

### Company A

TARKENTON, JOSEPH R., private: Previously served in Headquarters Company, 321st Infantry Regiment, 161st Infantry Brigade, 81st Division. Transferred to this company on October 22, 1917. Transferred to Company A, 1st Army Corps Headquarters Regiment on January 21, 1918.

## 161st INFANTRY BRIGADE

## 321st INFANTRY REGIMENT

## HEADQUARTERS COMPANY

POWELL, ALLEN THURMAN, private first class: Registered for Selective Service on June 5, 1917, at age 21; occupation — farmer. Inducted as a private at Windsor on September 5, 1917, and transported to Camp Jackson, Columbia, South Carolina. Assigned to this company. Promoted to private first class on October 29, 1917. Served overseas from July 30, 1918, until June 20, 1919. Honorably discharged on June 28, 1919, at Camp Lee, Petersburg, Virginia.

SPRUILL, MARTIN LUTHER, private: Registered for Selective Service on June 5, 1917, at age 21; occupation — farmer. Inducted as a private at Windsor on September 28, 1917, and transported to Camp Jackson, Columbia, South Carolina. Initially assigned to this company and transferred to Company E of this regiment on September 29, 1917.

TARKENTON, JOSEPH R., private: Registered for Selective Service on June 5, 1917, at age 22; occupation — laborer. Inducted as a private at Windsor on September 5, 1917, and transported to Camp Jackson, Columbia, South Carolina. Assigned to this company. Transferred to Company A, Military Police of this division on October 22, 1917.

## SUPPLY COMPANY

FORE, STONEWALL JACKSON, regimental supply sergeant: Registered for Selective Service on June 5, 1917, at age 30; occupation — bank cashier. Inducted as a private at Windsor on October 4, 1917, and transported to Camp Jackson, Columbia, South Carolina. Assigned to this company. Promoted to corporal on February 14, 1918, to sergeant on March 8, 1918, and to regimental supply sergeant on June 1, 1918. Served overseas from June 30, 1918, until June 20, 1919. Honorably discharged at Camp Lee, Petersburg, Virginia on June 27, 1919.

MITCHELL, ROBERT JUDSON, private: Registered for Selective Service as a Bertie County resident at Newport News, Virginia on June 5, 1917, at age 28; occupation — machinist's helper. Inducted as a private at Windsor on September 5, 1917, and transported to Camp Jackson, Columbia, South Carolina. Assigned to this company. Promoted to horseshoer on October 10, 1917, and reduced to private on December 9, 1917. Transferred to the 1st Company, 1st Air Service Mechanical Regiment on December 10, 1917.

## Company E

BAZEMORE, WILLIAM HOWARD, private: Registered for Selective Service on June 5, 1917, at age 24; occupation - farmer. Inducted as a private at Windsor on October 12, 1917, and transported to Camp Jackson, Columbia, South Carolina. Assigned to this company until transferred to Company K, 119th Infantry Regiment on an undisclosed date, but likely on October 16, 1917.

BRYANT, CLARENCE RUDOLPH, corporal: Registered for Selective Service on June 5, 1917, at age 23; occupation – sawmill foreman. Inducted as a private at Windsor on October 4, 1917, and transported to Camp Jackson, Columbia, South Carolina. Assigned to this company. Served overseas from December 1918 until April 3, 1919. Honorably discharged on April 7, 1919.

BURKETT, ERNEST EARL, corporal: Registered for Selective Service on June 5, 1917, at age 27; occupation – farmer. Inducted as a private at Windsor on September 20, 1917, and transported to Camp Jackson, Columbia, South Carolina. Assigned to this company and promoted to private first class on January 2, 1918. Transferred to the Machine Gun Company of this regiment on March 4, 1918. Transferred back to this company on June 23, 1918. Sent overseas on July 30, 1918, and promoted to corporal on September 1, 1918. Transferred to 287th Military Police Corps on May 30, 1919.

CASTELLOE, OBED, sergeant: Registered for Selective Service on June 5, 1917, at age 21; occupation – farmer. Inducted as a private at Windsor on October 4, 1917, and transported to Camp Jackson, Columbia, South Carolina. Assigned to this company. Promoted to corporal on October 11, 1917, and to sergeant on January 2, 1918. Transferred to the Central Officers Training School at Camp Gordon, Augusta, Georgia on March 19, 1918.

EARLY, JOHN FINCH, corporal: Registered for Selective Service on June 5, 1917, at age 23; occupation – farmer. Inducted as a private at Windsor on October 4, 1917, and transported to Camp Jackson, Columbia, South Carolina. Assigned to this company. Promoted to corporal on January 12, 1918, and served overseas from June 11, 1918, until April 11, 1919. Honorably discharged at Camp Jackson on April 14, 1919.

HALE, JOHN CLIFTON, supply sergeant: Registered for Selective Service as a Bertie County resident in Washington County, Georgia on or about June 5, 1917, at age 26; occupation – farmer. Inducted as a private at Windsor on September 20, 1917, and transported to Camp Jackson, Columbia, South Carolina. Assigned to this company. Promoted to corporal on October 10, 1917, to sergeant on May 20, 1918, and to supply sergeant on May 23, 1918. Sent overseas on July 31, 1918. Honorably discharged on October 31, 1918, to accept an officer's commission (in the 316th Infantry Regiment, 158th Infantry Brigade, 79th Division).

HARRELL, CLYDE B., private: Registered for Selective Service on June 5, 1917, at age 29; occupation – farmer. Inducted as a private at Windsor on September 5, 1917, and transported to Camp Jackson, Columbia, South Carolina. Assigned to this company. Transferred to Company M, 119th Infantry Regiment, 60th Infantry Brigade, 30th Division on October 16, 1917.

HARRELL, ROLAND, private: Registered for Selective Service on June 5, 1917, at age 23. Inducted as a private at Windsor on September 28, 1917, and transported to Camp Jackson, Columbia, South Carolina. Assigned to this company. Transferred to Company I, 119th Infantry Regiment, 60th Infantry Brigade, 30th Division on October 16, 1917.

HOGGARD, JOSEPH WRIGHT, private: Registered for Selective Service on June 5, 1917, at age 21; occupation – farmer. Inducted as a private at Windsor on October 4, 1917, and transported to Camp Jackson, Columbia, South Carolina. Assigned to this company. Transferred to Company K, 119th Infantry Regiment, 60th Infantry Brigade, 30th Division on October 16, 1917.

JERNIGAN, OSIE CLARENCE, private: Registered for Selective Service on June 5, 1917, at age 21; occupation – farmer. Inducted as a private at Windsor on September 28, 1917, and transported to Camp Jackson, Columbia, South Carolina. Assigned to this company. Transferred to Company H, 119th Infantry Regiment, 60th Infantry Brigade, 30th Division on October 16, 1917.

JONES, JESSE, private: Registered for Selective Service on June 5, 1917, at age 21; occupation – farmer. Inducted as a private at Windsor on September 28, 1917, and transported to Camp Jackson, Columbia, South Carolina. Assigned to this company. Transferred to Company M, 119th Infantry Regiment, 60th Infantry Brigade, 30th Division on October 16, 1917.

LEE, ROBERT EDWARD, private: Registered for Selective Service on June 5, 1917, at age 26; occupation – farmer. Inducted as a private at Windsor on October 4, 1917, and transported to Camp Jackson, Columbia, South Carolina. Assigned to this company. Transferred to Company I, 119th Infantry Regiment, 60th Infantry Brigade, 30th Division on October 16, 1917.

MILLER, ZEBULON THOMAS, private: Registered for Selective Service on June 5, 1917, at age 23; occupation – farmer. Inducted as a private at Windsor on September 28, 1917, and transported to Camp Jackson, Columbia, South Carolina. Assigned to this company. Transferred to Company I, 119th Infantry Regiment, 60th Infantry Brigade, 30th Division on October 16, 1917.

MITCHELL, CHARLES WALTER, corporal: Registered for Selective Service as a Bertie County resident in Newport News, Virginia on June 4, 1917, at age 24; occupation – fitter with a shipbuilder. Inducted as a private at Windsor on September 28, 1917, and transported to Camp Jackson, Columbia, South Carolina. Assigned to this company. Promoted to private first class on December 1, 1917, and to corporal on June 14, 1918. Served overseas from July 31, 1918, until June 20, 1919. Honorably discharged at Camp Lee, Petersburg, Virginia on June 28, 1919.

MITCHELL, WILLARD LEE, mess sergeant: Previously served as a noncommissioned officer in the army. Registered for Selective Service on June 5, 1917, at age 23; occupation – carpenter. Inducted as a private at Windsor on October 4, 1917, and transported to Camp Jackson, Columbia, South Carolina. Assigned to this company. Promoted to corporal on October 10, 1917, and to sergeant on December 7, 1917. Sent overseas on July 31, 1918. Promoted to mess sergeant on April 1, 1919. Honorably discharged on April 23, 1919, to accept an officer's commission in this regiment.

PARKER, CHARLES A., JR., sergeant: Registered for Selective Service on June 5, 1917, at age 24; occupation – laborer. Inducted as a private at Windsor on September 28, 1917, and transported to Camp Jackson, Columbia, South Carolina. Assigned to this company. Promoted to private first class on January 2, 1918, and to mechanic on April 19, 1918. Sent overseas on July 31, 1918. Promoted to corporal on September 1, 1918, and to sergeant on November 1, 1918. Returned from overseas on June 20, 1919, and honorably discharged at Camp Lee, Petersburg, Virginia on June 28, 1919.

PERRY, WILLIAM JOSEPH, private first class: Registered for Selective Service on June 5, 1917, at age 25; occupation – farmer. Inducted as a private at Windsor on September 28, 1917, and transported to Camp

Jackson, Columbia, South Carolina. Assigned to this company. Transferred to the Machine Gun Company, 119th Infantry Regiment, 60th Infantry Brigade, 30th Division on an undisclosed date, but likely on or about October 16, 1917.

PERRY, WILLIAM R., sergeant: Registered for Selective Service on June 5, 1917, at age 21; occupation – farmer. Inducted as a private at Windsor on September 28, 1917, and transported to Camp Jackson, Columbia, South Carolina. Assigned to this company. Promoted to private first class on June 14, 1918. Sent overseas on July 31, 1918, and promoted to sergeant on September 1, 1918. Returned from overseas on June 20, 1919, and honorably discharged at Camp Lee, Petersburg, Virginia on June 28, 1919.

QUINCY, ERNEST LINWOOD, private: Registered for Selective Service on June 5, 1917, at age 22; occupation – farmer. Inducted as a private at Windsor on September 28, 1917, and transported to Camp Jackson, Columbia, South Carolina. Assigned to this company. Transferred to Company M, 119th Infantry Regiment, 60th Infantry Brigade, 30th Division, October 16, 1917.

SPRUILL, MARTIN LUTHER, corporal: Previously served as a private in Headquarters Company of this regiment. Transferred to this company on September 29, 1917. Promoted to private first class on January 2, 1918, and to corporal on June 14, 1918. Served overseas from July 3, 1918, until June 20, 1919. Honorably discharged at Camp Lee, Petersburg, Virginia on June 28, 1919.

WADSWORTH (WARDSWORTH), VAN PERRY, private: Registered for Selective Service on June 5, 1917, at age 27; occupation – farmer. Inducted as a private at Windsor on October 4, 1917, and transported to Camp Jackson, Columbia, South Carolina. Assigned to this company. Transferred to Company M, 119th Infantry Regiment, 60th Infantry Brigade, 30th Di-

vision on October 16, 1917.

WALSTON, LESLIE, private: Registered for Selective Service on June 5, 1917, at age 26; occupation – farmer. Inducted as a private at Windsor on September 28, 1917, and transported to Camp Jackson, Columbia, South Carolina. Assigned to this company. Transferred to Company K, 119th Infantry Regiment, 60th Infantry Brigade, 30th Division on October 16, 1917.

WHITE, JAMES BINGHAM, private: Registered for Selective Service on June 5, 1917, at age 26; occupation – farmer. Inducted as a private at Windsor on October 4, 1917, and transported to Camp Jackson, Columbia, South Carolina. Assigned to this company. Transferred to Headquarters Company, 6th Infantry Regiment, 9th Infantry Brigade, 5th Division on February 16, 1918.

WHITE, LODOWICK H., first sergeant: Registered for Selective Service on June 5, 1917, at age 22; occupation – laborer. Inducted as a private at Windsor on September 28, 1917, and transported to Camp Jackson, Columbia, South Carolina. Assigned to this company. Promoted to corporal on October 11, 1917. Sent overseas on July 31, 1918. Promoted to sergeant on September 1, 1918. Slightly wounded on November 11, 1918. Promoted to first sergeant on January 15, 1919. Returned from overseas on June 20, 1919, and honorably discharged at Camp Lee, Petersburg, Virginia on June 28, 1919.

## Company F

JOHNSON, JOHNNIE, private: Registered for Selective Service on June 5, 1917, at age 21; occupation – farmer. Inducted as a private at Windsor on September 5, 1917, and transported to Camp Jackson, Columbia, South Carolina. Assigned to this company. Transferred to Company D, 6th Infantry Regiment, 9th Infantry Brigade, 5th Division on February 6, 1918.

## Company G

PUGH, EDWARD STEWART, sergeant: Previously served in Company H of this regiment. Transferred to this company on February 24, 1919, while serving overseas. Returned from overseas on June 20, 1919, and honorably discharged at Camp Lee, Petersburg, Virginia on June 28, 1919.

STALLINGS, CLIFTON, private: Registered for Selective Service on June 5, 1917, at age 22; occupation – farm laborer. Inducted as a private at Windsor on September 5, 1917, and transported to Camp Jackson, Columbia, South Carolina. Assigned to this company. Promoted to cook on October 2, 1917. Sent overseas on July 31, 1918. Reduced to private on September 2, 1918. Returned from overseas on June 20, 1919, and honorably discharged at Camp Lee, Petersburg, Virginia on June 28, 1919.

## Company H

PUGH, EDWARD STEWART, sergeant: Registered for Selective Service on June 5, 1917, at age 21; occupation – student. Inducted as a private at Windsor on September 5, 1917, and transported to Camp Jackson, Columbia, South Carolina. Assigned to this company. Promoted to corporal on October 13, 1917, and to sergeant on June 17, 1918. Sent overseas on July 31, 1918. Transferred to Company G of the regiment on February 24, 1919.

FOREHAND, JAMES B., sergeant: Registered for Selective Service on June 5, 1917, at age 24; occupation – farmer. Inducted as a private at Windsor on September 5, 1917, and transported to Camp Jackson, Columbia, South Carolina. Assigned to this company. Promoted to corporal on September 15, 1917 and to sergeant on October 13, 1917. Sent overseas on July 31, 1918, and transferred to 1st Battalion Army Officers Candidate School on October 5, 1918. Transferred back to this company on January 1, 1919. Returned from overseas on June 20,

1919, and honorably discharged at Camp Lee, Petersburg, Virginia on June 27, 1919.

HARDEN, LUTHER THOMAS, cook: Registered for Selective Service on June 5, 1917, at age 22; occupation – farmer. Inducted as a private at Windsor on September 5, 1917, and transported to Camp Jackson, Columbia, South Carolina. Assigned to this company. Promoted to cook on October 15, 1917, and transferred to the School for Bakers and Cooks at Camp Jackson on November 1, 1917. Transferred back to this company on January 7, 1918. Served overseas from July 30, 1918, until March 19, 1919. Honorably discharged at Camp Lee, Petersburg, Virginia on April 4, 1919.

## MACHINE GUN COMPANY

BURKETT, ERNEST EARL, private first class: Previously served in Company E of this regiment. Transferred to this company on March 4, 1918, and transferred back to Company E on June 23, 1918.

## MISCELLANEOUS (NO COMPANY IDENTIFIED)

MITCHELL, WILLARD LEE, second lieutenant: Previously served as an enlisted man in Company E of this regiment, from which he was honorably discharged on April 23, 1919, to accept an officer's commission. Appointed second lieutenant in this regiment on April 23, 1919, while serving overseas. Returned from overseas on June 20, 1919. Honorably discharged at Camp Stuart, Newport News, Virginia on July 11, 1919.

## 322nd INFANTRY REGIMENT

## SUPPLY COMPANY

WHITE, EDGAR, wagoner: Registered for Selective Service on June 5, 1917, at age 23;

occupation – farmer. Inducted as a private at Windsor on May 28, 1918, and transported to Camp Jackson, Columbia, South Carolina. Assigned to this company. Sent overseas on July 31, 1918. Promoted to wagoner on September 13, 1918. Returned from overseas on June 18, 1919, and honorably discharged on June 25, 1919.

## MACHINE GUN COMPANY

WHITE, ERNEST RUSSELL, private: Registered for Selective Service on June 5, 1917, at age 24; occupation – farmer. Inducted as a private at Windsor on May 28, 1918, and transported to Camp Jackson, Columbia, South Carolina. Assigned to this company. Sent overseas on July 31, 1918. Transferred to the 306th Engineers Regiment, 81st Division on April 19, 1919. Transferred back to this company on May 31, 1919. Returned from overseas on June 18, 1919, and honorably discharged at Camp Lee, Petersburg, Virginia on June 25, 1919.

WHITE, JESSE WEBSTER, private first class: Registered for Selective Service on June 5, 1917, at age 22; occupation – farmer. Inducted as a private at Windsor on May 28, 1918 and transported to Camp Jackson, Columbia, South Carolina. Initially assigned to the 156th Depot Brigade and transferred to this company on June 23, 1918. Sent overseas on July 31, 1918. Promoted to private first class on September 11, 1918. Returned from overseas and honorably discharged at Camp Lee, Petersburg, Virginia on June 25, 1919.

WHITE, TOMMIE, private: Registered for Selective Service on June 5, 1917, at age 27; occupation – farmer. Inducted as a private at Windsor on May 28, 1918, and transported to Camp Jackson, Columbia, South Carolina. Assigned to this company. Served overseas from July 31, 1918, until June 18, 1919. Honorably discharged at Camp Lee, Petersburg, Virginia on June 25, 1919.

WHITE, WILLIAM MCKINLEY, private: Registered for Selective Service on June 5, 1917, at age 21; occupation – farmer. Inducted as a private at Windsor on May 28, 1918, and transported to Camp Jackson, Columbia, South Carolina. Assigned to this company. Served overseas from July 31, 1918, until June 18, 1919. Honorably discharged on June 25, 1919.

WILLIAMS, ESSIE MERRIMAN, private: Registered for Selective Service on June 5, 1917, at age 22; occupation – farmer. Inducted as a private at Windsor on May 28, 1918, and transported to Camp Jackson, Columbia, South Carolina. Assigned to this company. Served overseas from July 31, 1918, until June 18, 1919. Honorably discharged on June 25, 1919.

## Company C

FRANCIS, WILLIAM T., private: Previously served in the 534th Engineers Service Battalion. Transferred to this company on June 2, 1918. Served overseas from July 31, 1918, until June 18, 1919. Honorably discharged at Camp Lee, Petersburg, Virginia on June 25, 1919.

## Company E

BEASLEY, CLARENCE WOOD, private: Registered for Selective Service on June 5, 1917, at age 25; occupation - salesman. Inducted as a private at Windsor on May 28, 1918, and transported to Camp Jackson, Columbia, South Carolina. Initially assigned to the 156th Depot Brigade and transferred to this company on June 23, 1918. Sent overseas on July 31, 1918. Transferred to Company G, 166th Infantry Regiment, 83rd Infantry Brigade, 42nd Division on August 26, 1918.

## Company F

ROBERTSON, WILLIAM JULIAN, private: Registered for Selective Service on June 5, 1917, at age 22; occupation – farmer. Inducted as a private at Windsor on May 28,

1918, and transported to Camp Jackson, Columbia, South Carolina. Assigned to this company. Served overseas from July 31, 1918, until April 15, 1919. Honorably discharged on April 26, 1919.

## Company L

SPIVEY, HENRY GODWIN, private: Registered for Selective Service on June 5, 1917, at age 21; occupation – farmer. Inducted as a private at Windsor on May 28, 1918, and transported to Camp Jackson, Columbia, South Carolina. Initially assigned to the 156th Depot Brigade and transferred to this company on June 23, 1918. Served overseas from July 31, 1918, until June 18, 1919. Honorably discharged on June 25, 1919.

STALLINGS, NOAH HENRY, JR., private: Registered for Selective Service on June 5, 1917, at age 23; occupation – farmer. Inducted as a private at Windsor on May 28, 1918, and transported to Camp Jackson, Columbia, South Carolina. Initially assigned to the 156th Depot Brigade and transferred to this company on June 23, 1918. Transferred back to the 156th Depot Brigade on July 11, 1918.

## Company M

TARKENTON, HERMAN E., corporal: Registered for Selective Service on June 5, 1917, at age 24; occupation – farmer. Inducted as a private at Windsor on May 28, 1918, and transported to Camp Jackson, Columbia, South Carolina. Initially assigned to the 156th Depot Brigade and transferred to this company on June 23, 1918. Sent overseas on July 30, 1918. Promoted to corporal on September 7, 1918. Wounded on November 10, 1918. Returned from overseas on December 17, 1918. Honorably discharged on January 19, 1919, with a disability rated as 5 percent.

THOMPSON, WILLIAM HENRY, private: Registered for Selective Service on June 5,

1917, at age 24; occupation – farmer. Inducted as a private at Windsor on May 28, 1918, and transported to Camp Jackson, Columbia, South Carolina. Assigned to this company. Served overseas from July 31, 1918, until May 19, 1919. Honorably discharged on May 20, 1919.

TODD, JOSEPH PENDER, corporal: Registered for Selective Service on June 5, 1917, at age 22; occupation – laborer. Inducted as a private at Windsor on May 28, 1918, and transported to Camp Jackson, Columbia, South Carolina. Initially assigned to the 156th Depot Brigade and transferred to this company on June 23, 1918. Sent overseas on July 31, 1918. Promoted to corporal on May 20, 1919. Returned from overseas and honorably discharged on June 25, 1919.

TRUMMEL, JOHN W., private: Registered for Selective Service on June 5, 1917, at age 23; occupation – farmer. Inducted as a private at Windsor on May 28, 1918, and transported to Camp Jackson, Columbia, South Carolina. Assigned to this company. Transferred to the 156th Depot Brigade on July 4, 1918.

# 317th MACHINE GUN BATTALION

## Company B

EARLY, WILLIAM THOMAS, first sergeant: Previously served in Company A, 318th Machine Gun Battalion, 162nd Infantry Brigade, 81st Division. Transferred as a sergeant to this company on March 31, 1919. Promoted to first sergeant and honorably discharged on April 23, 1919, to accept an officer's commission. Appointed second lieutenant on April 24, 1919, in Company C, 330th Machine Gun Battalion, 170th Infantry Brigade, 85th Division.

PRITCHARD, GROVER CLEVELAND, corporal: Registered for Selective Service on June 5, 1917, at age 30; occupation –

farmer. Inducted as a private at Windsor on November 16, 1917, and transported to Camp Jackson, Columbia, South Carolina. Initially assigned to the 156th Depot Brigade and transferred to this company on November 28, 1917. Promoted to private first class on June 1, 1918, and sent overseas on July 31, 1918. Promoted to corporal on September 1, 1918. Returned from overseas on June 19, 1919, and honorably discharged on July 1, 1919.

## MISCELLANEOUS (NO COMPANY IDENTIFIED)

EARLY, WILLIAM THOMAS, second lieutenant: Previously served in Company C, 330th Machine Gun Battalion, 170th Infantry Brigade, 85th Division. Transferred to this battalion on an undisclosed date while serving overseas. Returned from overseas on June 30, 1919, and honorably discharged at Camp Upton, Long Island, New York on July 24, 1919.

## 162nd INFANTRY BRIGADE

## 323rd INFANTRY REGIMENT

## MACHINE GUN COMPANY

WHITE, JOSEPH W., sergeant: Registered for Selective Service on June 5, 1917, at age 29; occupation – farmer. Inducted as a private at Windsor on November 16, 1917, and transported to Camp Jackson, Columbia, South Carolina. Initially assigned to the 156th Depot Brigade and transferred to this company on November 27, 1917. Promoted to sergeant on April 1, 1918. Served overseas from July 31, 1918, until June 19, 1919. Honorably discharged on July 1, 1919.

## Company L

MINTON, JOHN BAYARD, private: Registered for Selective Service on June 5, 1917, at age 24; occupation – mechanic/woodworker. Inducted as a private at Windsor on March 27, 1918, and transported to Camp Jackson, Columbia, South Carolina. Initially assigned to the 156th Depot Brigade and transferred to this company on June 28, 1918. Sent overseas on July 31, 1918. Transferred to Company D, 168th Infantry Regiment, 84th Infantry Brigade, 42nd Division on August 24, 1918.

## 324th INFANTRY REGIMENT

## Company D

SAUNDERS, JAMES P., private: Registered for Selective Service on June 5, 1917, at age 21; occupation – farmer. Inducted as a private at Windsor on April 26, 1918, and transported to Camp Jackson, Columbia, South Carolina. Assigned to this company. Transferred to Company M of this regiment on June 24, 1918.

## Company F

WATERS, CLYDE, private first class: Registered for Selective Service on June 5, 1917, at age 26; occupation – merchant. Inducted as a private at Windsor on April 26, 1918, and transported to Camp Jackson, Columbia, South Carolina. Assigned to this company. Served overseas from August 5, 1918, until February 28, 1919. Promoted to private first class on an undisclosed date. Honorably discharged on March 24, 1919.

## Company M

SAUNDERS, JAMES P., private: Previously served in Company D of this regiment. Transferred to this company on June 24, 1918. Served overseas from August 5, 1918, until June 18, 1919. Honorably discharged on June 25, 1919.

# 318th MACHINE GUN BATTALION

## Company A

DUNNING, GARFIELD, private: Registered for Selective Service on June 5, 1917, at age 22; occupation – farm laborer. Inducted as a private at Windsor on October 22, 1917, and transported to Camp Jackson, Columbia, South Carolina. Initially assigned to the 156th Depot Brigade and transferred to this company on an undisclosed date. Sent overseas on March 11, 1918, and transferred to Company G, 163rd Infantry Regiment, 82nd Infantry Brigade, 41st Division on May 21, 1918.

EARLY, WILLIAM THOMAS, sergeant: Registered for Selective Service on June 5, 1917, at age 28; occupation – building contractor. Inducted as a private at Windsor on October 22, 1917, and transported to Camp Jackson, Columbia, South Carolina. Assigned to this company. Promoted to corporal on January 7, 1918 and to sergeant on April 27, 1918. Transferred to Company B, 317th Machine Gun Battalion, 161st Infantry Brigade, 81st Division on March 31, 1919.

TAYLOR, BRODE, private: Registered for Selective Service on June 5, 1917, at age 26; occupation – farmer. Inducted as a private at Windsor on October 22, 1917, and transported to Camp Jackson, Columbia, South Carolina. Assigned to this company. Honorably discharged on July 29, 1918, having performed no overseas service. Reason for discharge not disclosed in military record.

## Company C

BAZEMORE, SETH R., private first class: Registered for Selective Service on June 5, 1917, at age 22; occupation – farm laborer. Inducted as a private at Windsor on October 22, 1917, and transported to Camp Jackson, Columbia, South Carolina. Assigned to

this company and promoted to private first class on January 1, 1918. Served overseas from July 31, 1918, until June 20, 1919, and honorably discharged on June 28, 1919.

EVANS, JAMES CLAUDIUS, sergeant: Registered for Selective Service as a Bertie County resident in Rockingham County, Virginia on or about June 5, 1917, at age 26; occupation – deputy for a fraternal society. Inducted as a private at Windsor on October 22, 1917, and transported to Camp Jackson, Columbia, South Carolina. Assigned to this company. Promoted to private first class on November 19, 1917, and to corporal on March 1, 1918. Sent overseas on July 31, 1918, and promoted to sergeant on September 21, 1918. Returned from overseas on July 18, 1919, and honorably discharged at Camp Upton, Long Island, New York on July 24, 1919.

NORFLEET, WILLIAM SMITH, private: Registered for Selective Service on June 5, 1917, at age 30; occupation – merchant and farmer. Inducted as a private at Windsor on October 22, 1917, and transported to Camp Jackson, Columbia, South Carolina. Assigned to this company. Transferred to the Machine Gun Company, 11th Infantry Regiment, 10th Infantry Brigade, 5th Division on February 6, 1918.

# 156th FIELD ARTILLERY BRIGADE

# 316th FIELD ARTILLERY REGIMENT

## HEADQUARTERS COMPANY

BAKER, WHEELER NURNEY, private first class: Registered for Selective Service on June 5, 1917, at age 21; occupation – railroad agent. Inducted as a private at Windsor on May 28, 1918, and transported to

Camp Jackson, Columbia, South Carolina. Assigned to this company and promoted to private first class on an undisclosed date. Served overseas from August 5, 1918, until March 18, 1919. Honorably discharged at Camp Lee, Petersburg, Virginia on March 29, 1919.

PRITCHARD, GEORGE HILL, private first class: Registered for Selective Service as a Bertie County resident in Richmond, Virginia on June 5, 1917, at age 27; occupation – machinist. Inducted as a private at Windsor on May 28, 1918, and transported to Camp Jackson, Columbia, South Carolina. Initially assigned to the 156th Depot Brigade and transferred to this company on June 15, 1918. Served overseas from August 5, 1918, until June 9, 1919. Honorably discharged at Camp Lee, Petersburg, Virginia on June 20, 1919.

## SUPPLY COMPANY

BASS, KADER WILLIAM, wagoner: Registered for Selective Service on June 5, 1917, at age 21; occupation – farmer. Inducted as a private at Windsor on May 28, 1918, and transported to Camp Jackson, Columbia, South Carolina. Initially assigned to the 156th Depot Brigade and transferred to this company on June 15, 1918. Promoted to wagoner on an undisclosed date. Served overseas from August 5, 1918, until June 9, 1919, and honorably discharged at Camp Lee, Petersburg, Virginia on June 20, 1919.

BYRD, HILARY LUTHER, sergeant: Registered for Selective Service on June 5, 1917, at age 24; occupation – farmer. Inducted as a private at Windsor on May 28, 1918, and transported to Camp Jackson, Columbia, South Carolina and assigned to this company. Promoted to wagoner on an undisclosed date and to sergeant on May 1, 1919. Served overseas from August 5, 1918, until June 9, 1919. Honorably discharged at Camp Lee, Petersburg, Virginia on June 20, 1919.

## Battery A

CASTELLOW, CULLEN WESLEY, private first class: Registered for Selective Service June 5, 1917, at age 24; occupation – laborer. Inducted as a private at Windsor on May 28, 1918, at age 25, and transported to Camp Jackson, Columbia, South Carolina. Assigned to this battery and sent overseas on August 5, 1918. Promoted to private first class on March 15, 1919. Returned from overseas on June 9, 1919, and honorably discharged at Camp Lee, Petersburg, Virginia on June 20, 1919,

CASTELLOW, ERNEST ELWOOD, private: Registered for Selective Service on June 5, 1917, at age 24; occupation – farmer. Inducted as a private at Windsor on May 26, 1918, and transported to Camp Jackson, Columbia, South Carolina. Assigned to this battery and served overseas from August 5, 1918, until June 9, 1919. Honorably discharged at Camp Lee, Petersburg, Virginia on June 20, 1919.

COBB, FRANK B., private: Registered for Selective Service on June 5, 1917, at age 23; occupation – farmer. Inducted as a private at Windsor on May 28, 1918, and transported to Camp Jackson, Columbia, South Carolina. Assigned to this battery and served overseas from August 5, 1918, until June 9, 1919. Honorably discharged at Camp Lee, Petersburg, Virginia on June 20, 1919.

COBB, STARKEY, private: Registered for Selective Service on June 5, 1918, at age 21; occupation – laborer. Inducted as a private at Windsor on August 25, 1918, and transported to Camp Jackson, Columbia, South Carolina. Assigned to the 156th Depot Brigade and transferred to this battery on an undisclosed date. Honorably discharged on December 10, 1918, having performed no overseas service.

DAVIS, WHIT TAYLOR, private: Registered for Selective Service on June 5, 1917, at age

22; occupation – farm laborer. Inducted as a private at Windsor on May 28, 1918, and transported to Camp Jackson, Columbia, South Carolina. Initially assigned to the 156th Depot Brigade and transferred to this battery on June 15, 1918. Served overseas from August 5, 1918, until March 24, 1919. Honorably discharged on April 25, 1919.

EARLY, SCARBOROUGH, private: Registered for Selective Service on June 5, 1917, at age 23; occupation – farmer. Inducted as a private at Windsor on May 28, 1918, and transported to Camp Jackson, Columbia, South Carolina. Initially assigned to the 156th Depot Brigade and transferred to this battery on an undisclosed date. Transferred back to 156th Depot Brigade on July 25, 1918.

EVANS, JAMES TESSIE, private: Registered for Selective Service on June 5, 1917, at age 23; occupation – farmer. Inducted as a private at Windsor on May 28, 1918, and transported to Camp Jackson, Columbia, South Carolina. Assigned to this battery. Served overseas from August 5, 1918, until June 9, 1919. Honorably discharged at Camp Lee, Petersburg, Virginia on June 20, 1919.

FARLESS, WILLIAM HAYWOOD, private: Registered for Selective Service on June 5, 1917, at age 23; occupation – farm laborer. Inducted as a private at Windsor on May 28, 1918, and transported to Camp Jackson, Columbia, South Carolina. Assigned to this battery and served overseas from August 5, 1918, until June 9, 1919. Honorably discharged at Camp Lee, Petersburg, Virginia on June 20, 1919.

FLOYD, GEORGE TURNER, wagoner: Registered for Selective Service on June 5, 1917, at age 21; occupation – laborer. Inducted as a private at Windsor on May 28, 1918, and transported to Camp Jackson, Columbia, South Carolina. Assigned to this battery and sent overseas on August 5, 1918. Promoted to wagoner on January 7, 1919. Returned from overseas on June 9, 1919, and honor-

ably discharged at Camp Lee, Petersburg, Virginia on June 20, 1919.

HOLDER, IRA A., private: Registered for Selective Service on June 5, 1917, at age 21; occupation – farmer. Inducted as a private at Windsor on May 28, 1918, and transported to Camp Jackson, Columbia, South Carolina. Assigned to this battery. Served overseas from August 5, 1918, until June 9, 1919. Honorably discharged at Camp Lee, Petersburg, Virginia on June 20, 1919.

PERRY, JOHN REDDICK, private: Registered for Selective Service on June 5, 1917, at age 22; occupation – farmer. Inducted as a private at Windsor on May 28, 1918, and transported to Camp Jackson, Columbia, South Carolina. Assigned to this battery. Served overseas from August 5, 1918, until June 9, 1919. Honorably discharged at Camp Lee, Petersburg, Virginia on June 20, 1919.

## Battery B

BROWN, LEWIS, EDGAR, private: Registered for Selective Service on June 5, 1917, at age 21; occupation – farmer. Inducted as a private at Windsor on May 26, 1918, and transported to Camp Jackson, Columbia, South Carolina. Assigned to this battery and served overseas from August 5, 1918, until June 9, 1919. Honorably discharged at Camp Lee, Petersburg, Virginia on June 20, 1919.

GREGORY, JOSEPH EDWARD, private: Registered for Selective Service on June 5, 1917, at age 26; occupation – farmer. Inducted as a private at Windsor on May 28, 1918, and transported to Camp Jackson, Columbia, South Carolina. Initially assigned to the 156th Depot Brigade and transferred to this battery on June 15, 1918. Served overseas from August 5, 1918, until June 9, 1919. Honorably discharged at Camp Lee, Petersburg, Virginia on June 20, 1919.

HARMON, JOSEPH W., private: Registered for Selective Service on June 5, 1917, at age

26; occupation – laborer, oil mill. Inducted as a private at Windsor on May 28, 1918, and transported to Camp Jackson, Columbia, South Carolina. Initially assigned to the 156th Depot Brigade and transferred to this battery on June 15, 1918. Served overseas from August 5, 1918, until June 9, 1919. Honorably discharged at Camp Lee, Petersburg, Virginia on June 20, 1919.

HARRELL, DAVID RIX, private: Registered for Selective Service on June 5, 1917, at age 22; occupation – farmer. Inducted as a private at Windsor on May 28, 1918, and transported to Camp Jackson, Columbia, South Carolina. Assigned to this battery. Served overseas from August 5, 1918, until June 9, 1919. Honorably discharged at Camp Lee, Petersburg, Virginia on June 20, 1919.

HARRELL, ROBERT HARTWELL, private: Registered for Selective Service on June 5, 1917, at age 25; occupation – farmer. Inducted as a private at Windsor on May 28, 1918, and transported to Camp Jackson, Columbia, South Carolina. Assigned to this battery. Served overseas from August 5, 1918, until June 9, 1919. Honorably discharged at Camp Lee, Petersburg, Virginia on June 20, 1919.

HARRELL, WESLEY P., private: Registered for Selective Service on June 5, 1917, at age 23; occupation – farmer. Inducted as a private at Windsor on May 28, 1918, and transported to Camp Jackson, Columbia, South Carolina. Initially assigned to the 156th Depot Brigade and transferred to this battery on June 15, 1918. Sent overseas on August 5, 1918. Died in France of "broncho pneumonia" on October 6, 1918.

HOGGARD, ARTHUR D., private: Registered for Selective Service on June 5, 1917, at age 21; occupation – laborer. Inducted as a private at Windsor on May 28, 1918, and transported to Camp Jackson, Columbia, South Carolina. Assigned to this battery. Transferred to the 156th Depot Brigade, Camp Jackson, on July 14, 1918.

HOGGARD, JAMES EDGAR, wagoner: Registered for Selective Service on June 5, 1917, at age 28; occupation – salesman. Inducted as a private at Windsor on May 28, 1918, and transported to Camp Jackson, Columbia, South Carolina. Assigned to this battery. Sent overseas on August 5, 1918. Promoted to wagoner on February 24, 1919. Returned from overseas on June 9, 1919, and honorably discharged at Camp Lee, Petersburg, Virginia on June 20, 1919.

HOGGARD, MARVIN, private: Registered for Selective Service on June 5, 1917, at age 26; occupation – farmer. Inducted as a private at Windsor on May 28, 1918, and transported to Camp Jackson, Columbia, South Carolina. Assigned to this battery. Honorably discharged at Camp Jackson on July 13, 1918, due to a service-connected disability. Degree of disability not disclosed in service record.

HOGGARD, WILLIAM LEVI, private: Registered for Selective Service on June 5, 1917, at age 22; occupation – farm laborer. Inducted as a private at Windsor on May 28, 1918, and transported to Camp Jackson, Columbia, South Carolina. Assigned to this battery. Served overseas from August 5, 1918, until June 9, 1919. Honorably discharged at Camp Lee, Petersburg, Virginia on June 20, 1919.

HOLDER, JOSEPH HILLARY, private first class: Registered for Selective Service on June 5, 1917, at age 23; occupation – farmer. Inducted as a private at Windsor on May 28, 1918, and transported to Camp Jackson, Columbia, South Carolina. Assigned to this battery. Served overseas from August 5, 1918, until June 9, 1919. Honorably discharged at Camp Lee, Petersburg, Virginia on June 20, 1919.

HOLLOMON, OTIS, private: Registered for Selective Service on June 5, 1917, at age 23; occupation – farmer. Inducted as a private at Windsor on May 28, 1918, and transported to Camp Jackson, Columbia, South Carolina. Initially assigned to the 156th Depot Brigade and transferred to this battery on June 15, 1918. Served overseas from August 5, 1918, until June 9, 1919. Honorably discharged at Camp Lee, Petersburg, Virginia on June 20. 1919.

HUGHES, ERNEST B., private: Registered for Selective Service on June 5, 1917, at age 24; occupation – farmer. Inducted as a private at Windsor on May 28, 1918, and transported to Camp Jackson, Columbia, South Carolina. Assigned to this battery. Honorably discharged on December 1, 1918, having performed no overseas service.

HUGHES, GURNIE PRESTON, private: Registered for Selective Service on June 5, 1917, at age 21; occupation – farmer. Inducted as a private at Windsor on May 28, 1918, and transported to Camp Jackson, Columbia, South Carolina. Assigned to this battery. Served overseas from August 5, 1918, until June 9, 1919. Honorably discharged at Camp Lee, Petersburg, Virginia on June 20, 1919.

ODER, WILLIAM H., private: Previously served in the July Automatic Replacement Draft, Camp Jackson. Transferred to this battery on an undisclosed date but likely prior to July 22, 1918. Served overseas from July 22, 1918, until September 22, 1919. Honorably discharged on September 27, 1919.

PARKER, JOHN BOND, private: Registered for Selective Service on June 5, 1917, at age 26; occupation – farmer. Inducted as a private at Windsor on May 28, 1918, and transported to Camp Jackson, Columbia, South Carolina. Assigned to this battery. Served overseas from August 5, 1918, until June 9, 1919. Honorably discharged at Camp Lee, Petersburg, Virginia on June 20, 1919.

PHELPS, WILLIAM MILES, private first class: Registered for Selective Service on June 5, 1917, at age 21; occupation – farmer. In-

ducted as a private at Windsor on May 28, 1918, and transported to Camp Jackson, Columbia, South Carolina. Initially assigned to the 156th Depot Brigade and transferred to this battery on June 15, 1918. Sent overseas on August 5, 1918. Promoted to private first class on March 29, 1919. Returned from overseas on June 9, 1919, and honorably discharged at Camp Lee, Petersburg, Virginia on June 20, 1919.

## Battery C

LASSITER, ALFRED G., private: Registered for Selective Service on June 5, 1917, at age 24; occupation – farmer. Inducted as a private at Windsor on May 28, 1918, and transported to Camp Jackson, Columbia, South Carolina. Assigned to this battery. Served overseas from August 5, 1918, until June 9, 1919. Honorably discharged at Camp Lee, Petersburg, Virginia on June 20, 1919.

LEE, NORMAN B., private: Registered for Selective Service on June 5, 1917, at age 23; occupation – farmer. Inducted as a private at Windsor on May 28, 1918, and transported to Camp Jackson, Columbia, South Carolina. Initially assigned to the 156th Depot Brigade and transferred to this battery on June 15, 1918. Sent overseas on August 5, 1918. Died of "broncho pneumonia" on October 5, 1918.

MIZELL, BALLIE DURHAM, private first class: Registered for Selective Service on June 5, 1917, at age 28; occupation – farmer. Inducted as a private at Windsor on May 28, 1918, and transported to Camp Jackson, Columbia, South Carolina. Assigned to this battery. Sent overseas on August 5, 1918. Promoted to private first class on March 19, 1919. Returned from overseas on June 9, 1919, and honorably discharged at Camp Lee, Petersburg, Virginia on June 20, 1919.

MIZELL, RHODEN LEE, private: Registered for Selective Service on June 5, 1917, at age 21; occupation – farmer. Inducted as a private at Windsor on May 28, 1918, and transported to Camp Jackson, Columbia, South Carolina. Assigned to this battery. Served overseas from August 5, 1918, until June 9, 1919. Honorably discharged at Camp Lee, Petersburg, Virginia on June 20, 1919.

NEWBERN, JOSEPH JAMES, private first class: Registered for Selective Service on June 5, 1917, at age 25; occupation – farmer. Inducted as a private at Windsor on May 28, 1918, and transported to Camp Jackson, Columbia, South Carolina. Initially assigned to the 156th Depot Brigade and transferred to this battery on June 15, 1918. Sent overseas on August 5, 1918. Promoted to private first class on May 1, 1919. Returned from overseas on June 9, 1919, and honorably discharged at Camp Lee, Petersburg, Virginia on June 20, 1919.

PARKER, JAMES NORMAN, private: Registered for Selective Service on June 5, 1917, at age 21; occupation – farmer. Inducted as a private at Windsor on May 28, 1918, and transported to Camp Jackson, Columbia, South Carolina. Assigned to this battery. Served overseas from August 5, 1918, until June 9, 1919. Honorably discharged at Camp Lee, Petersburg, Virginia on June 20, 1919.

POWELL, PAUL, private: Registered for Selective Service on June 5, 1917, at age 27; occupation – farmer. Inducted as a private at Windsor on May 28, 1918, and transported to Camp Jackson, Columbia, South Carolina. Initially assigned to the 156th Depot Brigade and transferred to this battery on June 15, 1918. Served overseas from August 5, 1918, until June 9, 1919. Honorably discharged at Camp Lee, Petersburg, Virginia on June 20, 1919.

## Battery D

BAKER, WALTER R., private: Registered for Selective Service on June 5, 1917, at age 25; occupation – farmer. Inducted as a private at Windsor on May 24, 1918, and transported to Camp Jackson, Columbia, South Carolina. Initially assigned to the 156th Depot Bri-

gade and transferred to this battery on June 15, 1918. Transferred to Battery C, 80th Field Artillery Regiment, 7th Field Artillery Brigade, 7th Division on August 13, 1918.

BROWN, RUFUS, private: Registered for Selective Service on June 5, 1917, at age 21; occupation – farmer. Inducted as a private at Windsor on May 28, 1918, and transported to Camp Jackson, Columbia, South Carolina. Assigned to this battery and served overseas from August 5, 1918, until April 17, 1919. Honorably discharged on July 10, 1919.

BUTLER, JERRY, private first class: Registered for Selective Service on June 5, 1917, at age 22; occupation – farmer. Inducted as a private at Windsor on May 28, 1918, and transported to Camp Jackson, Columbia, South Carolina. Initially assigned to the 156th Depot Brigade and transferred to this battery on June 15, 1918. Sent overseas on September 9, 1918. Promoted to private first class on June 7, 1919. Returned from overseas on July 11, 1919, and honorably discharged at Camp Lee, Petersburg, Virginia on July 20, 1919.

PHELPS, JAMES NORMAN, private: Registered for Selective Service on June 5, 1917, at age 23; occupation – farm laborer. Inducted as a private at Windsor on May 28, 1918, and transported to Camp Jackson, Columbia, South Carolina. Assigned to this battery. Served overseas from August 5, 1918, until June 9, 1919. Honorably discharged at Camp Lee, Petersburg, Virginia on June 20, 1919.

PHELPS, PERCY EVERETT, private: Registered for Selective Service on June 5, 1917, at age 27; occupation – farmer. Inducted as a private at Windsor on May 28, 1918, and transported to Camp Jackson, Columbia, South Carolina. Assigned to this battery. Served overseas from August 5, 1918, until June 9, 1919. Honorably discharged at Camp Lee, Petersburg, Virginia on June 20, 1919.

PRUDEN, EDMUND J., private: Registered for Selective Service on June 5, 1917, at age 22; occupation – farmer. Inducted as a private at Windsor on May 28, 1918, and transported to Camp Jackson, Columbia, South Carolina. Initially assigned to the 156th Depot Brigade and transferred to this battery on June 15, 1918. Served overseas from August 5, 1918, until June 9, 1919. Honorably discharged at Camp Lee, Petersburg, Virginia on June 20, 1919.

RAWLS, WILLIAM CLAUDE, private: Registered for Selective Service on June 5, 1917, at age 24; occupation – farmer. Inducted as a private at Windsor on May 28, 1918, and transported to Camp Jackson, Columbia, South Carolina. Initially assigned to the 156th Depot Brigade and transferred to this battery on June 15, 1918. Served overseas from August 5, 1918, until June 9, 1919. Honorably discharged at Camp Lee, Petersburg, Virginia on June 20, 1919.

## Battery E

BUTLER, JOSEPH ALLEN, private: Registered for Selective Service on June 5, 1917, at age 29; occupation – farmer. Inducted as a private at Windsor on May 28, 1918, and transported to Camp Jackson, Columbia, South Carolina. Assigned to this battery and served overseas from August 5, 1918, until June 9, 1919. Honorably discharged at Camp Lee, Petersburg, Virginia on June 20, 1919.

DAVIDSON, JESSE WILLARD, private: Registered for Selective Service on June 5, 1917, at age 23; occupation – mechanic and wood worker. Inducted as a private at Windsor on May 28, 1918, and transported to Camp Jackson, Columbia, South Carolina. Initially assigned to the 156th Depot Brigade and transferred to this battery on June 15, 1918. Transferred back to the 156th Depot Brigade on July 3, 1918.

HOLLOMON, THAD W., private: Registered for Selective Service at Detroit, Michigan, on May 29, 1917, at age 27; occupation – machinist at automobile manufacturer. Inducted as a private at Windsor on May 28, 1918, and transported to Camp Jackson, Columbia, South Carolina. Assigned to this battery. Transferred to the 156th Depot Brigade at Camp Jackson on July 3, 1918.

## Battery F

BYRD, JOSEPH LEVY, private: Registered for Selective Service on June 5, 1917, at age 27; occupation – salesman. Inducted as a private at Windsor on May 28, 1918, and transported to Camp Jackson, Columbia, South Carolina. Initially assigned to the 156th Depot Brigade and transferred to this battery on June 15, 1918. Served overseas from August 5, 1918, until June 9, 1919. Honorably discharged at Camp Lee, Petersburg, Virginia on June 20, 1919.

## MISCELLANEOUS (BATTERY NOT IDENTIFIED)

ASKEW, HUBERT F., private first class: Registered for Selective Service on June 5, 1917, at age 24; occupation – farmer. Inducted as a private at Windsor on May 28, 1918, and transported to Fort Jackson, Columbia, South Carolina. Initially assigned to the 156th Depot Brigade and transferred to this regiment (battery to which assigned not identified) on June 15, 1918. Promoted to private first class on March 15, 1919. Served overseas from August 5, 1918, until June 9, 1919, and honorably discharged at Camp Lee, Petersburg, Virginia on June 21, 1919.

## 83rd DIVISION

## 165th INFANTRY BRIGADE

# 330th INFANTRY REGIMENT

## Company C

HARDEN, NORMAN LOU, private: Previously served in Company F, 55th Pioneer Infantry Regiment. Transferred to this company on October 17, 1918, while serving overseas. Returned from overseas on January 30, 1919, and honorably discharged at Camp Lee, Petersburg, Virginia on February 16, 1919.

## Company H

HARDEN, FRANK HOBBS, private: Previously served in Company A, 57th Pioneer Infantry Regiment. Transferred to this company on November 8, 1918, while serving overseas. Returned from overseas on January 29, 1919, and honorably discharged at Camp Sherman, near Chillicothe, Ohio on February 10, 1919.

## MISCELLANEOUS (NO COMPANY IDENTIFIED)

LANGDALE, EDWARD JESSE, private: Previously served in Company G, 55th Infantry Regiment, 13th Infantry Brigade, 7th Division. Transferred to this regiment on November 2, 1918, while serving overseas. Transferred to Company M, 4th Infantry Regiment, 5th Infantry Brigade, 3rd Division on November 6, 1918.

# 166th INFANTRY BRIGADE

# 331st INFANTRY REGIMENT

## Company B

BRACY, ODIE LAWRENCE, private: Previously served in Company A, 57th Pioneer Infantry Regiment. Transferred to this company on December 5, 1918, while serving overseas. Subsequently transferred to Company A, 105th Engineers Regiment, 30th Division at an undisclosed date.

## MACHINE GUN COMPANY

FREEMAN, JOSEPH JOHN, private: Transferred to this company from the Camp Hancock, Georgia October Automatic Replacement Draft on November 24, 1918, while serving overseas. Returned from overseas on January 26, 1919, and honorably discharged at Camp Sherman, near Chillicothe, Ohio on February 8, 1919.

# 324th MACHINE GUN BATTALION

## Company D

HARRELL, WILLIAM GEORGE, private: Previously served in the Motor Transport Depot, Camp Hancock, Georgia. Transferred to this company on November 23, 1918, while serving overseas. Returned from overseas on January 31, 1919, and honorably discharged on February 13, 1919.

MIZELL, GEORGE TIMOTHY, private: Previously served in the October Automatic Replacement Draft, Camp Hancock, Georgia. Transferred to this company on November 23, 1918, while serving overseas. Returned from overseas on January 31, 1919, and transferred to the 155th Depot Brigade, Camp Lee, Virginia.

## 84th DIVISION

### 168th INFANTRY BRIGADE

### 336th INFANTRY REGIMENT

#### Company F

BAZEMORE, TURNER FRANKLIN, sergeant: Previously served in the 103rd Company, Coast Artillery Corps. Transferred as a corporal to this company on October 13, 1917, and promoted to sergeant on November 7, 1917. Transferred to Company I, 6th Infantry Regiment, 9th Infantry Brigade, 5th Division on February 16, 1918.

## 85th DIVISION

### DEPOT SERVICE COMPANY

WADSWORTH (WARDSWORTH), JAMES B., corporal: Previously served in Company E, 4th Provisional Regiment. Transferred as a private to this company on March 30, 1919, while serving overseas. Promoted to corporal on April 24, 1919. Returned from overseas on July 7, 1919, and honorably discharged at Camp Lee, Petersburg, Virginia on July 19, 1919.

### 169th INFANTRY BRIGADE

### 338th INFANTRY REGIMENT

#### MISCELLANEOUS (NO COMPANY IDENTIFIED)

HOLDER, JOHN E., sergeant first class: Registered for Selective Service on June 5, 1917, at age 27; occupation — farmer. Enlisted

as a private at Fort Thomas, Kentucky, on August 4, 1917, at age 27. Assigned to this regiment. Promoted to sergeant first class on May 11, 1918. Honorably discharged on January 9, 1919, having performed no overseas service.

### 170th INFANTRY BRIGADE

### 330th MACHINE GUN BATTALION

#### Company C

EARLY, WILLIAM THOMAS, second lieutenant: Honorably discharged as a first sergeant from Company B, 317th Machine Gun Battalion, 161st Infantry Brigade, 81st Division on April 23, 1919, to take an officer's appointment. Appointed second lieutenant and assigned to this company on April 24, 1919, and sent overseas. Transferred back to the 317th Machine Gun Battalion on an undisclosed date.

## 87th DIVISION

### 173rd INFANTRY BRIGADE

### 346th INFANTRY REGIMENT

#### Company A

PERRY, JOHN L.*, private: Registered for Selective Service on June 5, 1917, at age 24; occupation — farm laborer. Inducted as a private at Windsor on August 23, 1918, and transported to Camp Greene, Charlotte. Assigned to this company. Served overseas from September 30, 1918, until July 4, 1919. Honorably discharged at Camp Lee, Petersburg, Virginia on July 16, 1919.

## 88th DIVISION

### 176th INFANTRY BRIGADE

### 351st INFANTRY REGIMENT

#### Company E

MORRIS, TOMMIE T., private: Previously served in Company F, Casual Battalion at Camp Merritt, New Jersey. Transferred to this company on August 10, 1918. Served overseas from August 16, 1918, until May 31, 1919. Honorably discharged on June 12, 1919.

## 90th DIVISION

### 165th FIELD ARTILLERY BRIGADE

### 345th FIELD ARTILLERY REGIMENT

#### HEADQUARTERS COMPANY

HARRELL, JOHN THOMAS, private: Registered for Selective Service on June 5, 1917, at age 27; occupation – farmer. Inducted as a private at Windsor on June 28, 1918, and transported to Camp Jackson, Columbia, South Carolina. Initially assigned to the 56th Depot Brigade and transferred to this company on August 6, 1918. Served overseas from August 22, 1918, until June 7, 1919. Honorably discharged on June 21, 1919.

## 92nd DIVISION

### 317th AMMUNITION TRAIN (FIELD ARTILLERY)

#### Company F

HARDY, JAMES*, private: Registered for Selective Service on June 5, 1917, at age 21; occupation – farmer. Inducted as a private at Windsor on April 29, 1918, and transported to Camp Jackson, Columbia, South Carolina. Assigned to the 156th Depot Brigade and transferred to this company on July 21, 1918. Served overseas from August 22, 1918, until February 28, 1919. Honorably discharged at Camp Lee, Petersburg, Virginia on March 15, 1919.

### 183rd INFANTRY BRIGADE

### 365th INFANTRY REGIMENT

#### HEADQUARTERS COMPANY

BASS, ROBERT T.*, private: Registered for Selective Service on June 5, 1917, at age 21; occupation - laborer. Inducted as a private at Windsor on April 2, 1918, and transported to Camp Grant, Rockford, Illinois. Initially assigned to the 161st Depot Brigade and transferred to this company on April 20, 1918. Honorably discharged on July 3, 1918, having performed no overseas service. Discharged due to service-connected disability rated as 25 percent.

BUNCH, NATHANIEL*, private: Registered for Selective Service on June 5, 1917, at age 26; occupation – farmer. Inducted as a private at Windsor on April 2, 1918, and transported to Camp Grant, Rockford, Illinois. Initially assigned to the 161st Depot Brigade and transferred to this company on

April 20, 1918. Served overseas from June 10, 1918, until February 24, 1919. Honorably discharged at Camp Lee, Petersburg, Virginia on March 13, 1919.

DELOATCH, ISAAC*, private: Registered for Selective Service on June 5, 1917, at age 24; occupation – farmer. Inducted as a private at Windsor on April 2, 1918, and transported to Camp Grant, Rockford, Illinois. Assigned to this company and served overseas from June 10, 1918, until February 24, 1919. Honorably discharged at Camp Lee, Petersburg, Virginia on March 13, 1919.

HOLLEY, CLARENCE*, private: Previously served in Company D of this regiment. Transferred to this company on January 1, 1919, while serving overseas. Returned from overseas on April 18, 1919, and honorably discharged on May 12, 1919.

MITCHELL, WILLIE*, private: Registered for Selective Service on June 5, 1917, at age 23; occupation – farmer. Inducted as a private at Windsor on April 2, 1918, and transported to Camp Grant, Rockford, Illinois. Initially assigned to the 161st Depot Brigade and transferred to this company on April 20, 1918. Served overseas from June 10, 1918, until February 24, 1919. Honorably discharged at Camp Lee, Petersburg, Virginia on March 13, 1919.

ORR, SAMUEL EDWARD*, private: Registered for Selective Service on June 5, 1917, at age 30; occupation – brick mason. Inducted as a private at Windsor on April 2, 1918, and transported to Camp Grant, Rockford, Illinois. Assigned to this company. Served overseas from June 10, 1918, until February 24, 1919. Honorably discharged at Camp Lee, Petersburg, Virginia on March 13, 1919.

PETERSON, EDWARD B.*, private: Registered for Selective Service on June 5, 1917, at age 22; occupation – farmer. Inducted as a private at Windsor on April 2, 1918, and

transported to Camp Grant, Rockford, Illinois. Initially assigned to the 161st Depot Brigade and transferred to this company on April 20, 1918. Transferred to Headquarters Company, 323rd Service Battalion on May 23, 1918.

SANDERLIN, TOMMIE TURNER*, private: Registered for Selective Service on June 5, 1917, at age 23; occupation – laborer. Inducted as a private at Windsor on April 2, 1918, and transported to Camp Grant, Rockford, Illinois. Initially assigned to the 161st Depot Brigade and transferred to this company on April 20, 1918. Served overseas from June 10, 1918, until February 2, 1919. Honorably discharged at Camp Lee, Petersburg, Virginia on March 13, 1919.

WALKER, GARFIELD*, private: Registered for Selective Service on June 5, 1917, at age 26; occupation – farmer. Inducted as a private at Windsor on April 2, 1918, and transported to Camp Grant, Rockford, Illinois. Initially assigned to the 161st Depot Brigade and transferred to this company on April 20, 1918. Reassigned to the 161st Depot brigade on May 27, 1918.

## SUPPLY COMPANY

GILES, ALBERT*, private: Registered for Selective Service on June 5, 1917, at age 22; occupation – farmer. Inducted as a private at Windsor on April 2, 1918, and transported to Camp Grant, Rockford, Illinois. Assigned to this company. Promoted to wagoner on July 15, 1918, and reduced to private on October 11, 1918. Served overseas from June 10, 1918, until February 24, 1919. Honorably discharged at Camp Lee, Petersburg, Virginia on March 12, 1919.

HECKSTALL, THOMAS*, private: Registered for Selective Service on June 5, 1917, at age 21; occupation – farmer. Inducted as a private at Windsor on April 2, 1918, and transported to Camp Grant, Rockford, Illinois. Initially assigned to the 161st Depot Brigade and transferred to this company on an undisclosed date. Served overseas from June 10, 1918, until February 25, 1919. Honorably discharged at Camp Lee, Petersburg, Virginia on March 12, 1919.

WINBORNE, SAM*, wagoner: Registered for Selective Service on June 5, 1917, at age 22; occupation – logging. Inducted as a private at Windsor on April 2, 1918, and transported to Camp Grant, Rockford, Illinois. Assigned to this company. Sent overseas on June 10, 1918, and promoted to wagoner on June 15, 1918. Returned from overseas on February 23, 1919, and honorably discharged at Camp Lee, Petersburg, Virginia on March 12, 1919.

## MACHINE GUN COMPANY

BAZEMORE, BEN*, private: Registered for Selective Service on June 5, 1917, at age 26; occupation – farmer. Inducted as a private at Windsor on April 2, 1918, and transported to Camp Grant, Rockford, Illinois. Initially assigned to the 161st Depot Brigade and transferred to this company on April 20, 1918. Served overseas from June 10, 1918, until February 24, 1919, and honorably discharged at Camp Lee, Petersburg, Virginia on March 11, 1919.

BEASLEY, THOMAS E.*, private: Registered for Selective Service on June 5, 1917, at age 24; occupation – farmer. Inducted as a private at Windsor on April 2, 1918, and transported to Camp Grant, Rockford, Illinois. Initially assigned to the 161st Depot Brigade and transferred to this company on April 30, 1918. Served overseas from June 10, 1918, until February 24, 1919. Honorably discharged at Camp Lee, Petersburg, Virginia on March 11, 1919.

COOPER, FRANK R.*, private: Registered for Selective Service on June 5, 1917, at age 26; occupation – farmer. Inducted as a private at Windsor on April 22, 1918, and transported to Camp Grant, Rockford, Illinois.

Assigned to this company. Served overseas from June 10, 1918, until February 24, 1919. Honorably discharged at Camp Lee, Petersburg, Virginia on March 11, 1919.

JOHNSON, FLOYD*, private: Registered for Selective Service on June 5, 1917, at age 21; occupation – farm laborer. Inducted as a private at Windsor on April 2, 1918, and transported to Camp Grant, Rockford, Illinois. Assigned to this company. Served overseas from June 10, 1918, until February 24, 1919. Honorably discharged at Camp Lee, Petersburg, Virginia on March 11, 1919.

STEWART, NORMAN*, private: Registered for Selective Service on June 5, 1917, at age 21; occupation – farm laborer. Inducted as a private at Windsor on August 2, 1918, and transported to Camp Grant, Rockford, Illinois. Assigned to this company. Served overseas from June 10, 1918, until February 28, 1919. Honorably discharged at Camp Lee, Petersburg, Virginia on March 11, 1919.

WILLIAMS, FRANK B.*, private: Registered for Selective Service on June 5, 1917, at age 22; occupation – farmer. Inducted as a private at Windsor on April 2, 1918, and transported to Camp Grant, Rockford, Illinois. Initially assigned to the 161st Depot Brigade and transferred to this company. Sent overseas on June 16, 1918. Died of "broncho pneumonia & influenza" on March 17, 1919.

## Company D

HOLLEY, CLARENCE*, private: Registered for Selective Service on June 5, 1917, at age 22; occupation – farmer. Inducted as a private at Windsor on April 2, 1918, and transported to Camp Grant, Rockford, Illinois. Assigned to this company. Sent overseas on June 1, 1918. Transferred to Headquarters Company of the regiment on January 1, 1919.

## Company F

PERRY, LONNIE*, private: Previously served in the 20th Battery, August Automatic Replacement Draft (Field Artillery), Fort Jackson. Transferred to this company on September 24, 1918, while serving overseas. Returned from overseas on February 24, 1919, and honorably discharged at Camp Lee, Petersburg, Virginia on March 12, 1919.

## Company G

PARKER, CHARLES LEE*, private: Registered for Selective Service on June 5, 1917, at age 23; occupation – farmer. Inducted as a private at Windsor on April 2, 1918, and transported to Camp Grant, Rockford, Illinois. Initially assigned to the 10th Company, 3rd Training Battalion, until transferred to this company on an undisclosed date. Honorably discharged on May 9, 1918, due to a service-connected disability rated as 25 percent.

# 366th INFANTRY REGIMENT

## Company F

SMALL, JOHN B.*, private: Registered for Selective Service at Windsor, Connecticut on June 1, 1917, at age 24; occupation – farmer. Inducted as a private at Windsor, North Carolina on April 26, 1918, and transported to Camp Grant, Rockford, Illinois. Initially assigned to the 161st Depot Brigade and transferred to this company on May 15, 1918. Sent overseas on June 14, 1918. Slightly wounded on September 4, 1918, and severely wounded on November 11, 1918. Returned from overseas on January 18, 1919. Honorably discharged on March 29, 1919, with a disability rated as 25 percent.

## Company G

CRAIG, WILLIAM TURNER*, private: Registered for Selective Service on June 5, 1917, at age 30; occupation – lumbering. Inducted as a private at Windsor on April 26, 1918, and transported to Camp Grant, Rockford, Illinois. Initially assigned to the 161st Depot Brigade and transferred to this company on May 24, 1918. Served overseas from June 15, 1918, until February 28, 1919. Honorably discharged at Fort Oglethorpe, Chickamauga Park, Georgia on March 19, 1919.

## Company H

CHERRY, OLIVER*, private: Registered for Selective Service on June 5, 1917, at age 29; occupation – farmer. Inducted as a private at Windsor on April 26, 1918, and transported to Camp Grant, Rockford, Illinois. Assigned to this company. Served overseas from June 15, 1918, until February 28, 1919. Honorably discharged at Fort Oglethorpe, Chickamauga Park, Georgia on March 19, 1919.

## Company I

WILLIAMS, WHITTIE*, private: Registered for Selective Service on June 5, 1917, at age 21; occupation – farm laborer. Inducted as a private at Windsor on April 26, 1918, and transported to Camp Grant, Rockford, Illinois. Initially assigned to the 161st Depot Brigade. Transferred to this company on May 24, 1918. Died at Camp Grant of "Cerebro spinal meningitis" on July 17, 1918.

## Company M

MELTON, WILLIAM*, private: Registered for Selective Service on June 5, 1917, at age 21; occupation – farm laborer. Inducted as a private at Windsor on April 26, 1918, and transported to Camp Grant, Rockford, Illinois. Initially assigned to the 161st Depot Brigade and transferred to this company in May 1918. Sent overseas on June 15, 1918. Slightly wounded on October 1, 1918. Returned from overseas on February 28,

1919, and honorably discharged on March 19, 1919.

# 350th MACHINE GUN BATTALION

## Headquarters Company

SANDERLIN, JOSEPH*, private first class: Registered for Selective Service on June 5, 1917, at age 21; occupation – presser. Inducted as a private at Windsor on April 28, 1918, and transported to Camp Grant, Rockford, Illinois. Initially assigned to the 161st Depot Brigade and transferred to this company on May 9, 1918. Sent overseas on June 10, 1918, and promoted to private first class on July 1, 1918. Returned from overseas on March 6, 1919, and honorably discharged at Camp Upton, Long Island, New York on March 20, 1919.

## Company A

CHAVIS, JESSE*, private first class: Registered for Selective Service at Richmond, Virginia on or about June 5, 1917, at age 21; occupation – employee of locomotive company. Inducted as a private at Windsor on April 26, 1918, and transported to Camp Grant, Rockford, Illinois. Assigned to this company and served overseas from June 10, 1918. Promoted to private first class on July 1, 1918. Returned from overseas on March 6, 1919, and honorably discharged at Camp Upton, Long Island, New York on March 22, 1919.

PHILLIPS, COLUMBUS*, private: Registered for Selective Service on June 5, 1917, at age 21; occupation – farmer. Inducted as a private at Windsor on April 28, 1918, and transported to Camp Grant, Rockford, Illinois. Assigned to this company. Transferred to Company B, 329th Labor Battalion, Quartermaster Corps, on May 21, 1918.

THOMPSON, LEO O.*, private first class: Registered for Selective Service on June 5, 1917, at age 21; occupation – farmer. Inducted as a private at Windsor on April 28, 1918, and transported to Camp Grant, Rockford, Illinois. Initially assigned to the 161st Depot Brigade and transferred to this company on May 9, 1918. Promoted to private first class on April 15, 1918. Served overseas from June 10, 1918, until March 6, 1919. Honorably discharged at Camp Upton, Long Island, New York on March 20, 1919.

WHITFIELD, JOHN FRANK*, private: Registered for Selective Service on June 5, 1917, at age 21; occupation – laborer, log woods. Inducted as a private at Windsor on April 28, 1918, and transported to Camp Grant, Rockford, Illinois. Assigned to this company. Served overseas from June 10, 1918, until March 6, 1919. Honorably discharged at Camp Upton, Long Island, New York on March 20, 1919.

## Company B

BASNETT, LEWIS*, private: Registered for Selective Service on June 5, 1917, at age 21; occupation – farmer. Inducted as a private at Windsor on April 26, 1918, and transported to Fort Grant, Rockford, Illinois. Initially assigned to the 161st Depot Brigade. Transferred to this company on May 9, 1918. Served overseas from June 16, 1918, until March 6, 1919, and honorably discharged at Camp Upton, Long Island, New York on March 20, 1919.

BOND, ELY (EALIE)*, private: Registered for Selective Service on June 5, 1917, at age 23; occupation – farmer. Inducted as a private at Windsor on April 26, 1918, and transported to Camp Grant, Rockford, Illinois. Initially assigned to the 161st Depot Brigade and transferred to this company on May 9, 1918. Served overseas from June 10, 1918, until March 6, 1919. Honorably discharged at Camp Upton, Long Island, New York on March 20, 1919.

HARMON, WALTER RALEIGH*, private first class: Registered for Selective Service on June 5, 1917, at age 24; occupation – farmer. Inducted as a private at Windsor on April 28, 1918, and transported to Camp Grant, Rockford, Illinois. Assigned to this company. Sent overseas on June 10, 1918. Promoted to private first class on March 1, 1919. Returned from overseas on March 6, 1919, and honorably discharged at Camp Upton, Long Island, New York on March 20, 1919.

HOGGARD, LEAVIE (LEVI)*, private: Registered for Selective Service on June 5, 1917, at age 25; occupation – farm laborer. Inducted as a private at Windsor on April 28, 1918, and transported to Camp Grant, Rockford, Illinois. Assigned to this company. Served overseas from June 10, 1918, until March 16, 1919. Honorably discharged at Camp Upton, Long Island, New York on March 20, 1919.

## Company C

HECKSTALL, HARRY*, private: Registered for Selective Service on June 5, 1917, at age 21; occupation – farm laborer. Inducted as a private at Windsor on April 28, 1918, and transported to Camp Grant, Rockford, Illinois. Assigned to Company C. Served overseas from June 10, 1918, until March 6, 1919. Honorably discharged at Camp Upton, Long Island, New York on March 20, 1919.

HUX, JAMES ANDREW*, private: Registered for Selective Service on June 5, 1917, at age 23; occupation – farmer. Inducted as a private at Windsor on April 26, 1918, and transported to Camp Grant, Rockford, Illinois. Initially assigned to the 161st Depot Brigade and transferred to this company on May 9, 1918. Sent overseas on June 10, 1918. Slightly wounded about September 6, 1918. Returned from overseas on May 7, 1919, and honorably discharged on May 9, 1919.

LEE, JOHN*, private: Registered for Selective Service as a Bertie County resident in Ches-ter County, Pennsylvania on June 5, 1918, at age 23; occupation – hospital orderly. Inducted as a private at Windsor on April 26, 1918, and transported to Camp Grant, Rockford, Illinois. Assigned to this company. Served overseas from June 10, 1918, until March 6, 1919. Honorably discharged at Camp Upton, Long Island, New York on March 20, 1919.

MANLY, LORENZO*, private: Registered for Selective Service on June 5, 1917, at age 22; occupation – laborer, log woods. Inducted as a private at Windsor on April 26, 1918, and transported to Camp Grant, Rockford, Illinois. Initially assigned to the 161st Depot Brigade and transferred to this company on May 9, 1918. Served overseas from June 10, 1918, until March 6, 1919. Honorably discharged at Camp Upton, Long Island, New York on March 20, 1919.

WHITE, ARTHUR*, private: Registered for Selective Service on June 5, 1917, at age 23; occupation – laborer, log woods. Inducted as a private at Windsor on April 26, 1918, and transported to Camp Grant, Rockford, Illinois. Assigned to this company and served overseas from June 10, 1918, until March 6, 1919. Honorably discharged at Camp Upton, Long Island, New York on March 20, 1919.

# 93rd DIVISION

# 185th INFANTRY BRIGADE

# 370th INFANTRY REGIMENT

## Company K

COLLINS, CHARLES*, private: Registered for Selective Service on June 5, 1917, at age 23; occupation – laborer. Inducted as a private at Windsor on July 16, 1918, and transported to Camp Dix, near Trenton, New Jersey.

Assigned to this company and served overseas from August 22, 1918, until February 9, 1919. Honorably discharged at Camp Grant, Rockford, Illinois on March 6, 1919.

# 186th INFANTRY BRIGADE

# 371st INFANTRY REGIMENT

## Medical Detachment

HYMAN, DANIEL C.*, sergeant: Registered for Selective Service as a Bertie County resident in Chester County, Pennsylvania on May 30, 1917, at age 24; occupation – employee at commissary restaurant. Inducted as a private at Windsor on December 17, 1917, and transported to Camp Jackson, Columbia, South Carolina. Assigned to this detachment. Promoted to sergeant on March 25, 1918. Served overseas from August 26, 1918, until February 11, 1919. Honorably discharged on February 27, 1919.

## Company C

HECKSTALL, JOHNNIE*, private: Registered for Selective Service on June 5, 1917, at age 21; occupation – farmer. Inducted as a private at Windsor on December 18, 1917, and transported to Camp Jackson, Columbia, South Carolina. Assigned to this company. Sent overseas on April 7, 1918. Severely wounded about September 28, 1918. Returned from overseas on February 12, 1919, and honorably discharged on April 7, 1919.

PARKER, KINLEY*, private: No Selective Service registration found for this individual; however, he was inducted as a private at Windsor on December 6, 1917, at age 23, and transported to Camp Jackson, Columbia, South Carolina. Assigned to this company. Honorably discharged on December 26, 1918, having performed no overseas service.

SKINNER, PETER*, private: Registered for Selective Service on June 5, 1917, at age 25; occupation – laborer. Inducted as a private at Windsor on December 18, 1917, and transported to Camp Jackson, Columbia, South Carolina. Assigned to this company. Transferred to Company A, 328th Service Battalion on March 6, 1918.

STEWART, JAMES*, private: Registered for Selective Service as a Bertie County resident in Chester County, Pennsylvania on June 1, 1917, at age 28; occupation – clerk. Inducted as a private at Windsor on December 18, 1917, and transported to Camp Jackson, Columbia, South Carolina. Assigned to this company. Sent overseas on April 7, 1918. Wounded on August 28, 1918. Returned from overseas on February 12, 1919, and honorably discharged on February 28, 1919.

# 96th DIVISION

# 192nd INFANTRY BRIGADE

# 363rd MACHINE GUN BATTALION

# MISCELLANEOUS (NO COMPANY IDENTIFIED)

WINBORNE, WILLIAM CHESTER, private: Registered for Selective Service on June 5, 1917, at age 24; occupation – farmer. Inducted as a private at Windsor on July 22, 1918, and transported to Camp Hancock, near Augusta, Georgia. Initially assigned to the Machine Gun Training Center and transferred to this battalion on October 30, 1918. Honorably discharged on December 18, 1918, having performed no overseas service.

## NON-DIVISIONAL UNITS

## 2nd CAVALRY REGIMENT

RHODES, HERBERT C., private: Enlisted as a private at Fort Slocum, Davids Island, New York on April 23, 1917, at age 20. Assigned to this regiment. Promoted to private first class on July 17, 1917, and to corporal on November 26, 1917. Reduced to private on February 13, 1918. Served overseas from March 22, 1918, until June 29, 1919. Honorably discharged on July 15, 1919.

## 25th INFANTRY REGIMENT

### Headquarters Company

GILLAM, DAVID C.*, color sergeant: Previously served in Company E of this regiment. Transferred to this company on September 22, 1917, while serving in Hawaii. Promoted to color sergeant on September 22, 1917. Honorably discharged on March 30, 1919, having performed no overseas service in Europe.

### Company E

GILLAM, DAVID C.*, color sergeant: Enlisted at Schofield Barracks, Hawaii on February 13, 1914, at age 41. Served in this company and promoted to corporal and sergeant on undisclosed dates. Transferred to Headquarters Company of this regiment on September 22, 1917.

## 27th INFANTRY REGIMENT

### Company B

PIERCE, GEORGE W., sergeant: Enlisted as a private at Columbus, Ohio on November 14, 1914, at age 18. Assigned to this company. Promoted to private first class on Oc-

tober 12, 1916, and to corporal on August 26, 1917. Sent overseas on August 7, 1918 and served until honorably discharged on July 16, 1919. Date of return to the United States not disclosed in military record.

## PIONEER INFANTRY

## 1st PIONEER INFANTRY REGIMENT

### Company C

BELL, FRANK, private: Previously served in Company E, 116th Infantry Regiment. Transferred to this company on April 6, 1918. Arrested and jailed by Sheriff John W. Cooper in Bertie County on May 21, 1918, for being a deserter. No additional information regarding this incident. Transferred to Company H, 51st Pioneer Infantry Regiment on June 29, 1918.

## 51st PIONEER INFANTRY REGIMENT

### Company H

BELL, FRANK, private: Previously served in Company C, 1st Pioneer Infantry Regiment. Transferred to this company on June 29, 1918. Served overseas from July 26, 1918, until July 6, 1919. Honorably discharged at Camp Upton, Long Island, New York on July 11, 1919, "for re-enlistment." No information found regarding Bell's re-enlistment.

## 53rd PIONEER INFANTRY REGIMENT

## Supply Company

HAYES, LEMUEL PARKER, wagoner: Previously served in Company K of this regiment. Transferred as a private to this company on September 10, 1918, while serving overseas. Promoted to wagoner on November 27, 1918. Returned from overseas on May 4, 1919, and honorably discharged at Camp Lee, Petersburg, Virginia on May 12, 1919.

## Company K

HAYES, LEMUEL PARKER, private: Registered for Selective Service on June 5, 1917, at age 30; occupation – mill laborer. Inducted as a private at Windsor on June 28, 1918, and transported to Camp Jackson, Columbia, South Carolina. Initially assigned to the 156th Depot Brigade and transferred to this company on July 25, 1918. Sent overseas on August 6, 1918. Transferred to Supply Company of this regiment on September 10, 1918.

# 55th PIONEER INFANTRY REGIMENT

## Company F

BURKETT, JAMES ANDREW, private: Previously served in Company A, 57th Pioneer Infantry Regiment. Transferred to this company on August 20, 1918. Transferred to the 56th Guard Company, Army Service Corps on November 1, 1918.

HARDEN, NORMAN LOU, private: Previously served in Company A, 57th Pioneer Infantry Regiment. Transferred to this company on August 28, 1918. Sent overseas on September 22, 1918, and transferred to Company C, 330th Infantry Regiment, 165th Infantry Brigade, 83rd Division on October 17, 1918.

MIZELL, DAVID ROBERT, cook: Previously served in Company A, 57th Pioneer Infantry Regiment. Transferred as a private to this company on August 27, 1918. Promoted to cook on September 6, 1918. Sent overseas on September 14, 1918. Transferred to the 59th Guard Company, Army Service Corps on an undisclosed date.

MIZELL, WILLIAM WESLEY, private: Registered for Selective Service on June 5, 1917, at age 25; occupation – farmer. Inducted as a private at Windsor on August 5, 1918, and transported to Camp Wadsworth, Spartanburg, South Carolina. Assigned to this company. Served overseas from September 15, 1918, until April 27, 1919. Honorably discharged at Camp Lee, Petersburg, Virginia on May 5, 1919.

SMITHWICK, JOSEPH EDWARD, private: Registered for Selective Service on June 5, 1917, at age 21; occupation – farmer. Inducted as a private at Windsor on August 5, 1918, and transported to Camp Wadsworth, Spartanburg, South Carolina. Assigned to this company. Sent overseas on September 15, 1918. Transferred to Company I, 107th Infantry, 54th Infantry Brigade, 27th Division on November 11, 1918.

WHITE, ASA W., private: Registered for Selective Service on June 5, 1917, at age 26; occupation – farmer. Inducted as a private at Windsor on August 5, 1918, and transported to Camp Wadsworth, Spartanburg, South Carolina. Assigned to this company. Sent overseas on September 15, 1918. Transferred to 308th Motor Supply Train on November 15, 1918.

# MISCELLANEOUS (NO COMPANY IDENTIFIED)

PIERCE, SAMUEL WHITE., private: Previously served in Company A, 57th Pioneer Infantry Regiment. Transferred to this regiment on August 27, 1918. Sent overseas on September 15, 1918, and transferred to Company L, 106th Infantry Regiment, 53rd Infantry Brigade, 27th Division on December 9, 1918.

# 57th PIONEER INFANTRY REGIMENT

## MEDICAL DEPARTMENT

NORFLEET, EDGAR POWELL, first lieutenant: "Called into service" and appointed first lieutenant in the Medical Department at Fort Oglethorpe, Chickamauga Park, Georgia on October 8, 1917. Assigned to Ambulance Number 22 of this regiment. Served overseas from July 26, 1918, until July 3, 1919. Also served on undisclosed dates at Camp Wadsworth, South Carolina; Camp Merritt, New Jersey; and Camp Mills, New York. Honorably discharged on July 25, 1919.

## Company A

BRACY, ODIE LAWRENCE, private: Registered for Selective Service on June 5, 1917, at age 21; occupation – farmer. Inducted as a private at Windsor on August 5, 1918, and transported to Camp Wadsworth, Spartanburg, South Carolina. Per his military service record, he enlisted as a private in the Enlisted Reserve Corps in Bertie County on August 5, 1918, and was assigned to this company on that date. Sent overseas on September 15, 1918. Transferred to Company B, 331st Infantry Regiment, 166th Infantry Brigade, 83rd Division on December 5, 1918.

BURKETT, JAMES ANDREW, private: Registered for Selective Service on June 5, 1918, at age 21. Inducted as a private at Windsor on August 5, 1918, and transported to Camp Wadsworth, Spartanburg, South Carolina. Assigned to this company and transferred to Company F, 55th Pioneer Infantry Regiment on August 20, 1918.

BYRD, COLA JOHN, private: Registered for Selective Service on June 5, 1917, at age 29; occupation – contractor and builder. Inducted as a private at Windsor on August 5, 1918, and transported to Camp Wadsworth, Spartanburg, South Carolina. Assigned to this company and transferred to Company B, Provisional Engineers Battalion on August 28, 1918.

HARDEN, FRANK HOBBS, private: Registered for Selective Service on June 5, 1917, at age 21; occupation – farmer. Inducted as a private at Windsor on August 5, 1918, and transported to Camp Wadsworth, Spartanburg, South Carolina. Assigned to this company. Sent overseas on September 15, 1918, and transferred to Company H, 330th Infantry Regiment, 165th Infantry Brigade, 83rd Division on November 8, 1918.

HARDEN, NORMAN LOU, private: Registered for Selective Service on June 5, 1917, at age 29; occupation – farm laborer. Inducted as a private at Windsor on August 5, 1918, and transported to Camp Wadsworth, Spartanburg, South Carolina. Assigned to this company and transferred to Company F, 55th Pioneer Infantry Regiment on August 28, 1918.

MIZELL, DAVID ROBERT, private: Registered for Selective Service on June 5, 1917, at age 26; occupation – farmer. Inducted as a private at Windsor on August 5, 1918, and transported to Camp Wadsworth, Spartanburg, South Carolina. Initially assigned to this company and transferred to Company F, 55th Pioneer Infantry Regiment on August 27, 1918.

MORRIS, LEROY, private: Registered for Selective Service on June 5, 1917, at age 22; occupation – farmer. Inducted as a private at Windsor on August 5, 1918, and transported to Camp Wadsworth, Spartanburg, South Carolina. Assigned to this company. Transferred to Company A, 107th Infantry Regiment, 54th Infantry Brigade, 27th Division on August 27, 1918.

PERRY, JAMES L., private: Registered for Selective Service on June 5, 1917, at age 21; occupation – farmer. Name appears on a list of men inducted at Windsor on May 28, 1918, who were transported to Camp Jackson, Columbia, South Carolina; however, the entry for Perry was lined through. Inducted as a private at Windsor on August 5, 1918, and transported to Camp Wadsworth, Spartanburg, South Carolina. Assigned to this company. Served overseas from October 3, 1918, until April 21, 1919. Honorably discharged at Camp Jackson on May 12, 1919.

PERRY, WILLIAM LEWIS, private: Registered for Selective Service on June 5, 1917, at age 25; occupation – farmer. Inducted as a private at Windsor on August 5, 1918, and transported to Camp Wadsworth, Spartanburg, South Carolina. Assigned to this company. Transferred to the Artillery Park, 4th Army Corps on August 27, 1918.

PHELPS, NORMAN HENSON, private: Registered for Selective Service as a Bertie County resident in Norfolk County, Virginia on May 24, 1917, at age 24; occupation – farmer. Inducted as a private at Windsor on August 5, 1918, and transported to Camp Wadsworth, Spartanburg, South Carolina. Assigned to this company. Transferred to Headquarters Company, Artillery Park, 4th Army Corps on August 27, 1918.

PHELPS, WILLIAM GRADY, private: Registered for Selective Service on June 5, 1917, at age 26; occupation – farmer. Inducted as a private at Windsor on August 5, 1918, and transported to Camp Wadsworth, Spartanburg, South Carolina. Assigned to this company. Transferred to Company B, 107th Infantry Regiment, 54th Infantry Brigade, 27th Division on August 27, 1918.

PIERCE, SAMUEL WHITE., private: Registered for Selective Service on June 5, 1917, at age 26; occupation – farmer. Inducted as

a private at Windsor on August 5, 1918, and transported to Camp Wadsworth, Spartanburg, South Carolina. Assigned to this company. Transferred to the 55th Pioneer Infantry Regiment on August 27, 1918.

SUTTON, WILLIAM MOORING, JR., private: Previously served in the Air Service Enlisted Reserve Corps from which he was honorably discharged on February 10, 1918. Inducted as a private at Windsor on August 5, 1918, and transported to Camp Wadsworth, Spartanburg, South Carolina. Assigned to this company. Sent overseas on September 23, 1918.

THURSTON, FRED WARD, private: Registered for Selective Service on June 5, 1917, at age 26; occupation – farm laborer. Inducted as a private at Windsor on August 5, 1918, and transported to Camp Wadsworth, Spartanburg, South Carolina. Assigned to this company. Sent overseas on September 15, 1918. Transferred to Company I, 107th Infantry Regiment, 54th Infantry Brigade, 27th Division on December 7, 1918.

# 62ND PIONEER INFANTRY REGIMENT

## MISCELLANEOUS (NO COMPANY IDENTIFIED)

CASTELLOE, OBED, second lieutenant: Appointed second lieutenant at the Central Officers Training School, Camp Gordon, Augusta, Georgia on August 26, 1918. Assigned to this regiment at Camp Wadsworth, Spartanburg, South Carolina on an undisclosed date. Honorably discharged on December 11, 1918, having performed no overseas service.

# 63rd PIONEER INFANTRY REGIMENT

## Company H

WILSON, WILLOUGHBY*, private: Previously served in the 153rd Depot Brigade, Camp Dix, New Jersey. Transferred to this company on October 22, 1918. Honorably discharged on December 19, 1918, having performed no overseas service.

## Company K

KING, CHARLIE*, private: Registered for Selective Service on June 5, 1917, at age 30; occupation – laborer, log woods. Inducted as a private at Windsor on July 16, 1918, and transported to Camp Dix, near Trenton, New Jersey. Assigned to the 153rd Depot Brigade and transferred to this Company on October 29, 1918. Honorably discharged on December 13, 1918, having performed no overseas service.

## 801st PIONEER INFANTRY REGIMENT

### Company A

SAVAGE, DUDLEY*, private: Registered for Selective Service on June 5, 1917, at age 21; occupation – laborer, log woods. Inducted as a private at Windsor on June 21, 1918, and transported to Camp Taylor, Louisville, Kentucky. Initially assigned to the 159th Depot Brigade and transferred to this company on July 15, 1918. Served overseas from September 8, 1918, until June 5, 1919. Honorably discharged on June 13, 1919.

### Company F

LIVERMAN, SPURGEON*, private: Registered for Selective Service on June 5, 1917, at age 27; occupation – farmer. Name appears on a list of men inducted at Windsor on April 28, 1918, and transported to Camp Grant, Rockford, Illinois, but Liverman was "sick when called" and was not inducted. Subsequently inducted as a private at Wind-

sor on July 3, 1918, and transported to Camp Taylor, Louisville, Kentucky. Initially assigned to the 159th Depot Brigade and transferred to this company on August 17, 1918. Served overseas from September 8, 1918, until June 19, 1919. Honorably discharged on July 20, 1919.

## MISCELLANEOUS (NO COMPANY IDENTIFIED)

PARKER, HENRY*, private: Registered for Selective Service on June 5, 1917, at age 27; occupation – laborer. Inducted as a private at Windsor on July 3, 1918, and transported to Camp Taylor, Louisville, Kentucky. Assigned to this regiment. Honorably discharged on June 13, 1919, having performed no overseas service.

## 805th PIONEER INFANTRY REGIMENT

### Company A

CHERRY, JOE ALLEN*, private: Previously served in Company A, 330th Labor Battalion, Quartermaster Corps. Transferred to this company on November 27, 1918, while serving overseas. Returned from overseas on June 27, 1919, and honorably discharged at Camp Lee, Petersburg, Virginia on July 12, 1919.

EBRON, JOSEPH*, private: Previously served in the 344th Labor Battalion, Quartermaster Corps. Transferred to this company on March 4, 1919, while serving overseas. Returned from overseas on June 27, 1919, and honorably discharged at Camp Lee, Petersburg, Virginia on July 12, 1919.

### Company B

TYNER, PLUMMER G.* private: Registered for Selective Service on June 5, 1917, at age 22; occupation – farmer. Inducted as a private at Windsor on August 1, 1918, and transported to Camp Jackson, Columbia, South Carolina. Assigned to this company. Served overseas from September 25, 1918, until June 27, 1919. Honorably discharged at Camp Lee, Petersburg, Virginia on July 12, 1919.

# 807th PIONEER INFANTRY REGIMENT

## Company L

CARTER, WILL*, private: Registered for Selective Service on June 5, 1917, at age 26; occupation – laborer at lumber company. Inducted as a private at Windsor on July 16, 1918, and transported to Camp Dix, near Trenton, New Jersey. Initially assigned to the 153rd Depot Brigade and transferred to this company on August 29, 1918. Served overseas from August 1918, until January 3, 1919. Honorably discharged on February 27, 1919.

JOHNSON, ARCHIE S.*, private: Registered for Selective Service on June 5, 1917, at age 22; occupation – laborer. Inducted as a private at Windsor on July 16, 1918, and transported to Camp Dix, near Trenton, New Jersey. Initially assigned to the 153rd Depot Brigade and transferred to this company on August 291, 1918. Served overseas from September 4, 1918, until July 3, 1919. Honorably discharged on July 16, 1919.

# 810TH PIONEER INFANTRY REGIMENT

## HEADQUARTERS COMPANY

WILLIAMS, JAMES AUGUSTUS*, private: Registered for Selective Service on June 5, 1917, at age 21; occupation – farmer. Inducted as a private at Windsor on Au-

gust 23, 1918, and transported to Camp Greene, Charlotte. Assigned to this company. Transferred to 423rd Labor Battalion on December 3, 1918.

## Company A

DEANS, JAMES W.*, private: Registered for Selective Service on June 5, 1917, at age 23; occupation – farm laborer. Inducted as a private at Windsor on July 29, 1918, and transported to Camp Greene, Charlotte, where he was assigned to this company. Honorably discharged on January 13, 1919, having performed no overseas service.

MIZELL, WILLIE*, private: Registered for Selective Service on June 5, 1917, at age 24; occupation – farmer. Inducted as a private at Windsor on July 29, 1918, and transported to Camp Greene, Charlotte. Assigned to this company. Died at of lobar pneumonia at Camp Greene on October 14, 1918.

MOORE, JOHN C.*, private: Registered for Selective Service on June 5, 1917, at age 28; occupation – laborer. Inducted as a private at Windsor on July 29, 1918, and transported to Camp Greene, Charlotte. Assigned to this company. Honorably discharged on December 11, 1918, having performed no overseas service.

## Company D

RUFFIN, NED*, private: Registered for Selective Service on June 5, 1917, at age 21; occupation – farmer. Inducted as a private at Windsor on August 23, 1918, and transported to Camp Greene, Charlotte. Initially assigned to Recruit Camp Number 3 and transferred to this company on September 18, 1918. Transferred to the 423rd Reserve Labor Battalion, Quartermaster Corps, on December 13, 1918.

WATFORD, DAVID*, private: Registered for Selective Service on September 12, 1918, at age 21; occupation – farm laborer. Inducted as a private at Windsor on August 23, 1918, and transported to Camp Greene, Charlotte. Assigned to this company. Honorably discharged on December 23, 1918, having performed no overseas service.

## Company I

BROWN, LEE*, private: Registered for Selective Service on June 5, 1917, at age 21; occupation – farmer. Inducted as a private at Windsor on August 23, 1918, and transported to Camp Greene, Charlotte. Assigned to this company and honorably discharged at Camp Greene on December 12, 1918, having performed no overseas service.

CHERRY, JOSEPH RALEIGH*, private: Registered for Selective Service on June 5, 1917, at age 27; occupation – farmer. Inducted as a private at Windsor on August 23, 1918, and transported to Camp Greene, Charlotte. Assigned to this company and honorably discharged at Camp Greene on January 31, 1919, having performed no overseas service.

COTTON, WILLIAM*, private: Registered for Selective Service on June 5, 1917, at age 21; occupation – farm laborer. Inducted as a private at Windsor on August 23, 1918, and transported to Camp Greene, Charlotte. Assigned to this company and died of pneumonia on October 17, 1918, having performed no overseas service.

HOLLEY, OSCAR*, private: Registered for Selective Service on June 5, 1917, at age 22; occupation – farmer. Inducted as a private at Windsor on August 23, 1918, and transported to Camp Greene, Charlotte. Served in this company. Honorably discharged at Camp Greene on January 13, 1919, having performed no overseas service.

JAMES, THOMAS*, private: Registered for Selective Service on June 5, 1917, at age 22; occupation – farmer. Inducted as a private at Windsor on August 23, 1918, and

transported to Camp Greene, Charlotte. Assigned to this company. Honorably discharged on December 10, 1918, having performed no overseas service.

SESSOMS, OSCAR*, private: Registered for Selective Service on June 5, 1917, at age 21; occupation – farmer. Inducted as a private at Windsor on August 23, 1918, and transported to Camp Greene, Charlotte. Assigned to this company. Honorably discharged on January 31, 1919, with a service-connected disability rated as 50 percent, having performed no overseas service.

WESSON, ARCHIE GLENN*, private: Registered for Selective Service on June 5, 1917, at age 26; occupation – farmer. Inducted as a private at Windsor on August 23, 1918, and transported to Camp Greene, Charlotte. Assigned to this company. Honorably discharged at Camp Greene on December 10, 1918, having performed no overseas service.

WILLIAMS THOMAS*, private: Registered for Selective Service on June 5, 1917, at age 23; occupation – farmer. Inducted as a private at Windsor on August 23, 1918, and transported to Camp Greene, Charlotte. Assigned to this company. Honorably discharged on December 10, 1918, having performed no overseas service.

## Company L

PRITCHARD, ANDREW JACKSON*, private: Registered for Selective Service on June 5, 1917, at age 22; occupation – hotel cook. Inducted as a private at Windsor on July 29, 1918, and transported to Camp Greene, Charlotte. Assigned to Recruit Camp Number 3. Transferred to this company on October 20, 1918. Transferred to Company D, 423rd Reserve Labor Battalion, Quartermaster Corps on December 3, 1918.

THOMPSON, JACOB*, private: A Selective Service registrant who transferred from

Norfolk, Virginia. Inducted as a private at Windsor on August 23, 1918, and transported to Camp Greene, Charlotte. Assigned to this company. Transferred to Company D, 423rd Reserve Labor Battalion on December 3, 1918.

# LOUISIANA NATIONAL GUARD

## 1st INFANTRY REGIMENT

### Company B

PERRY, JOSEPH CLEE, private: Enlisted at Crawley, Louisiana as a private in the Louisiana National Guard on June 20, 1916. Served in this company. Honorably discharged on April 27, 1917, with a service-connected disability. Registered for Selective Service in Bertie County on June 5, 1917, and was subsequently inducted.

# NORTH CAROLINA NATIONAL GUARD

## 2nd INFANTRY REGIMENT NORTH CAROLINA NATIONAL GUARD

### Company G

JONES, RUBIN, private: Enlisted as a private at Goldsboro on June 6, 1917, at age 21. Served in this company. Transferred to Company C, 117th Engineers Regiment, 42nd Division on August 20, 1917. (Subsequent to Pvt. Jones's service, this regiment was re-designated the 119th Infantry Regiment in September 1917.)

### Company I

LAWRENCE, ROBERT WHIT, corporal: Enlisted as a private at an undisclosed location on July 20, 1916. Served in this company while the regiment was in Federal service along the United States–Mexico border. Promoted to corporal on an undisclosed date. Honorably discharged on June 15, 1917. (Subsequent to Corporal Lawrence's service, this regiment was re-designated the 119th Infantry Regiment on September 1917.)

# VIRGINIA NATIONAL GUARD

## 2nd INFANTRY REGIMENT

### Company C

HAIGHT, THOMAS EDWIN, private: Registered for Selective Service on or about June 5, 1917, at age 21. Enlisted as a private in the Virginia National Guard at Petersburg, Virginia on July 19, 1917. Assigned to this company. Transferred to Company C, 118th Infantry Regiment, 59th Infantry Brigade, 30th Division on August 17, 1917.

## 4TH INFANTRY REGIMENT

## MACHINE GUN COMPANY

CLEATON, JOHN THOMAS, private: Enlisted as a private in the Virginia National Guard at Norfolk, Virginia on May 28, 1917. Assigned to this company. Transferred to Company B, 112th Machine Gun Battalion, 58th Infantry Brigade, 29th Division on September 27, 1917.

MCDANIEL, THOMAS, private: Enlisted as a private at Norfolk, Virginia on May 28, 1917. Assigned to this company (subsequently designated as Company B, 112th Machine Gun Battalion, 58th Infantry Brigade, 29th Division). Promoted to mess sergeant on March 19, 1918, and reduced to private on May 11, 1918. Transferred to the Sanitation Detachment, Company B, 112th Machine Gun Battalion, 54th Field Artillery Brigade, 29th Division on June 1, 1918.

WILLIAMS, THOMAS L., private: Enlisted as a private at Norfolk, Virginia on June 6, 1917. Assigned to this company, subsequently designated as Company B, 112th Machine Gun Battalion, 58th Infantry Brigade, 29th Division.

## Company F

BELL, FRANK, private: Enlisted as a private in the Virginia National Guard at Suffolk, Virginia on July 31, 1917. Assigned to this company. Transferred to Company E, 116th Infantry Regiment, 58th Infantry Brigade, 29th Division on October 4, 1917.

DAVIDSON, CLAUDE D., private: Registered for Selective Service on June 5, 1917, at age 28; occupation – farm laborer. Enlisted at Norfolk, Virginia as a private on May 12, 1917 or June 16, 1917. Assigned to this company. Transferred to Company E, 116th Infantry Regiment, 58th Infantry Brigade, 29th Division on an undisclosed date.

## Company I

CASPER, ROY ADSON, private: Registered for Selective Service on June 5, 1917, at age 23; occupation – farm laborer. Enlisted as a private in the Virginia National Guard at Franklin on July 31, 1917, at age 25. Assigned to this company. Transferred to Headquarters Company, 111th Field Artillery Regiment on October 10, 1917.

HARRINGTON, JAMES O., private: Enlisted as a private at Franklin, Virginia on July 27, 1917. Assigned to this company. Transferred to Headquarters Company, 111th Field Artillery Regiment, 54th Field Artillery Brigade, 29th Division on October 10, 1917.

HUGHES, DAVID AARON, private: Enlisted as a private at Franklin, Virginia on July 31, 1917. Assigned to this company. Transferred to Headquarters Company, 111th Field Artillery Regiment, 54th Field Artillery Brigade, 29th Division on October 10, 1917.

JACOCKS, JESSE CARTER, private: Enlisted as a private at Franklin, Virginia on June 5, 1917. Assigned to this company. Transferred to Company C, 104th Field Signal Battalion, Signal Corps on November 8, 1917.

THOMAS, JOHN ALEXANDER, private: Enlisted at Franklin, Virginia as a private in the Virginia National Guard on July 3, 1917, at age 19. Assigned to this company. Transferred to Headquarters Company, 111th Field Artillery Regiment, 54th Field Artillery Brigade, 29th Division on October 10, 1917.

WILLIAMS, ABNER WRIGHT, private: Registered for Selective Service on June 5, 1917, at age 24; occupation – farm laborer. Enlisted at Franklin, Virginia, as a private in the Virginia National Guard on July 31, 1917, at age of 24. Assigned to this company. Transferred to Headquarters Company, 111th Field Artillery Regiment, 54th Field Artillery Brigade, 29th Division on October 10, 1917.

## Company M

MINTON, PATRICK WINSTON, private: Enlisted as a private at Suffolk, Virginia on July 31, 1917. Assigned to this company. Transferred to the Machine Gun Company, 115th Infantry Regiment, 58th Infantry Brigade, 29th Division on November 8, 1917.

## CORPS OF ENGINEERS

## 15th ENGINEERS REGIMENT

### Company F

ALEXANDER, SEATON NORWOOD, private first class: Previously served in the 19th Engineers Regiment. Transferred as a private to this company on April 28, 1918, while serving overseas. Promoted to private first class on August 1, 1918. Returned to the United States from overseas service on April 27, 1919, and honorably discharged at Camp Sherman, near Chillicothe, Ohio on May 9, 1919.

## 17th ENGINEERS REGIMENT

## MISCELLANEOUS (NO COMPANY IDENTIFIED)

ADAMS, WILLIAM FRANKLIN, private first class: Registered for Selective Service on June 5, 1917, at age 28; occupation – railroad bridge watchman. Enlisted as a private at Wilmington on June 22, 1917, and assigned to the 7th Reserve Engineers Regiment, subsequently the 17th Engineers Regiment, at Atlanta, Georgia. Promoted to private first class on May 1, 1918. Served overseas from July 28, 1917 until March 25, 1919, and honorably discharged at Camp Gordon, Augusta, Georgia on April 5, 1919.

## 19th ENGINEERS REGIMENT

## MISCELLANEOUS (NO COMPANY IDENTIFIED)

ALEXANDER, SEATON NORWOOD, private: Previously served in Company B, 316th Machine Gun Battalion, 81st Division. Transferred to this regiment on February 21, 1918, and sent overseas on March 14, 1918. Transferred to Company F, 15th Engineers Regiment on April 28, 1918.

## 71st ENGINEERS REGIMENT

## MISCELLANEOUS (NO COMPANY IDENTIFIED)

CASTELLOW, HERBERT CLYDE, private: Previously served in the 3rd Company, 7th Engineers Training Regiment. Transferred to this regiment October 21, 1918. Honorably discharged on December 28, 1918, having performed no overseas service.

## 118th ENGINEERS REGIMENT

RAYNER, THOMAS AUGUSTUS, first lieutenant: Served in this regiment on undisclosed dates. Also served in 218th Engineers Regiment, 18th Division, and in the 19th Division.

## HEADQUARTERS COMPANY

ROUNTREE, LONNIE NORFLEET, private: Registered for Selective Service on June 5, 1917, at age 27; occupation – engineer. Inducted as a private at Windsor on August 25, 1918, and transported to Camp Jackson, Columbia, South Carolina. Assigned to this company. Honorably discharged on December 9, 1918, having performed no overseas service.

## 128th ENGINEERS REGIMENT

### Company B

COX, WILLIAM LEE, private first class: Previously served in the 116th Engineers Regiment, 41st Division. Transferred as a private to this company on November 20, 1918, while serving overseas. Promoted to private first class on December 28, 1918. Returned from overseas on July 12, 1919, and honorably discharged at Camp Dix, near Trenton, New Jersey on July 23, 1919.

## 131st ENGINEERS REGIMENT

### Company B

BYRD, COLA JOHN, private first class: Previously served in Company B, Provisional Engineers Battalion. Transferred as a private to this company on March 16, 1919, while serving overseas. Promoted to private first class on May 1, 1919, and returned from overseas on July 15, 1919. Honorably discharged at Camp Lee, Petersburg, Virginia on July 23, 1919.

## 532nd ENGINEERS SERVICE BATTALION

### Company B

WHITE, CANSEY (COSSIE)*, private: Registered for Selective Service on June 5, 1917, at age 21; occupation – laborer. Inducted as a private at Windsor on June 21, 1918, and transported to Camp Taylor, Louisville, Kentucky. Assigned to this company. Served overseas from August 22, 1918, until June 20, 1919. Honorably discharged on July 15, 1919.

## Company C

WINBORNE, ROBERT LEE*, mechanic: Registered for Selective Service on June 5, 1917, at age 23; occupation – blacksmith. Inducted as a private at Windsor on June 21, 1918, and transported to Camp Taylor, Louisville, Kentucky. Initially assigned to the 159th Depot Brigade and transferred to this company on July 12, 1918. Promoted to private first class on August 1, 1918. Sent overseas August 22, 918. Promoted to mechanic on September 7, 1918. Returned from overseas on February 28, 1919. Honorably discharged on March 19, 1919, with a service-connected disability rated as 15 percent.

## Company D

COFFIELD, WILLIE*, private: Registered for Selective Service on June 5, 1917, at age 23; occupation – farmer. Inducted as a private at Windsor on June 2, 1918, and transported to Camp Taylor, Louisville, Kentucky. Assigned to the 159th Depot Brigade until July 12, 1918, when he was transferred to this company. Sent overseas on August 22, 1918. Died of "peritonitis and tuberculosis suspect" on March 14, 1919.

WATSON, ALBERT DAVID*, private first class: Registered for Selective Service on June 5, 1917, at age 21; occupation – farmer. Inducted as a private at Windsor on June 21, 1918, and transported to Camp Taylor, Louisville, Kentucky. Initially assigned to the 159th Depot Brigade and transferred to this company on July 12, 1918. Sent overseas on August 22, 1918. Promoted to private first class on January 1, 1919. Returned from overseas on July 12, 1919, and honorably discharged at Camp Taylor on July 21, 1919.

# 534th ENGINEERS SERVICE BATTALION

## Company A

HOGGARD, BENJAMIN FRANKLIN, sergeant: Registered for Selective Service on June 5, 1917, at age 21; occupation – farm laborer. Inducted as a private at Windsor on April 26, 1918, and transported to Camp Jackson, Columbia, South Carolina. Assigned to this company. Promoted to private first class on June 1, 1918, to corporal on June 16, 1918, and to sergeant on July 1, 1918. Served overseas from August 29, 1918, until July 3, 1919. Honorably discharged on July 18, 1919.

## Company B

PEELE, THOMAS N., first sergeant: Registered for Selective Service on June 5, 1917, at age 27; occupation – bank manager. Inducted as a private at Windsor on May 28, 1918, and transported to Camp Jackson, Columbia, South Carolina. Initially assigned to the 156th Depot Brigade and transferred to this company on June 13, 1918. Promoted to private first class on June 16, 1918, and to sergeant on August 1, 1918. Sent overseas on August 29, 1918. Promoted to first sergeant on February 11, 1919. Returned from overseas on July 4, 1919, and honorably discharged on July 14, 1919.

# MISCELLANEOUS (NO COMPANY IDENTIFIED)

FRANCIS, WILLIAM THOMAS, private: Registered for Selective Service on June 5, 1917, at age 22; occupation – farmer. Inducted as a private at Windsor on April 26, 1918, and transported to Camp Jackson, Columbia, South Carolina. Initially assigned to the 156th Depot Brigade and transferred to this battalion on May 24, 1918. Trans-ferred to Company C, 322nd Infantry Regiment, 161st Infantry Brigade, 81st Division on June 2, 1918.

# 536th ENGINEERS SERVICE BATTALION

## Company A

BUNCH, FRED JUNIUS*, private: Registered for Selective Service on June 5, 1917, at age 30; occupation –farmer. Inducted as a private at Windsor on July 16, 1918, and transported to Camp Dix, near Trenton, New Jersey. Assigned to this company on an undisclosed date. Served overseas from August 26, 1918, until July 30, 1919. Honorably discharged at Camp Jackson, Columbia, South Carolina on August 6, 1919.

## Company D

FREEMAN, DAVID*, private: Registered for Selective Service on June 5, 1917, at age 21; occupation – farmer. Inducted as a private at Windsor on July 16, 1918, and transported to Camp Dix, near Trenton, New Jersey. Initially assigned to the 153rd Depot Brigade and transferred to this company on August 16, 1918. Served overseas from August 3, 1918, until July 31, 1919. Honorably discharged at Camp Jackson, Columbia, South Carolina on August 16, 1919.

GILLAM, GEORGE BRETT*, private first class: Registered for Selective Service on June 5, 1917, at age 22; occupation – laborer. Inducted as a private at Windsor on July 16, 1918, and transported to Camp Dix, near Trenton, New Jersey. Assigned to this company and sent overseas on August 26, 1918. Promoted to private first class on May 22, 1919. Returned from overseas on July 30, 1919, and honorably discharged at Camp Jackson, Columbia South Carolina on August 6, 1919.

HARRELL, HENRY*, private first class: Registered for Selective Service on June 5, 1917, at age 23; occupation – farmer. Inducted as a private at Windsor on July 16, 1918, and transported to Camp Dix, near Trenton, New Jersey. Initially assigned to the 153rd Depot Brigade and transferred to this company on August 18, 1918. Sent overseas on August 26, 1918. Promoted to private first class on December 13, 1918. Returned from overseas on July 30, 1919, and honorably discharged on August 6, 1919.

MORRIS, NORMAN*, corporal: Registered for Selective Service on June 5, 1917, at age 21; occupation – farmer. Inducted as a private at Windsor on July 16, 1918, and transported to Camp Dix, near Trenton, New Jersey. Assigned to this company. Promoted to private first class on September 7, 1918, and to corporal on May 27, 1919. Served overseas from August 26, 1918, until July 30, 1919. Honorably discharged on August 6, 1919.

RYAN, CLEVELAND*, private: Registered for Selective Service on June 5, 1917, at age 21; occupation – laborer. Inducted as a private at Windsor on July 16, 1918, and transported to Camp Dix, near Trenton, New Jersey. Assigned to this company. Served overseas from August 26, 1918, until July 30, 1919. Honorably discharged on August 6, 1919.

SESSOMS, JONAH*, private: Registered for Selective Service on June 5, 1917, at age 21; occupation – farm laborer. Inducted as a private at Windsor on July 16, 1918, and transported to Camp Dix, near Trenton, New Jersey. Assigned to this company. Served overseas from August 26, 1918, until July 30, 1919. Honorably discharged on August 6, 1919.

## 541st ENGINEERS REGIMENT

### Company A

SMALLWOOD, FRANK H.*, private: Was "delinquent in registering" for Selective Service when he registered on June 28, 1918, at age 25; occupation – undisclosed. Inducted as a private at Windsor on July 3, 1918, and transported to Camp Taylor, Louisville, Kentucky. Initially assigned to the 159th Depot Brigade and transferred to this company on August 22, 1918. Served overseas from September 20, 1918, until July 28, 1919. Honorably discharged at Camp Lee, Petersburg, Virginia on August 1, 1919.

## 605th ENGINEERS REGIMENT

### Company D

BURDEN, WALTER JACKSON, private: Inducted as a private at Windsor on May 16, 1918, and purportedly assigned to the Student Army Training Corps but no subsequent record(s) found to confirm such assignment. Instead, he was assigned to this company and transferred to Company F of this regiment on August 3, 1918.

### Company F

BURDEN, WALTER JACKSON, private: Previously served in Company D of this regiment. Transferred to this company on August 3, 1918. Transferred to the October Automatic Replacement Draft (Engineers) at Washington Barracks, Washington, D.C. on September 16, 1918.

## MISCELLANEOUS ENGINEERS UNITS

BYRD, COLA JOHN, private: Previously served in Company A, 57th Pioneer Infantry Regiment. Transferred to Company B, Provisional Engineers Battalion on August 28, 1918. Sent overseas on September 15, 1918. Transferred to Company B, 131st Engineers Regiment on March 16, 1919.

CASTELLOW, HERBERT CLYDE, private: Registered for Selective Service in Salem County, New Jersey on an undisclosed date, but likely on or about June 5, 1917, at age 25; occupation – munitions worker. Inducted as a private at Windsor on September 5, 1918, and transferred to Camp Humphries, Fairfax County, Virginia. Assigned to the 3rd Company, 7th Engineers Training Regiment and transferred to 71st Engineers Regiment on October 21, 1918.

SMITH, OSCAR RHODES, private: Registered for Selective Service on June 5, 1917, at age 24; occupation – automobile mechanic. Inducted as a private at Windsor on September 5, 1918, and transported to Camp Humphries, Fairfax County, Virginia. Assigned to the Engineers Training Regiment. Honorably discharged on December 27, 1918, having performed no overseas service.

# QUARTERMASTER CORPS

# 301st STEVEDORE REGIMENT

## Company C

BELL, GEORGE*, private: Registered for Selective Service on June 5, 1917, at age 21; occupation – farmer. Inducted as a private at Windsor on April 2, 1918, and transported to Camp Grant, Illinois. Initially assigned to the 161st Depot Brigade and transferred to the 140th Company Draft Labor Battalion, Quartermaster Corps, Camp Grant on April 20, 1918. Sent overseas on May 8, 1918, and transferred to this company on June 15, 1918. Transferred to the 801st Stevedore Battalion on an undisclosed date.

BUNCH, ARTHUR*, private: Registered for Selective Service on June 5, 1917, at age 21; occupation – farmer. Inducted as a private at Windsor on April 2, 1918, and transport-

ed to Camp Grant, Rockford, Illinois. Initially assigned to the 161st Depot Brigade and transferred to this company on June 15, 1918. Sent overseas on May 8, 1918, and transferred to the 803rd Transportation Company, Transportation Corps on an undisclosed date while serving overseas.

## Company D

GATLING, IRVING*, private: Registered for Selective Service on June 5, 1917, at age 29; occupation – laborer. Inducted as a private at Windsor on April 2, 1918, and transported to Camp Grant, Rockford, Illinois. Initially assigned to the 161st Depot Brigade and sent overseas on May 8, 1918. Transferred to this company on June 15, 1918. Transferred to the 804th Stevedore Battalion on an undisclosed date.

HOLLOMON, ED*, private: Registered for Selective Service on June 5, 1917, at age 21; occupation – farmer. Inducted as a private at Windsor on April 2, 1918, and transported to Camp Grant, Rockford, Illinois. Initially assigned to the 161st Depot Brigade and transferred to this company on April 25, 1918. Subsequently transferred to the 812th Transportation Company, Transportation Corps on an undisclosed date.

LIVERMAN, TOM*, private: Registered for Selective Service on June 5, 1917, at age 21; occupation – farmer. Inducted as a private at Windsor on April 2, 1918, and transported to Camp Grant, Rockford, Illinois. Initially assigned to the 161st Depot Brigade and transferred to this company on April 25, 1918. Sent overseas on May 8, 1918. Transferred to the 803rd Company of this corps on April 5, 1919.

## Company E

MIDGETTE, JAMES H.*, corporal: Registered for Selective Service on June 5, 1917, at age 28; occupation – laborer, log woods. Inducted as a private at Windsor on April 2, 1918, and transported to Camp Grant, Rockford,

Illinois. Assigned to this company. Sent overseas o May 8, 1918. Promoted to corporal on January 4, 1919. Returned from overseas on June 29, 1919, and honorably discharged on July 13, 1919.

PETERSON, ARTHUR*, private first class: Registered for Selective Service on June 5, 1917, at age 27; occupation – farm laborer. Inducted as a private at Windsor on April 2, 1918, and transported to Camp Grant, Rockford, Illinois. Likely assigned to this company and subsequently assigned to the 805th Company of this corps.

## Company K

COFFIELD, JOHN LUSTER*, private: Registered for Selective Service before the Bertie County Clerk of Superior Court on June 28, 1917, at age 21; occupation – farm laborer. Inducted as a private at Windsor on April 2, 1918, and transported to Camp Grant, Rockford, Illinois. Assigned to the 161st Depot brigade until April 28, 1918, when he was transferred to the 13th Company, Camp Grant Reinforcement Draft. Transferred to this company on June 15, 1918, while serving overseas. Served overseas from May 8, 1918, until June 18, 1919. Honorably discharged on July 1, 1919.

SAVAGE, ESTON*, private: Registered for Selective Service on June 5, 1917, at age 21; occupation – farmer. Inducted as a private at Windsor on April 2, 1918, and transported to Camp Grant, Rockford, Illinois. Assigned to this company. Served overseas from May 8, 1918, until July 9, 1919. Honorably discharged on July 16, 1919.

## SUPPLY TRAINS

## 305TH MOTOR SUPPLY TRAIN

FREEMAN, REDDICK N., private first class: Registered for Selective Service on June 5,

1917, at age 24; occupation – blacksmith and automobile repair. Inducted as a private at Windsor on May 28, 1918, and transported to Camp Jackson, Columbia, South Carolina. Initially assigned to the 156th Depot Brigade and transferred to the 5th Company of this Motor Supply Train on June 23, 1918. Sent overseas on August 5, 1918. Promoted to private first class on March 15, 1919. Returned from overseas on June 24, 1919, and honorably discharged on July 9, 1919.

## 306TH SUPPLY TRAIN

STOKES, JOSEPH W., private first class: Registered for Selective Service on June 5, 1917, at age 22; occupation – automobile mechanic. Inducted as a private at Windsor on May 28, 1918, and transported to Camp Jackson, Columbia, South Carolina. Assigned to the 5th Company of this supply train. Sent overseas on August 5, 1918. Promoted to private first class on March 15, 1919. Returned from overseas on June 24, 1919, and honorably discharged on July 9, 1919.

WARD, HENRY CLINTON, private: Registered for Selective Service on June 5, 1917, at age 22; occupation – farmer. Inducted as a private at Windsor on May 28, 1918, and transported to Camp Jackson, Columbia, South Carolina. Assigned to this supply train. Served overseas from August, 1918, until June 20, 1919. Honorably discharged at Camp Lee, Petersburg, Virginia on June 29, 1919.

## 308TH MOTOR SUPPLY TRAIN

WHITE, ASA W., private: Previously served in Company F, 55th Pioneer Infantry Regiment. Transferred to this supply train on November 15, 1918, while serving overseas. Transferred to Company C, Mechanical Unit, Army Service Corps on March 11, 1919.

## MOTOR TRANSPORT CORPS

BURDEN, WILLIAM E., private: Enlisted as a private at Jacksonville, Florida on January 29, 1918, at age 33. Assigned to the Quartermaster Corps at Camp Johnston, Jacksonville, Florida. Transferred to Company B, Motor Supply Battalion, Motor Transport Corps at Camp Holabird, Baltimore, Maryland on an undisclosed date. Honorably discharged on October 14, 1918, due to service-connected disability rated as 25 percent. Performed no overseas service.

COWAND, JOHN WESLEY, private: Registered for Selective Service on June 5, 1917, at age 22; occupation – farmer. Inducted as a private at Windsor on July 22, 1918, and transported to Camp Hancock, near Augusta, Georgia. Assigned to the 51st Company, Motor Truck Division. Honorably discharged at Camp Hancock on December 20, 1918, having performed no overseas service.

HARRELL, WILLIAM GEORGE, private: Registered for Selective Service on June 5, 1917, at age 21; occupation – farmer. Inducted as a private at Windsor on July 22, 1918, and transported to Camp Hancock, near Augusta, Georgia. Assigned to the Motor Transport Depot and sent overseas on November 10, 1918. Transferred to Company D, 324th Machine Gun Battalion, 166th Infantry Brigade, 83rd Division on November 23, 1918.

HOGGARD, JOSEPH ROGER, private: Registered for Selective Service on June 5, 1917, at age 23; occupation – farmer. Inducted as a private at Windsor on July 22, 1918, and transported to Camp Hancock, near Augusta, Georgia. Initially assigned to the 3rd Company, Recruit Receiving Depot and transferred to the 51st Company, Motor Transport Depot, Camp Hancock on August 23, 1918. Transferred to the Camp Hancock October Automatic Replacement draft on October 21, 1918.

HOUSTON, LEOPOLD H.*, private: Registered for Selective Service on June 5, 1917, at age 22; occupation – farmer. Inducted as a private at Windsor on June 30, 1918, and transported to Camp Hancock, near Augusta, Georgia. Assigned to the 7th Group Motor Truck Detachment and sent overseas on September 29, 1918. Died in France of pneumonia on October 18, 1918. Buried in Oise-Aisne American Cemetery at Fere-en-Tardenois, France.

SESSOMS, JOSEPH W., corporal: Enlisted as a private at Fort Thomas, Kentucky, on June 3, 1918, at age 21. Assigned to this company. Promoted to private first class on October 22, 1918, and to corporal on June 9, 1919. Honorably discharged on July 12, 1919, having performed no overseas service.

## AUXILIARY REMOUNT DEPOTS

## 306TH AUXILIARY REMOUNT DEPOT

WHITE, LUTHER G., private: Registered for Selective Service on June 5, 1917, at age 29; occupation – blacksmith. Inducted as a private at Windsor on August 31, 1918, and transported to Camp Greene, Charlotte. Assigned to this remount depot. Honorably discharged on March 8, 1919, having performed no overseas service.

## 309TH AUXILIARY REMOUNT DEPOT

MINTON, PATRICK WINSTON, private: Previously served in the Machine Gun Company, 115th Infantry Regiment, 58th Infantry Brigade, 29th Division. Transferred to this remount depot on November 25, 1917. Transferred to the 104th Motor Ordnance Repair Depot on December 1, 1917.

## 315TH AUXILIARY REMOUNT DEPOT

DEANS, CLARENCE WILLIAM, private: Registered for Selective Service as a Bertie County resident at Portsmouth, Virginia on June 1, 1917, at age 22; occupation – dairy farm worker. Inducted as a private at Windsor on March 29, 1918, and transported to Camp Jackson, Columbia, South Carolina. Assigned to this remount depot. Honorably discharged at Camp Jackson on April 17, 1919, with a service-connected disability rated as 33-1/3 percent. Performed no overseas service.

## LABOR BATTALIONS

## 318th LABOR BATTALION

### Company B

BARNES, WILLIAM CLINGMAN, captain: Previously served as a private in the Coast Artillery Corps, Fort Amador, Panama Canal Zone, and in Student Company No. 8, Camp Johnston, Jacksonville, Florida. Appointed second lieutenant in the Quartermaster Corps at Camp Johnston on June 1, 1918, and assigned to this company. Sent overseas on June 30, 1918. Promoted to captain on August 13, 1918. Returned from overseas on June 27, 1919, and honorably discharged on July 23, 1919.

## 321st LABOR BATTALION

### Company C

RUFFIN, JOHN HARDY*, private: Registered for Selective Service on June 5, 1917, at age 23; occupation – farmer. Inducted as a private at Windsor on April 29, 1918, and

transported to Camp Jackson, Columbia, South Carolina. Initially assigned to the 156th Depot Brigade and transferred to this company on May 23, 1918. Sent overseas on July 31, 1918. Died of tuberculosis on January 9, 1919.

WILSON, JOSEPH BENJAMIN*, private: Registered for Selective Service on June 5, 1917, at age 21; occupation – farm laborer. Inducted as a private at Windsor on April 29, 1918, and transported to Camp Jackson, Columbia, South Carolina. Assigned to this company. Transferred to Company A, 305th Service Battalion of this corps on August 22, 1918.

## 323rd LABOR BATTALION

### Company A

MITCHELL, THOMAS BRYANT*, private first class: Previously served in Company A, 329th Service Battalion of this corps. Transferred as a private to this company on July 2, 1918. Sent overseas on July 11, 1918. Promoted to private first class on August 1, 1918. Returned from overseas on May 24, 1919, and honorably discharged on June 9, 1919.

### Company B

WILDER, THOMAS STEWART*, private: Registered for Selective Service on June 5, 1917, at age 26; occupation – laborer. Inducted as a private at Windsor on April 2, 1918, and transported to Camp Grant, Rockford, Illinois. Initially assigned to the 161st Depot Brigade and transferred to this company on May 27, 1918. Transferred to the 329th Labor Battalion on July 3, 1918.

### Company C

BALLARD, GEORGE*, private: Registered for Selective Service on June 5, 1917, at age 25; occupation – farmer. Inducted as a private at Windsor on April 26, 1918, and transported to Camp Grant, Rockford, Illinois. Initially assigned to the 161st Depot Brigade and transferred to this company on May 26, 1918. Served overseas from July 10, 1918, until June 18, 1919, and honorably discharged on July 10, 1919.

BAZEMORE, TOMMIE*, private: Registered for Selective Service on June 5, 1917, at age 26; occupation - farmer. Inducted as a private at Windsor on April 26, 1918, and transported to Camp Grant, Rockford, Illinois. Assigned to this company, in which he served until he died of "Cerebro-Spinal Meningitis" on June 3, 1918.

BIGGS, WALTER MAINE*, private: Registered for Selective Service on June 5, 1917, at age 22; occupation – laborer. Inducted as a private at Windsor on April 26, 1918, and transported to Camp Grant, Rockford, Illinois. Initially assigned to the 161st Depot Brigade and transferred to this company on May 26, 1918. Promoted to sergeant on June 15, 1918, and reduced in rank to private on November 16, 1918. Served overseas from July 9, 1918, until June 3, 1919. Honorably discharged in June 1919.

JONES, LEANDER*, private: Registered for Selective Service on June 5, 1917, at age 23; occupation – farmer. Inducted as a private at Windsor on April 28, 1918, and transported to Camp Grant, Rockford, Illinois. Initially assigned to the 161st Depot Brigade and transferred to this company on May 26, 1918. Sent overseas on July 10, 1918. Died of "broncho pneumonia" on February 23, 1919.

RAZOR, WILLIAM*, private: Registered for Selective Service on June 5, 1917, at age 23; occupation – laborer. Inducted as a private at Windsor on April 28, 1918, and transported to Camp Grant, Rockford, Illinois. Assigned to this company. Honorably discharged on June 21, 1918, with a service-connected disability rated as 33-1/3 percent.

SESSOMS, SONNIE*, private: Registered for Selective Service on June 5, 1917, at age 21; occupation – farm laborer. Inducted as a private at Windsor on April 26, 1918, and transported to Camp Grant, Rockford, Illinois. Initially assigned to the 161st Depot Brigade and transferred to this company on May 26, 1918. Served overseas from July 9, 1918, until July 4, 1919. Honorably discharged on July 17, 1919.

WALTON, WILLIE, JACKSON*, private: Registered for Selective Service on June 5, 1917, at age 26; occupation – farmer. Inducted as a private at Windsor on April 28, 1918, and transported to Camp Grant, Rockford, Illinois. Assigned to this company. Honorably discharged on January 11, 1919, having performed no overseas service.

WILLIFORD, WILLIE*, private: Previously served in the 358th Casual Detachment, Camp Grant, Illinois. Transferred to this company on an undisclosed date. Served overseas from June 24, 1918, until July 15, 1919. Honorably discharged on April 28, 1920, with a service-connected disability rated as 100 percent.

# 329th LABOR BATTALION

## Company B

PHILLIPS, COLUMBUS*, private: Previously served in Company A, 350th Machine Gun Battalion, 183rd Infantry Brigade, 92nd Division. Transferred to this company on May 21, 1918. Honorably discharged on June 6, 1919, having performed no overseas service. Discharged with a service-connected disability rated as 33-1/3 percent.

WILLIAMS, BEN H.*, private: Registered for Selective Service on June 5, 1917, at age 21; occupation – farmer. Inducted as a private at Windsor on April 2, 1918, and transported to Camp Grant, Rockford, Illinois. Assigned to the 161st Depot Brigade. Transferred to this company on July 16, 1918. Transferred to Company A, 416th Service Battalion on August 3, 1918.

## Company D

HOGGARD, JAMES LUTHER*, private: Registered for Selective Service on June 5, 1917, at age 21; occupation – farmer. Inducted as a private at Windsor on April 28, 1918, and transported to Camp Grant, Rockford, Illinois. Assigned to this company. Transferred to Company B, 323rd Service Battalion on July 2, 1918.

## 329th LABOR BATTALION

## MISCELLANEOUS (NO COMPANY IDENTIFIED)

WILDER, THOMAS STEWART*, private: Previously served in Company B, 323rd Labor Battalion of this corps on May 27, 1918. Transferred to this battalion on July 3, 1918. Transferred to the 161st Depot Brigade, Camp Grant, Rockford, Illinois on July 11, 1918.

## 330th LABOR BATTALION

## Company A

CHERRY, JOE ALLEN*, private: Registered for Selective Service on June 5, 1917, at age 22; occupation – farmer. Inducted as a private at Windsor on April 16, 1918, and transported to Camp Jackson, Columbia, South Carolina. Initially assigned to the 156th Depot Brigade and transferred to this company on June 12, 1918. Sent overseas on September 16, 1918. Transferred to Company A, 805th Pioneer Infantry Regiment on November 27, 1918.

JOHNSON, DEAREST*, private: Registered for Selective Service on June 5, 1917, at age 26; occupation – laborer. Inducted as a private at Windsor on April 29, 1918, and transported to Camp Jackson, Columbia, South Carolina. Assigned to this company. Transferred to Company A, 422nd Labor Battalion on August 14, 1918.

## 337th LABOR BATTALION

## Company C

COOPER, WILLIE*, private: Enlisted as a private at Fort Monroe, Hampton, Virginia on April 24, 1918, at age 18. Assigned to Company I, Provisional Labor Battalion, Camp Hill, Newport News, Virginia and transferred to this company on May 17, 1918. Transferred to Company B, 404th Reserve Labor Battalion, on June 3, 1918.

## 339th LABOR BATTALION

## Company B

HOGGARD, ELMORE DUKE*, private: Registered for Selective Service on June 5, 1917, at age 23; occupation - engineer. Noted by the Bertie County Local Board as a Selective Service delinquent who was arrested and jailed by Sheriff John W. Cooper in Bertie County on June 17, 1918. Charged with being a "slacker" (someone seeking to avoid military service). Released from jail and inducted as a private at Windsor on June 19, 1918. Transported to Camp Jackson, Columbia, South Carolina. Initially assigned to the 156th Depot Brigade and transferred to this company. Transferred to Company C of this battalion on September 5, 1918.

## Company C

HOGGARD, ELMORE DUKE*, mechanic: Previously served in Company B of this battalion, Transferred as a private to this company September 5, 1918. Sent overseas on September 8, 1918, and promoted to mechanic on November 5, 1918. Returned from overseas on August 20, 1919, and honorably discharged on August 26, 1919.

# 344th LABOR BATTALION

## Company A

LEARY, WILLIAM*, private: Registered for Selective Service on June 5, 1917, at age 21; occupation – hotel porter. Inducted as a private at Windsor on July 29, 1918, and transported to Camp Greene, Charlotte. Assigned to this company. Honorably discharged at Camp Greene on January 1, 1919, having performed no overseas service.

SESSOMS, SAMUEL*, private: Registered for Selective Service on June 5, 1917, at age 25; occupation – farmer. Inducted as a private at Windsor on July 29, 1918, and transported to Camp Greene, Charlotte. Assigned to this company. Served overseas from September 25, 1918, until July 10, 1919. Honorably discharged at Camp Lee, Petersburg, Virginia on July 19, 1919.

VEALE, BEN*, private: Registered for Selective Service on June 5, 1917, at age 23; occupation – farmer. Inducted as a private at Windsor on July 29, 1918, and transported to Camp Greene, Charlotte. Assigned to this company. Served overseas from September 28, 1918, until December 18, 1918. Honorably discharged at Camp Greene on January 14, 1919.

## Company B

BAZEMORE, LONNIE*, private: Registered for Selective Service on June 5, 1917, at age 21; occupation – farmer. Inducted as a private at Windsor on August 1, 1918, and transported to Camp Greene, Charlotte. Assigned to this company on an undisclosed date and served overseas from September

25, 1919, until March 24, 1919. Wounded "severely" on an undisclosed date. Honorably discharged on April 9, 1919.

CHERRY, ESSIE SIDNEY*, private first class: Registered for Selective Service on June 5, 1917, at age 28; occupation – farmer. Inducted as a private at Windsor on August 1, 1918, and transported to Camp Greene, Charlotte. Assigned to this company and promoted to private first class on April 1, 1919. Served overseas from September 25, 1918, until July 12, 1919. Honorably discharged at Camp Lee, Petersburg, Virginia on July 19, 1919.

DAVIS, CHARLIE*, private: Registered for Selective Service on June 5, 1917, at age 23; occupation – farmer. Inducted as a private at Windsor on August 1, 1918, and transported to Camp Greene, Charlotte. Assigned to this company. Sent overseas on September 25, 1918, and transferred to the Casual Depot, Army Post Office (APO) 910 of this corps on October 26, 1918.

HERITAGE, ROSCOE GREEN*, private: Registered for Selective Service on June 5, 1917, at age 30; occupation – barber. Inducted as a private at Windsor on August 1, 1918, and transported to Camp Grant, Rockford, Illinois. Assigned to this company. Served overseas from September 25, 1918, until December 18, 1918. Honorably discharged on January 14, 1919.

HYMAN, ALEXANDER*, private: Registered for Selective Service on June 5, 1917, at age 21; occupation – farmer. Inducted as a private at Windsor on August 1, 1918, and transported to Camp Greene, Charlotte. Assigned to this company. Sent overseas on September 25, 1918, and died of pneumonia while on board the transport ship on October 4, 1918.

JOHNSON, CORNELIUS*, private: Registered for Selective Service on June 5, 1917, at age 24; occupation – laborer, log woods. Inducted as a private at Windsor on August

1, 1918, and transported to Camp Greene, Charlotte, Assigned to this company. Sent overseas on September 25, 1918, and died of pneumonia on October 21, 1918.

JONES, ARIE*, private: Registered for Selective Service on June 5, 1917, at age 22; occupation — farm laborer. Inducted as a private at Windsor on August 1, 1918, and transported to Camp Greene, Charlotte. Assigned to this company. Served overseas from September 25, 1918, until July 12, 1919. Honorably discharged on July 19, 1919.

WINSTON, MOSES C.*, private: Registered for Selective Service on June 5, 1917, at age 24; occupation — farmer. Inducted as a private at Windsor on August 1, 1918, and transported to Camp Greene, Charlotte. Assigned to this company. Transferred to Transportation Train Meal Service, Army Post Office (APO) 717 on an undisclosed date.

## Company C

MILLER, WILLIE*, private: Registered for Selective Service on June 5, 1917, at age 21; occupation — laborer. Inducted as a private at Windsor on August 14, 1918, and transported to Camp Greene, Charlotte. Assigned to this company. Served overseas from September 25, 1918, until December 23, 1918. Honorably discharged at Camp Greene on January 14, 1919.

OUTLAW, JAMES*, private: Registered for Selective Service on June 5, 1917, at age 25; occupation — farm laborer. Inducted as a private at Windsor on July 29, 1918, and transported to Camp Greene, Charlotte. Initially assigned to Recruit Camp Number 1 and transferred to this company on September 6, 1918. Transferred to the 152nd Depot Brigade, Camp Upton, Long Island, New York on September 24, 1918.

WILLIAMS, FRANK*, private: Registered for Selective Service on June 5, 1917, at age 21; occupation — farmer. Inducted as a private

at Windsor on July 29, 1918, and transported to Camp Greene, Charlotte. Assigned to Recruit Camp Number 1. Transferred to this company on September 7, 1918. Sent overseas on September 25, 1918, and died of pneumonia on October 5, 1918.

## Company D

HECKSTALL, JOHN WILLIAM*, private: Registered for Selective Service on June 5, 1917, at age 22; occupation — farmer. Inducted as a private at Windsor on July 29, 1918, and transported to Camp Greene, Charlotte. Assigned to this company. Served overseas from September 25, 1918, until December 18, 1918. Transferred to a convalescent center (location not disclosed) on an undisclosed date and honorably discharged at on February 24, 1919.

JAMES, JOE*, private: Registered for Selective Service on June 5, 1917, at age 25; occupation — laborer, county roads. Inducted as a private at Windsor on July 29, 1918, and transported to Camp Greene, Charlotte. Assigned to this company. Served overseas from September 25, 1918, until July 12, 1919. Honorably discharged at Camp Lee, Petersburg, Virginia on July 20, 1919.

## MISCELLANEOUS (NO COMPANY IDENTIFIED)

EBRON, JOSEPH*, private: Registered for Selective Service on June 5, 1917, at age 21; occupation — farmer. Inducted as a private at Windsor on August 1, 1918, and transported to Camp Greene, Charlotte, Assigned to this battalion. Sent overseas on September 20, 1918. Transferred to Company A, 805th Pioneer Infantry Regiment on March 4, 1919.

# 346th LABOR BATTALION

## Company A

CLARK, WILLIAM*, private: Registered for Selective Service on June 5, 1917, at age 21; occupation – farm laborer. Inducted as a private at Windsor on August 23, 1918, and transported to Camp Lee, Petersburg, Virginia. Assigned to the 565th Casual Camp Training Center until transferred to this company on an undisclosed date. Honorably discharged at Camp Lee on December 7, 1918, having performed no overseas service.

FREEMAN, RALEIGH (ROLLIE)*, private: Registered for Selective Service on June 5, 1917, at age 23; occupation – farmer. Inducted as a private at Windsor on August 23, 1918, and transported to Camp Greene, Charlotte. Assigned to this company, in which he served until dying of "Broncho pneumonia & influenza" at Camp Greene on October 16, 1918.

## MISCELLANEOUS (NO COMPANY IDENTIFIED)

SPELLER, FAYTON*, private: Registered for Selective Service on June 5, 1917, at age 21; occupation – farmer. Inducted as a private at Windsor on August 23, 1918, and transported to Camp Greene, Charlotte. Assigned to this battalion. Honorably discharged on January 21, 1919, having performed no overseas service.

# 347th LABOR BATTALION

## Company A

COOPER, EDWARD*, private: Registered for Selective Service on June 23, 1917, at age 21; occupation – farm laborer. Name appears on a list of Bertie County men induct-ed on July 2, 1918, who were transported to Camp Greene, Charlotte, but the entry for Cooper was lined through. Inducted as a private at Windsor on July 29, 1918, and transported to Camp Greene. Assigned to this company. Honorably discharged at Camp Greene on December 14, 1918, with a service-connected disability rated as 25 percent.

## Company C

BOND, ARMSTEAD*, private: Previously served in Company C, 355th Service Battalion of this corps. Transferred to this company on October 17, 1918. Served overseas from October 21, 1918, until he died on February 11, 1919, of lobar pneumonia.

MILLER, WILLIAM MCKINLEY*, private: Previously served in Company C, 355th Labor Battalion. Transferred to this company on October 14, 1918. Served overseas from October 21, 1918, until June 29, 1919. Honorably discharged on July 14, 1919.

## MISCELLANEOUS (NO COMPANY IDENTIFIED)

DEANS, KELLY*, private: Registered for Selective Service on June 5, 1917, at age 25; occupation – farmer. Inducted as a private at Windsor on August 1, 1918, and transported to Camp Greene, Charlotte. Assigned to this battalion and honorably discharged at Camp Greene on December 19, 1918, having performed no overseas service.

# 348th LABOR BATTALION

## Company C

RIDDICK, WHIT D.*, private: Registered for Selective Service on June 5, 1917, at age 21; occupation – farmer. Inducted as a private at Windsor on August 23, 1918, and transported to Camp Greene, Charlotte. Initially assigned to Recruit Camp Number 3 and transferred to this company on September 25, 1918. Died at Camp Greene of lobar pneumonia on October 14, 1918.

SEVERE, WILLIE*, private: Registered for Selective Service on June 5, 1917, at age 25; occupation — farmer. Inducted as a private at Windsor on August 23, 1918, and transported to Camp Greene, Charlotte. Assigned to this company. Served overseas from September 16, 1918, until March 31, 1919. Honorably discharged at Camp Lee, Petersburg, Virginia on April 10, 1919.

## 349th LABOR BATTALION

### Company A

GILLAM, LEWIS*, sergeant: Registered for Selective Service on June 5, 1917, at age 22; occupation — laborer. Inducted as a private at Windsor on August 1, 1918, and transported to Camp Greene, Charlotte. Initially assigned to the 51st Depot Brigade and transferred to this company on September 27, 1918. Promoted to sergeant on November 1, 1918. Honorably discharged at Camp Greene on December 191, 1918, having performed no overseas service.

### Company B

FREEMAN, Granville*, private: Registered for Selective Service on June 5, 1917, at age 21; occupation — farm laborer. Inducted as a private at Windsor on July 29, 1918, and transported to Camp Greene, Charlotte. Assigned to this company. Honorably discharged on April 15, 1919, having performed no overseas service.

### Company C

JONES, BEN*, private: Registered for Selective Service on June 5, 1917, at age 24; occupation — laborer. Inducted as a private at Windsor on August 1, 1918, and transported to

Camp Greene, Charlotte. Assigned to this company. Honorably discharged on April 15, 1919, having performed no overseas service.

OUTLAW, WALTON W.*, private: Registered for Selective Service on June 5, 1917, at age 27; occupation — farmer. Inducted as a private at Windsor on August 1, 1918, and transported to Camp Greene, Charlotte. Assigned to this company. Deserted at Camp Greene on October 10, 1918.

RUFFIN, THAD*, private: Registered for Selective Service on June 5, 1917, at age 21; occupation — farmer. Inducted as a private at Windsor on July 29, 1918, and transported to Camp Greene, Charlotte. Assigned to this company. Honorably discharged at Charleston, South Carolina on April 16, 1919, having performed no overseas service.

## 350th LABOR BATTALION

### Company C

JONES, CULLEN*, private: Registered for Selective Service on June 5, 1917, at age 21; occupation — farm laborer. Inducted as a private at Windsor on July 29, 1918, and transported to Camp Greene, Charlotte. Assigned to the 51st Depot Brigade and transferred to this company on November 10, 1918. Honorably discharged on March 5, 1919, having performed no overseas service.

## MISCELLANEOUS (NO COMPANY IDENTIFIED)

WARD, SCOTT*, private: Registered for Selective Service on June 5, 1917, at age 25; occupation — farmer. Inducted as a private at Windsor on August 23, 1918, and transported to Camp Greene, Charlotte. Assigned to this battalion. Honorably discharged on March 24, 1919, having performed no overseas service.

## 355th LABOR BATTALION

### Company C

MILLER, WILLIAM MCKINLEY*, private: Registered for Selective Service on June 5, 1918, at age 21; occupation – farmer. Inducted as a private at Windsor on September 4, 1918, and transported to Camp Lee, Petersburg, Virginia. Assigned to this company. Transferred to Company C, 347th Service Battalion of this corps on October 14, 1918.

### Company D

SMITH, JAMES ROBERT*, private: Registered for Selective Service on June 5, 1917, at age 21; occupation – farmer. Inducted as a private at Windsor on July 29, 1918, and transported to Camp Greene, Charlotte. Initially assigned to the 154th Depot Brigade and transferred to this company on October 19, 1918. Transferred to the 860th Company, Transportation Corps, on October 29, 1918.

## 404th RESERVE LABOR BATTALION

### Company B

COOPER, WILLIE*, private: Previously served in Company C, 337th Labor Battalion. Transferred to this company on June 3, 1918. Deserted at Camp Alexander, Newport News, Virginia on September 15, 1918. Returned to service, since he was honorably discharged on June 30, 1919, having performed no overseas service.

## 406th RESERVE LABOR BATTALION

### Company C

GURLEY, WILLIE*, private: Registered for Selective Service on June 5, 1917, at age 23; occupation – farmer. Inducted as a private at Windsor on June 19, 1918, and transported to Camp Jackson, Columbia, South Carolina. Assigned to this company. Honorably discharged at Camp Jackson on March 27, 1919, having performed no overseas service.

## 407th RESERVE LABOR BATTALION

### Company B

RUFFIN, PETER*, private: Previously served in the 155th Depot Brigade, Camp Lee, Petersburg, Virginia. Transferred to this company on July 20, 1918, and transferred back to the 155th Depot Brigade on October 21, 1918.

SMALLWOOD, JESSE*, private: Registered for Selective Service on June 5, 1918, at age 21; occupation – undisclosed. Inducted as a private at Windsor on September 4, 1918, and transported to Camp Lee, Petersburg, Virginia. Initially assigned to the 155th Depot Brigade and transferred to this company on October 21, 1918. Honorably discharged on April 2, 1919, having performed no overseas service.

## 411th RESERVE LABOR BATTALION

### Company D

COX, JAMES*, private: Registered for Selective Service on June 5, 1917, at age 23; occupation – laborer. Inducted as a private at Windsor on June 21, 1918, and transported to Camp Taylor, Louisville, Kentucky. Assigned to the 159th Depot Brigade and transferred to this company on September 9, 1918. Transferred back to the 159th Depot Brigade on October 17, 1918. Honorably discharged on December 17, 1918, having performed no overseas service.

## 413th RESERVE LABOR BATTALION

### Company B

SANDERLIN, LOUIS*, private: Registered for Selective Service on June 5, 1917, at age 22; occupation – laborer. Inducted as a private at Windsor on July 16, 1918, and transported to Camp Dix, near Trenton New Jersey. Initially assigned to the 155th Depot Brigade and transferred to this company on September 16, 1918. Honorably discharged on July 12, 1919, having performed no overseas service.

### Company C

ROULHAC, NED*, private first class: Registered for Selective Service on June 5, 1917, at age 23; occupation – laborer. Inducted as a private at Windsor on July 16, 1918, and transported to Camp Dix, near Trenton, New Jersey. Assigned to this company. Promoted to private first class on December 1, 1918. Transferred to Company B, 413th Service Battalion of this corps on May 6, 1919. Honorably discharged at Camp Lee, Petersburg, Virginia on July 13, 1919, having performed no overseas service.

## 422nd LABOR BATTALION

### Company A

JOHNSON, DEAREST*, private: Previously served in Company A, 330th Labor Battalion. Transferred to this company on August 14, 1918. Honorably discharged on March 11, 1919, having performed no overseas service.

## 423rd RESERVE LABOR BATTALION

### Company A

MITCHELL, ROBERT EARL*, private: Registered for Selective Service on June 5, 1917, at age 21; occupation – farmer. Inducted as a private at Windsor on August 1, 1918, and transported to Camp Greene, Charlotte. Assigned to this company. Honorably discharged on March 4, 1919, having performed no overseas service.

WILLIAMS, JUNIUS*, private: Registered for Selective Service on June 5, 1917, at age 24; occupation – farmer. Inducted as a private at Windsor on July 29, 1918, and transported to Camp Greene, Charlotte. Assigned to this company. Honorably discharged on December 16, 1918, having performed no overseas service.

WHITE, WILLIAM*, private: Registered for Selective Service on June 5, 1917, at age 22; occupation – farm laborer. Inducted as a private at Windsor on August 23, 1918, and transported to Camp Greene, Charlotte. Initially assigned to the Development Battalion and transferred to this company on December 2, 1918. Honorably discharged on March 4, 1919, having performed no overseas service.

## Company B

BOND, WILLIE T.*, private: Registered for Selective Service on June 5, 1917, at age 26; occupation – farmer. Inducted as a private at Windsor on August 23, 1918, and transported to Camp Greene, Charlotte. Assigned to this company with which he served until honorably discharged on April 4, 1919, having performed no overseas service.

GILLAM, WILLIE*, private: Registered for Selective Service on June 5, 1917, at age 23; occupation – farmer. Inducted as a private at Windsor on August 1, 1918, and transported to Camp Greene, Charlotte. Assigned to this company. Honorably discharged at Camp Greene on March 3, 1919, having performed no overseas service.

REDDICK, MOSES*, private: Registered for Selective Service on June 5, 1917, at age 21; occupation – farm laborer. Inducted as a private at Windsor on August 1, 1918, and transported to Camp Greene, Charlotte. Assigned to this company. Honorably discharged at Camp Greene on March 4, 1919, having performed no overseas service.

## Company C

PEELE, ROY MCKINLEY*, private: Registered for Selective Service on June 5, 1918, at age 21; occupation – farmer. Inducted as a private at Windsor on August 23, 1918, and transported to Camp Greene, Charlotte. Assigned to this company. Honorably discharged on March 6, 1919, having performed no overseas service.

## Company D

PRITCHARD, ANDREW JACKSON*, private: Previously served in Company L, 810th Pioneer Infantry Regiment. Transferred to this company on December 3, 1918. Honorably discharged on March 4, 1919, having performed no overseas service.

THOMPSON, JACOB*, private: Previously served in Company I, 810th Pioneer Infantry Regiment. Transferred to this company on December 3, 1918. Honorably discharged on March 4, 1919, having performed no overseas service.

## MISCELLANEOUS (NO COMPANY IDENTIFIED)

RUFFIN, NED*, private: Previously served in Company D, 810th Pioneer Infantry Regiment. Transferred to this battalion on December 13, 1918. Honorably discharged on March 4, 1919, having performed no overseas service.

WILLIAMS, JAMES AUGUSTUS*, private: Previously served in Headquarters Company, 810th Pioneer Infantry Regiment. Transferred to this battalion on December 3, 1918. Honorably discharged on March 3, 1919, having performed no overseas service.

## 424th RESERVE LABOR BATTALION

## Company B

MOUNTAIN, AUGUSTUS*, private first class: Registered for Selective Service on June 5, 1917, at age 21; occupation – farm laborer. Inducted as a private at Windsor on July 16, 1918, and transported to Camp Dix, near Trenton, New Jersey. Assigned to this company. Promoted to private first class on April 1, 1919. Transferred to the 155th Depot Brigade, Camp Lee, Petersburg, Virginia on May 6, 1919.

## 441st RESERVE LABOR BATTALION

### Company B

HARDY, CHARLIE*, corporal: Registered for Selective Service on June 5, 1917, at age 24; occupation – farmer. Inducted as a private at Windsor on August 23, 1918, and transported to Camp Greene, Charlotte. Assigned to this company. Promoted to corporal on Nov. 13, 1918, and honorably discharged at Camp Polk, near Leesville, Louisiana, on April 3, 1919, having performed no overseas service.

### Company C

TAYLOR, DAVID E.*, cook: Registered for Selective Service on June 5, 1917, at age 30; occupation – farmer. Inducted as a private at Windsor on August 23, 1918, and transported to Camp Greene, Charlotte. Assigned to this company. Promoted to cook on December 1, 1918. Honorably discharged at Camp Polk, Raleigh on April 3, 1919, having performed no overseas service.

## SERVICE BATTALIONS

## 305th SERVICE BATTALION

### Company A

WILSON, JOSEPH BENJAMIN*, private: Previously served in Company C, 321st Labor Battalion of this corps. Transferred to this company on August 22, 1918. Served overseas from September 20, 1918, until July 15, 1919. Honorably discharged on July 18, 1919.

## 308th SERVICE BATTALION

### Company A

BOND, JOHN ("JOHNNIE")*, private: Registered for Selective Service on an undisclosed date, but likely on or about June 5, 1917, at age 25; occupation – laborer. Inducted as a private at Windsor on April 2, 1918, and transported to Camp Grant, Rockford, Illinois. Initially assigned to the 161st Depot Brigade and transferred to the 14th Company, Replacement Draft on April 28, 1918. Served overseas from July 30, 1918, until July 18, 1919, during which he was assigned to the Gas and Oil Station, American Expeditionary Forces, on an undisclosed date. Transferred to the Garden Service of this corps on March 5, 1919, and to this company on May 23, 1919. Honorably discharged on July 24, 1919.

## 321st SERVICE BATTALION

### Company C

ASKEW, CHARLIE EDWARD*, private: Registered for Selective Service on June 5, 1917, at age 21; occupation – laborer. Arrested and jailed by Sheriff John W. Cooper in Bertie County on June 18, 1918, for being a "slacker." Released from jail and "Carried to the Camp" on June 21, 1918, having been inducted as a private at Windsor on June 20, 1918, and transported to Camp Jackson, Columbia, South Carolina. Initially assigned to the 156th Depot Brigade and transferred to this company on July 6, 1918. Served overseas from July 31, 1918, until July 7, 1919, and honorably discharged at Camp Lee, Petersburg, Virginia on July 18, 1919.

PILMAN, WILEY*, private first class: Registered for Selective Service on June 5, 1917, at age 25; occupation – farmer. Inducted as a private at Windsor on April 29, 1918, and transported to Camp Jackson, Columbia, South Carolina. Assigned to this company. Sent overseas on July 31, 1918. Promoted to private first class on September 1, 1918. Returned from overseas on July 9, 1919, and honorably discharged on July 18, 1919.

RUFFIN, MOSES*, private first class: Registered for Selective Service on June 5, 1917, at age 30; occupation – minister. Name appears on a list of men inducted at Windsor on April 29, 1918, with the notation "delinquent." Subsequently inducted as a private on May 2, 1918, and transported to Camp Jackson, Columbia, South Carolina. Initially assigned to the 156th Depot Brigade and transferred to this company on May 23, 1918. Sent overseas on July 31, 1918, and promoted to private first class on September 1, 1918. Returned from overseas on July 7, 1919, and honorably discharged on July 18, 1919.

# 323rd SERVICE BATTALION

## HEADQUARTERS COMPANY

PETERSON, EDWARD B.*, private: Previously served in Headquarters Company, 365th Infantry Regiment, 183rd Infantry Brigade, 92nd Division. Transferred to this company on May 23, 1918. Served overseas from July 9, 1918, until July 4, 1919. Honorably discharged on July 8, 1919, for immediate re-enlistment.

## Company B

HOGGARD, JAMES LUTHER*, private: Previously served in Company D, 329th Labor Battalion of this corps. Transferred to this company on July 2, 1918, and sent overseas on July 10, 1918. Returned from overseas on August 8, 1919, and honorably discharged on August 15, 1919.

## Company C

BAZEMORE, HENRY*, private first class: Registered for Selective Service on June 5, 1917, at age 21; occupation – log woods laborer. Inducted as a private at Windsor on April 26, 1918, and transported to Camp Grant, Rockford, Illinois. Initially assigned to the 161st Depot Brigade and transferred to this company on May 26, 1918. Promoted to private first class on August 1, 1918. Served overseas from July 9, 1918, until July 4, 1919, and honorably discharged on July 17, 1919.

CHERRY, LESLIE*, private first class: Registered for Selective Service on June 5, 1917, at age 21; occupation – farmer. Inducted as a private at Windsor on April 26, 1918, and transported to Camp Grant, Rockford, Illinois. Initially assigned to the 161st Depot Brigade and transferred to this company on May 26, 1918. Promoted to private first class on August 1, 1918. Served overseas from July 10, 1918, until August 3, 1919. Honorably discharged at Camp Dix, near Trenton, New Jersey on August 5, 1919.

HOLLEY, NATHANIEL H.*, private first class: Registered for Selective Service on June 5, 1917, at age 21; occupation – farmer. Inducted as a private at Windsor on April 26, 1918, and transported to Camp Grant, Rockford, Illinois. Initially assigned to the 161st Depot Brigade and transferred to this company on May 26, 1918. Served overseas from July 9, 1918, until October 20, 1918. Promoted to private first class on March 16, 1919. Honorably discharged on November 22, 1919.

HOLLEY, RICHARD*, private first class: Registered for Selective Service on June 5, 1917, at age 23; occupation – farm laborer. Inducted as a private at Windsor on April 28, 1918, and transported to Camp Grant, Rockford, Illinois. Assigned to this company. Sent overseas on July 9, 1918. Promoted to private first class on August 1, 1918. Returned from overseas on July 4, 1919, and honorably discharged on July 17, 1919.

LEE, GURLEY*, private first class: Registered for Selective Service on June 5, 1917, at age 21; occupation – farmer. Arrested and jailed by Sheriff John W. Cooper in Bertie County on May 20, 1918, for being a "slacker." Released from jail by order of the Bertie County Local Board and inducted as a private at Windsor on May 21, 1918. Transported to Camp Grant, Rockford, Illinois, and initially assigned to the 161st Depot Brigade. Assigned to this company on July 2, 1918, and sent overseas on July 9, 1918. Promoted to private first class on August 1, 1918. Returned from overseas on July 4, 1919, and honorably discharged on July 17, 1919.

RYAN, JOHN*, private: Registered for Selective Service on June 5, 1917, at age 27; occupation – farmer. Inducted as a private at Windsor on Aril 26, 1918, and transported to Camp Grant, Rockford, Illinois. Assigned to this company. Served overseas from July 9, 1918, until July 4, 1919. Honorably discharged on July 17, 1919.

RYAN, WELTON*, private: Registered for Selective Service on June 5, 1917, at age 23; occupation – farmer. Inducted as a private at Windsor on April 28, 1918, and transported to Camp Grant, Rockford, Illinois. Initially assigned to the 161st Depot Brigade and transferred to this company on May 26, 1918. Served overseas from July 9, 1918, until July 4, 1919. Honorably discharged on July 17, 1919.

SPIVEY, JOSEPH*, corporal: Registered for Selective Service on June 5, 1917, at age 25; occupation – laborer. Inducted as a private at Windsor on April 26, 1918, and transported to Camp Grant, Rockford, Illinois. Assigned to this company. Sent overseas on July 10, 1918. Promoted to corporal November 16, 1918. Returned from overseas on October 20, 1919, and honorably discharged on November 26, 1919.

WHITE, WILLIAM DREW*, private: Registered for Selective Service on June 5, 1917, at age 23; occupation – laborer. Inducted as a private at Windsor on April 28, 1918, and transported to Camp Grant, Rockford, Illinois. Initially assigned to the 161st Depot Brigade and transferred to this company on May 26, 1918. Served overseas from July 9, 1918, until July 4, 1919. Honorably discharged on July 16, 1919.

## MISCELLANEOUS (NO COMPANY IDENTIFIED)

KEEMER, JOE BURLEY*, private first class: Registered for Selective Service on June 5, 1917, at age 21; occupation – farmer. Inducted as a private at Windsor on April 26, 1918, and transported to Camp Grant, Rockford, Illinois. Assigned to this battalion. Sent overseas from July 9, 1918, and promoted to private first class on August 1, 1918. Returned from overseas on July 4, 1919, and honorably discharged at Camp Lee, Petersburg, Virginia on July 17, 1919.

## 328th SERVICE BATTALION

## Company A

SKINNER, PETER*, private: Previously served in Company C, 371st Infantry Regiment, 186th Infantry Brigade, 93rd Division. Transferred to this company on March 6, 1918. Transferred to the 88th Prison Military Police on July 22, 1918.

## 329th SERVICE BATTALION

## Company A

HOLLEY, OSCAR*, private: Registered for Selective Service as a Bertie County resident incarcerated in the Beaufort County jail on June 5, 1917, at age 22; occupation –

"county convict force." Inducted as a private at Washington, Beaufort County, on July 16, 1918, and transported to Camp Grant, Rockford, Illinois. Assigned to this company. Served overseas from August 23, 1918, until April 23, 1919. Honorably discharged on June 27, 1919.

MITCHELL, THOMAS BRYANT*, private: Registered for Selective Service on June 5, 1917, at age 23; occupation – farmer. Inducted as a private at Windsor on April 2, 1918, and transported to Camp Grant, Rockford, Illinois. Initially assigned to the 161st Depot Brigade and transferred to this company on June 27, 1918. Transferred to Company A, 323rd Labor Battalion of this corps on July 2, 1918.

## 330th SERVICE BATTALION

## Company A

MELTON, JULE*, private: Registered for Selective Service on June 5, 1917, at age 30; occupation – farm laborer. Inducted as a private at Windsor on April 29, 1918, and transported to Camp Jackson, Columbia, South Carolina. Initially assigned to the 156th Depot Brigade and transferred to this company on June 12, 1918. Promoted to cook on August 6, 1918. Sent overseas on September 15, 1918. Reduced to private on February 3, 1919. Returned from overseas on October 28, 1919, and honorably discharged on October 31, 1919.

WILLIAMS, HENRY CHEATHAM*, private: Registered for Selective Service on June 5, 1917 June 5, 1917, at age 21; occupation – saw mill laborer. Inducted as a private at Windsor on April 29, 1918, and transported to Camp Jackson, Columbia, South Carolina. Assigned to this company. Served overseas from September 15, 1918, until September 20, 1919. Honorably discharged on September 25, 1919.

## 338th SERVICE BATTALION

## Company B

BOND, THOMAS SIDWOOD*, private: Registered for Selective Service on June 5, 1917, at age 27; occupation – laborer. Inducted as a private at Williamston, Martin County, on June 20, 1918, and transported to Camp Dix, near Trenton, New Jersey. Initially assigned to the 155th Depot Brigade and transferred to this company on August 14, 1918. Served overseas from August 22, 1918, until July 18, 1919. Honorably discharged on August 24, 1919.

## 343rd SERVICE BATTALION

## Company B

BROWN, JOHN WILLIAM*, private: Registered for Selective Service on June 5, 1917, at age 24; occupation – laborer. Inducted as a private at Windsor on August 1, 1918, and transported to Camp Greene, Charlotte. Assigned to this company and served overseas from October 20, 1918, until August 4, 1919. Honorably discharged on September 4, 1919.

## 344th SERVICE BATTALION

## Company B

HARDY, WILLIAM*, private first class: Registered for Selective Service on June 5, 1917, at age 21; occupation – laborer, log woods. Inducted as a private at Windsor on August 1, 1918, and transported to Camp Greene, Charlotte. Assigned to this company. Sent overseas on September 28, 1918, and promoted to private first class on April 1, 1919. Returned from overseas on July 12, 1919, and honorably discharged at Camp Lee, Petersburg, Virginia on July 19, 1919.

NEWSOME, LENWOOD*, corporal: Registered for Selective Service on June 5, 1917, at age 27; occupation – farmer. Inducted as a private at Windsor on August 1, 1918, and transported to Camp Greene, Charlotte. Assigned to this company. Promoted to corporal on September 13, 1918. Served overseas from September 18, 1919, until July 10, 1919. Honorably discharged on July 18, 1919.

OUTLAW, JOHN*, private: Registered for Selective Service on June 5, 1917, at age 29; occupation – farmer. Inducted as a private at Windsor on August 8, 1918, and transported to Camp Greene, Charlotte. Assigned to this company. Served overseas from September 22, 1918, until July 5, 1919. Honorably discharged at Camp Lee, Petersburg, Virginia on July 11, 1919.

RAYNER, SAM*, private: Registered for Selective Service on June 5, 1917, at age 21; occupation – laborer. Inducted as a private at Windsor on August 1, 1918, and transported to Camp Green, Charlotte. Assigned to this company. Served overseas from September 25, 1918, until July 12, 1919. Honorably discharged at Camp Lee, Petersburg, Virginia on July 19, 1919.

RYAN, MELTON*, sergeant: Registered for Selective Service on June 5, 1917, at age 21; occupation – farmer. Inducted as a private at Windsor on August 1, 1918, and transported to Camp Greene, Charlotte. Assigned to this company. Promoted to sergeant on September 13, 1918. Served overseas from September 25, 1918, until July 12, 1919. Honorably discharged at Camp Lee, Petersburg, Virginia on July 19, 1919.

## Company D

BEECHER, HENRY*, private: Registered for Selective Service on June 5, 1917, at age 21; occupation – public work. Inducted as a private at Windsor on July 29, 1918, and transported to Camp Greene, Charlotte. Assigned to this company and served over-

seas from September 25, 1918, until July 12, 1919. Honorably discharged at Camp Lee, Petersburg, Virginia on July 20, 1919.

HOGGARD, ARCILIOUS*, private: Registered for Selective Service on June 5, 1917, at age 22; occupation – farmer. Inducted as a private at Windsor on July 29, 1918, and transported to Camp Greene, Charlotte. Assigned to this company and served overseas from September 25, 1918, until July 12, 1919. Honorably discharged at Camp Lee, Petersburg, Virginia on July 20, 1919.

# 346th SERVICE BATTALION

## Company A

CLARK, SAMUEL*, private: Registered for Selective Service on June 5, 1917, at age 22; occupation – farm laborer. Inducted as a private at Windsor on August 23, 1918, and transported to Camp Greene, Charlotte. Assigned to this company and served overseas from September 30, 1918, until July 4, 1919. Honorably discharged on July 10, 1919.

# 347th SERVICE BATTALION

## Company A

JAMES, WILLIE*, private: Registered for Selective Service on June 5, 1917, at age 21; occupation – farm laborer. Inducted as a private at Windsor on August 1, 1918, and transported to Camp Greene, Charlotte. Initially assigned to Recruit Camp Number 1 and transferred to this company on September 6, 1918. Served overseas from October 24, 1918, until July 18, 1919. Honorably discharged at Camp Lee, Petersburg, Virginia on July 24, 1919.

STEWART, JOHN M.*, corporal: Registered for Selective Service on June 5, 1917, at age 25; occupation – farmer. Inducted as a private at Windsor on August 1, 1918, and transported to Camp Greene, Charlotte. Assigned to this company. Sent overseas on October 21, 1918. Promoted to mechanic on January 1, 1919, and to corporal on May 1, 1919. Returned from overseas on June 29, 1919. Honorably discharged at Camp Lee, Petersburg, Virginia on July 15, 1919.

## 348th SERVICE BATTALION

### Company B

COFFIELD, CLAUDE*, private: Registered for Selective Service on June 5, 1917, at age 21; occupation – laborer, logging. Inducted as a private at Windsor on July 29, 1918, and transported to Camp Greene, Charlotte. Assigned to the 51st Separation Brigade until September 23, 1918, when he was transferred to this company. Served overseas from October 20, 1918, until August 5, 1919. Honorably discharged at Camp Lee, Petersburg, Virginia on August 11, 1919.

JORDAN, ERNEST*, private: Registered for Selective Service on June 5, 1917, at age 22; occupation – farmer. Inducted as a private at Windsor on July 29, 1918, and transported to Camp Greene, Charlotte. Assigned to this company. Served overseas from October 20, 1918, until August 5, 1919. Honorably discharged on August 12, 1919.

### Company C

RICE, JOHN GUTHRIE*, private first class: Registered for Selective Service on June 5, 1917, at age 24; occupation – farmer. Inducted as a private at Windsor on August 23, 1918, and transported to Camp Greene, Charlotte. Assigned to this company. Sent overseas on September 30, 1918, and promoted to private first class on November 1, 1918. Returned from overseas on July 4, 1919, and honorably discharged on July 16, 1919.

## 355th SERVICE BATTALION

### Company C

BOND, ARMSTEAD (ARMSTRONG)*, private: Registered for Selective Service on an undisclosed date, but likely on or about June 5, 1917, in Martin County at age 30; occupation – road builder. Inducted as a private at Windsor on September 4, 1918, at age 31, and transported to Camp Dix, near Trenton, New Jersey. Initially assigned to the 155th Depot Brigade and transferred to this company on October 14, 1918. Transferred to Company C, 347th Labor Battalion of this corps on October 17, 1918.

## 413th SERVICE BATTALION

### Company A

LEE, EDGAR*, private: Registered for Selective Service on June 5, 1917, at age 23; occupation – laborer, log woods. Inducted as a private at Windsor on July 16, 1918, and transported to Camp Dix, near Trenton, New Jersey. Initially assigned to the 153rd Depot Brigade and transferred to this company on September 20, 1918. Honorably discharged on July 1, 1919, having performed no overseas service.

### Company B

ROULHAC, NED*, private first class: Previously served in Company C, 413th Reserve Labor Battalion of this corps. Transferred as a private first class to this company on May 6, 1919. Honorably discharged at Camp Lee, Petersburg, Virginia on July 13, 1919, having performed no overseas service.

## 416th SERVICE BATTALION

### Company A

WALKER, GARFIELD*, private: Previously served in the 161st Depot Brigade, Camp Grant, Rockford, Illinois. Transferred to this company on April 11, 1919. Jailed in the Camp Grant Stockade on October 6, 1919. Dishonorably discharged on April 23, 1921, pursuant to the order of a general court martial.

WILLIAMS, BEN H.*, private: Previously served in to Company B, 329th Labor Battalion. Transferred to this company on August 3, 1918. Honorably discharged on May 21, 1919, having performed no overseas service.

## MISCEALLANEOUS QUARTERMASTER CORPS

HARDY, GENERAL*, private: Registered for Selective Service on June 5, 1917, at age 30; occupation – laborer. Inducted as a private at Windsor on April 2, 1918, and transported to Camp Grant, Rockford, Illinois. Assigned to this corps (no unit specified). Served overseas from May 8, 1918, until July 13, 1919. Honorably discharged on July 22, 1919.

HASSELL, MCKINLEY*, private: Registered for Selective Service on June 5, 1917, at age 22; occupation – laborer. Inducted as a private at Windsor on April 2, 1918, and transported to Camp Grant, Rockford, Illinois. Initially assigned to the 161st Depot Brigade and transferred to this corps (no unit specified), Camp Merritt, New Jersey on April 28, 1918. Honorably discharged at Camp Merritt on August 24, 1918, having performed no overseas service. Discharged due to service-connected disability rated as 5 percent.

HOGGARD, LYMAN B., private: Enlisted as a private at Fort Thomas, Kentucky, on June 30, 1917, at age 20. Assigned to this corps (no unit specified). Honorably discharged on December 26, 1918, having performed no overseas service.

ODOM, GERTHA, private: Registered for Selective Service on June 5, 1917, at age 22; occupation – clerk. Inducted as a private at Windsor on August 31, 1918, and transported to Camp Greene, Charlotte. Assigned to this corps (no unit specified). Honorably discharged on December 30, 1918, having performed no overseas service.

## SIGNAL CORPS

## 104th FIELD SIGNAL BATTALION

### Company C

JACOCKS, JESSE CARTER, private first class: Previously served in Company I, 4th Infantry Regiment, Virginia National Guard. Transferred as a private to this company on November 8, 1917. Sent overseas on June 19, 1918. Wounded on October 16, 1918; severity of wound not disclosed in military record. Promoted to private first class on April 1, 1919. Returned from overseas on May 20, 1919, and honorably discharged on May 22, 1919, for immediate re-enlistment. Re-enlisted on May 23, 1919, and honorably discharged on May 22, 1920.

## 325th FIELD SIGNAL BATTALION

## Company B

RAWLS, HARVEY LEE*, private: Registered for Selective Service on June 5, 1917, at age 22; occupation – laborer with ship builder. Inducted as a private at Windsor on April 29, 1918, and transported to Camp Jackson, Columbia, South Carolina. Assigned to this company. Served overseas from July 31, 1918, until February 27, 1919. Honorably discharged on March 19, 1919.

# TRANSPORTATION CORPS

## STEVEDORE BATTALIONS

### 801st STEVEDORE BATTALION

BELL, GEORGE*, private: Previously served in Company C, 301st Stevedore Regiment, Quartermaster Corps. Transferred to this battalion on an undisclosed date while serving overseas. Transferred to the 810th Transportation Company of this corps on March 30, 1919.

### 804th STEVEDORE BATTALION

EASON, DONNIE*, private: Registered for Selective Service on June 5, 1917, at age 21; occupation – laborer, log woods. Inducted as a private at Windsor on April 2, 1918, and transported to Camp Grant, Rockford, Illinois. Initially assigned to the 161st Depot Brigade and transferred to this battalion on April 28, 1918. Sent overseas on May 8, 1918, and transferred to 812th Stevedore Battalion on April 7, 1919.

EATON, JASPER*, private: Registered for Selective Service on June 5, 1917, at age 23; occupation – farmer. Inducted as a private at Windsor on April 2, 1918, and transported to Camp Grant, Rockford, Illinois. Initially assigned to this battalion and transferred to the 812th Transportation Company of this corps on April 7, 1918.

GATLING, IRVING*, private: Previously served in Company D, 301st Stevedore Regiment, Quartermaster Corps. Transferred to this battalion on an undisclosed date while serving overseas. Transferred to the 812th Stevedore Battalion on April 7, 1919.

LEE, NELSON*, private: Registered for Selective Service on June 5, 1917, at age 23; occupation – farmer. Inducted as a private at Windsor on April 2, 1918, and transported to Camp Grant, Rockford, Illinois. Initially assigned to the 161st Depot Brigade and sent overseas on May 8, 1918. Transferred to this battalion on June 15, 1918. Transferred to 812th Stevedore Battalion on April 7, 1919.

## 812th STEVEDORE BATTALION

EASON, DONNIE*, private: Previously served in the 804th Stevedore Battalion. Transferred to this battalion on April 7, 1919, while serving overseas. Returned from overseas on July 24, 19 19, and honorably discharged on July 28, 1919.

GATLING, IRVING*, private: Previously served in the 804th Stevedore Battalion. Transferred to this battalion on April 7, 1919, while serving overseas. Returned from overseas on July 24, 1919, and honorably discharged on July 28, 1919.

LEE, NELSON*, private: Previously served in the 804th Stevedore Battalion. Transferred to this battalion on April 7, 1919, while serving overseas. Returned from overseas on July 24, 1919, and honorably discharged on July 28, 1919.

# TRANSPORTATION COMPANIES

## 801st COMPANY

COOPER, FRED D.*, private: Previously served in the 803rd Transportation Company. Transferred to this company on February 11, 1919, while serving overseas. Returned from overseas on April 18, 1919. Honorably discharged at Camp Lee, Petersburg, Virginia on May 2, 1919.

COTTON, WILLIE*, private first class: Registered for Selective Service on June 5, 1917, at age 22; occupation – farmer. Inducted as a private at Windsor on April 2, 1918, and transported to Camp Grant, Rockford, Illinois. Initially assigned to the 161st Depot Brigade and transferred to the Camp Grant April Automatic Replacement Draft on April 28, 1918. Sent overseas on June 5, 1918, and transferred to this company on June 15, 1918. Promoted to private first class on September 12, 1918. Transferred to the 805th Transportation Company on February 21, 1919.

## 802nd COMPANY

SESSOMS, BRODE*, private first class: Previously served in the 806th Transportation Company. Transferred as a private to this company on May 15, 1918, while serving overseas. Promoted to private first class on November 1, 1918. Returned from overseas on July 24, 1919, and honorably discharged on July 27, 1919.

## 803rd COMPANY

BUNCH, ARTHUR*, private: Previously served in Company C, 301st Stevedore Regiment, Quartermaster Corps. Transferred to this company on June 15, 1918, while serving overseas. Transferred to the 810th Transportation Company on March 30, 1919.

COOPER, FRED D.*, private: Registered for Selective Service on June 5, 1917, at age 25; occupation – farmer. Inducted as a private at Windsor on April 2, 1918, and transported to Camp Grant, Rockford, Illinois. Initially assigned to the 161st Depot Brigade and transferred to this company on April 28, 1918. Sent overseas on May 8, 1918. Transferred to the 801st Transportation Company on February 11, 1919, while serving overseas.

LIVERMAN, TOM*, private: Previously served in Company D, 301st Stevedore Regiment, Quartermaster Corps. Transferred to this company on April 5, 1919, while serving overseas. Returned from overseas on June 28, 1919, and honorably discharged on July 16, 1919.

## 805th COMPANY

COTTON, WILLIE*, private first class: Previously served in the 801st Transportation Company. Transferred to this company on February 21, 1919, while serving overseas. Transferred to the 812th Transportation Company on May 7, 1919.

PETERSON, ARTHUR*, private first class: Likely served in Company E, 301st Stevedore Regiment, Quartermaster Corps prior to be assigned to this company. Sent overseas on May 8, 1918. Transferred to the 812th Company, Transportation Corps, on May 7, 1919.

SIMON, BENNIE, private first class: Enlisted as a private at Washington Barracks, District of Columbia on September 22, 1917, at age 24. Assigned to this company. Promoted to sergeant on October 10, 1917, and sent overseas on October 17, 1917. Reduced to private on November 1, 1917, and promoted to private first class on December 1, 1918. Returned from overseas on June 28, 1919, and honorably discharged on July 11, 1919.

## 806th COMPANY

SESSOMS, BRODE*, private: Registered for Selective Service on June 5, 1917, at age 23; occupation – laborer. Inducted as a private at Windsor on April 2, 1918, and transported to Camp Grant, Rockford, Illinois. Assigned to this company. Sent overseas on April 5, 1918, and transferred to the 802nd Transportation Company on May 15, 1918.

## 807th COMPANY

GURLEY, BEN*, private: Registered for Selective Service on June 5, 1917, at age 21; occupation – laborer. Inducted as a private at Windsor on April 2, 1918, and transported to Camp Grant, Rockford, Illinois. Assigned to the 14th Company, Camp Grant Labor Battalion, and sent overseas on May 8, 1918. Transferred to this company on June 18, 1918. Returned from overseas on July 8, 1919, and honorably discharged on July 16, 1919.

RUFFIN, MANUEL*, private: Registered for Selective Service on June 5, 1917, at age 24; occupation – farmer. Inducted as a private at Windsor on April 2, 1918, and transported to Camp Grant, Rockford, Illinois. Initially assigned to the 161st Depot Brigade and transferred to this company on April 25, 1918. Served overseas from May 7, 1918, until April 27, 1919. Honorably discharged on May 23, 1919.

## 809th COMPANY

ROBBINS, TRIM*, private first class: Registered for Selective Service on June 5, 1917, at age 23; occupation – farmer. Inducted as a private at Windsor on April 2, 1918, and transported to Camp Grant, Rockford, Illinois. Assigned to this company. Sent overseas on May 8, 1918, and promoted to private first class on October 1, 1918. Returned from overseas on July 24, 1919, and honorably discharged on July 23, 1919.

## 810th COMPANY

BELL, GEORGE*, private: Previously served in the 801st Stevedore Battalion. Transferred to this company on March 30, 1919, while serving overseas. Returned from overseas on July 7, 1919, and honorably discharged on July 19, 1919.

BUNCH, ARTHUR*, private: Previously served in the 803rd Transportation Company. Transferred to this company on March 30, 1919, while serving overseas. Returned from overseas on July 7, 1919, and was honorably discharged on July 19, 1919.

## 812th COMPANY

COTTON, WILLIE*, private first class: Previously served in the 805th Transportation Company. Transferred to this company on May 7, 1919, while serving overseas. Returned from overseas on July 24, 1919, and honorably discharged on July 28, 1919.

EATON, JASPER*, corporal: Previously served in the 804th Stevedore Battalion. Transferred as a private to this company on April 7, 1918. Sent overseas on May 8, 1918. Promoted to corporal on June 4, 1919. Returned from overseas on July 21, 1919, and honorably discharged on August 12, 1919.

HOLLOMON, ED*, private: Previously served in Company D, 301st Stevedore Regiment, Quartermaster Corps. Transferred to this company on an undisclosed date. Served overseas from May 5, 1918, until July 24, 1919. Honorably discharged on July 28, 1919.

PETERSON, ARTHUR*, private first class: Previously served in the 805th Company, Transportation Corps. Transferred to this company on May 7, 1919, while serving overseas. Returned from overseas on July 24, 191, and honorably discharged on July 2, 1919.

## 814th COMPANY

MITCHELL, LLOYD*, private: Registered for Selective Service on June 5, 1917, at age 21; occupation – farmer. Inducted as a private at Windsor on April 2, 1918, and transported to Camp Grant, Rockford, Illinois. Initially assigned to the 161st Depot Brigade and sent overseas on May 8, 1918. Transferred to this company on June 15, 1918. Returned from overseas on July 16, 1919, and honorably discharged on July 22, 1919.

## 833rd COMPANY

AMBERS, GEORGE M.*, private first class: Registered for Selective Service on June 5, 1917, at age 23; occupation – laborer. Inducted as a private at Windsor on April 2, 1918, and transported to Camp Grant, Rockford, Illinois. Initially assigned to the 161st Depot Brigade and transferred to this company on April 28, 1918. Promoted to private first class on February 1, 1919. Served overseas from May 8, 1918 until May 3, 1919, and honorably discharged on May 6, 1919.

## 860th COMPANY

SMITH, JAMES ROBERT*, private: Previously served in Company D, 355th Labor Battalion, Quartermaster Corps. Transferred to this company, Transportation Corps, on October 29, 1918. Served overseas from November 12, 1918, until July 5, 1919. Honorably discharged for re-enlistment on July 9, 1919.

## AIR SERVICE

## 8th AERO SQUADRON

BAZEMORE, VERNON, private first class: Enlisted as a private at Fort Thomas, Kentucky, on April 27, 1917, at age 26. Assigned to the Signal Corps, Air Service until transferred to the 8th Aero Squadron, Signal Corps on June 21, 1917. Promoted to private first class on October 1, 1918. Served overseas from November 22, 1917, until May 1, 1919, and honorably discharged on May 20, 1919.

## 474TH AERO SQUADRON

BARNES, JAMES CROSS, corporal: Registered for Selective Service on June 5, 1917, at age 21; occupation - salesman. Enlisted as a private at Fort Thomas, Kentucky, on December 7, 1917. Promoted to corporal on March 1, 1918. Assigned to the 62nd Aero Squadron (Provisional), subsequently re-designated as the 474th Aero Squadron. Served overseas from March 4, 1918, until January 18, 1919. Honorably discharged on January 31, 1919.

## 1st AIR SERVICE MECHANICAL REGIMENT

## 1ST COMPANY

MITCHELL, ROBERT JUDSON, sergeant: Previously served in Supply Company, 321st Infantry Regiment, 161st Infantry Brigade, 81st Division. Transferred as a private to this company on December 10, 1917. Promoted to sergeant on January 1, 1918. Served overseas from February 10, 1918, until June 18, 1919. Honorably discharged at Camp Jackson, South Carolina on July 1, 1919.

## AIR SERVICE ENLISTED
## RESERVE CORPS

SUTTON, WILLIAM MOORING, JR., private: Registered for Selective Service as a Bertie County resident in Walker County, Georgia on June 5, 1917, at age 24; occupation – railroad office worker. Enlisted at Toronto, Canada, on August 15, 1917 in this corps. Honorably discharged on February 10, 1918, with a service-connected disability, the degree of which not disclosed in his military record. Inducted as a private at Windsor on August 5, 1918, and transported to Camp Wadsworth, Spartanburg, South Carolina. Assigned to Company A, 57th Pioneer Infantry Regiment.

## DEPOT BRIGADES

## 51st DEPOT BRIGADE

## CAMP GREENE,
## NORTH CAROLINA

CHERRY, BENNIE*, private: Registered for Selective Service on June 5, 1917, at age 21; occupation – farmer. Inducted as a private at Windsor on July 29, 1918, and transported to Camp Greene, Charlotte. Initially assigned to an unspecified recruit camp and transferred to this depot brigade on September 24, 1918. Honorably discharged at Camp Greene on December 10, 1918, having performed no overseas service.

FREEMAN, HOBART*, private: Registered for Selective Service on June 5, 1917, at age 21; occupation – butler. Inducted as a private at Windsor on July 29, 1918, and transported to Camp Greene, Charlotte. Assigned to Recruit Camp Number 1 and transferred to this depot brigade on September 18, 1918. Honorably discharged at Camp Greene on December 10, 1918, having performed no overseas service.

JOHNSON, ISAAC P.*, private: Registered for Selective Service on June 5, 1917, at age 21; occupation – farmer. Inducted as a private at Windsor on August 23, 1918, and transported to Camp Greene, Charlotte. Assigned to this depot brigade. Honorably discharged at Camp Greene on January 22, 1919, having performed no overseas service.

MITCHELL, RHODEN LEE*, private: Registered for Selective Service on June 5, 1917, at age 25; occupation – laborer. Inducted as a private at Windsor on August 1, 1918, and transported to Camp Greene, Charlotte. Assigned to this depot brigade. Honorably discharged at Camp Greene on January 13, 1919, having performed no overseas service.

PUGH, GEORGE*, private: Registered for Selective Service on June 5, 1917, at age 24; occupation – farmer. Inducted as a private at Windsor on August 23, 1918, and transported to Camp Greene, Charlotte. Assigned to this depot brigade. Honorably discharged on January 30, 1919, having performed no overseas service.

WIGGINS, SELMA*, private: Registered for Selective Service on June 5, 1917, at age 22; occupation – laborer. Inducted as a private at Windsor on July 29, 1918, and transported to Camp Greene, Charlotte. Assigned to this depot brigade. Honorably discharged on January 13, 1919, having performed no overseas service.

WILKINS, ALEXANDER*, private: Registered for Selective Service on June 5, 1917, at age 21; occupation – farm laborer. Inducted as a private at Windsor on August 1, 1918, and transported to Camp Greene, Charlotte. Assigned to this depot brigade. Honorably discharged on December 10, 1918, having performed no overseas service.

## 53rd DEPOT BRIGADE

## CAMP HANCOCK, GEORGIA

RAWLS, CLARENCE, private: Registered for Selective Service on June 5, 1917, at age 22; occupation – farmer. Inducted as a private at Windsor on July 22, 1918, and transported to Camp Hancock, near Augusta, Georgia. Assigned to this depot brigade. Transferred to the Camp Hancock Automatic Replacement Draft (machine gun) on October 21, 1918.

## 55th DEPOT BRIGADE

## CAMP SEVIER, SOUTH CAROLINA

WHITE, WILLIE DAVID, private: Previously served in Company D, 105th Ammunition Train, 30th Division. Transferred to this depot brigade on May 13, 1918. Honorably discharged on December 7, 1018, having performed no overseas service.

## 152nd DEPOT BRIGADE

## CAMP UPTON, NEW YORK

OUTLAW, HARVEY*, private: Registered for Selective Service on June 5, 1917, at age 23; occupation – farmer. Inducted as a private at Windsor on April 26, 1918, and transported to Camp Grant, Rockford, Illinois. Transferred to this depot brigade on an undisclosed date. Honorably discharged on November 15, 1918, due to a service-connected disability rated as 25 percent.

OUTLAW, JAMES*, private: Previously served in Company C, 344th Labor Battalion, Quartermaster Corps. Transferred to this depot brigade on September 24, 1918. Honorably discharged on December 9, 1918, having performed no overseas service.

## 153rd DEPOT BRIGADE

## CAMP DIX, NEW JERSEY

BELL, JIM*, private: Registered for Selective Service on June 5, 1917, at age 23; occupation – laborer, log woods. Inducted as a private at Windsor on July 16, 1918, and transported to Camp Dix, near Trenton, New Jersey. Assigned to this depot brigade. Died of pneumonia on September 27, 1918.

JONES, HOWARD*, private: Registered for Selective Service on June 5, 1917, at age 21; occupation – farmer. Inducted as a private at Windsor on July 16, 1918, and transported to Camp Dix, near Trenton, New Jersey. Assigned to this depot brigade. Transferred to the 156th Depot Brigade, Camp Jackson, Columbia, South Carolina on October 31, 1918.

LEE, TOMMIE*, private: Registered for Selective Service on June 5, 1917, at age 23; occupation – foreman on a log train. Inducted as a private at Windsor on July 16, 1918, and transported to Camp Dix, near Trenton, New Jersey. Assigned to this depot brigade. Honorably discharged on December 13, 1918, having performed no overseas service.

SANDERLIN, ASA*, private: Registered for Selective Service on June 5, 1917, at age 23; occupation – painter. Inducted as a private at Windsor on July 16, 1918, and transported to Camp Dix, near Trenton, New Jersey. Assigned to this depot brigade. Honorably discharged on September 28, 1918, with a service-connected disability rated as 8 ½ percent.

WILSON, WILLOUGHBY*, private: Registered for Selective Service on June 5, 1917, at age 21; occupation – laborer. Inducted as a private at Windsor on July 22, 1918, and transported to Camp Dix, near Trenton, New Jersey. Assigned to this depot brigade. Transferred to Company H, 63rd Pioneer Infantry Regiment on October 22, 1918.

## 155th DEPOT BRIGADE

## CAMP LEE, VIRGINIA

JONES, ISAIAH*, private: Registered for Selective Service on June 5, 1917, at age 21; occupation – farmer. Inducted as a private at Windsor on September 4, 1918, and transported to Camp Lee, Petersburg, Virginia. Assigned to this depot brigade. Honorably discharged on January 14, 1919, having performed no overseas service.

MIZELL, GEORGE TIMOTHY, private: Previously served in Company D, 324th Machine Gun Battalion, 166th Infantry Brigade, 83rd Division. Transferred to this depot brigade on February 5, 1919. Honorably discharged at Camp Lee, Petersburg, Virginia on February 17, 1919.

MOUNTAIN, AUGUSTUS*, private first class: Previously served in Company B, 424th Reserve Labor Battalion, Quartermaster Corps. Transferred to this depot brigade on May 6, 1919. Honorably discharged at Camp Lee on May 22, 1919, having performed no overseas service.

PARKER, GENERAL GRANT*, private: Registered for Selective Service on June 5, 1917, at age 21; occupation – laborer. Inducted as a private at Windsor on August 31, 1918, and transported to Camp Lee, Petersburg, Virginia. Assigned to this depot brigade. Honorably discharged for re-enlistment on May 9, 1919, having performed no overseas service.

RUFFIN, PETER*, private: Registered for Selective Service on June 5, 1917, at age 21; occupation – farmer. Inducted as a private at Portsmouth, Virginia on April 27, 1918, and transported to Camp Lee, Petersburg, Virginia. Assigned to this depot brigade. Transferred to Company B, 407th Reserve Labor Battalion, Quartermaster Corps on July 20, 1918. Transferred back to this depot brigade on October 21, 1918. Honorably discharged on December 11, 1918, having performed no overseas service.

SMALLWOOD, WILLIE H., private: Registered for Selective Service on June 5, 1917, at age 23; occupation – farmer. Name appears on a list of men inducted at Windsor on August 3, 1918, and transported to Camp Greene, Charlotte, but the entry for Smallwood was lined through. Subsequently inducted as a private at Windsor on August 31, 1918, and transported to Camp Lee, Petersburg, Virginia. Assigned to this depot brigade. Honorably discharged on December 17, 1918, having performed no overseas service.

WILKINS, OTIS*, private: Registered for Selective Service on June 5, 1917, at age 25; occupation – farmer. Inducted as a private at Windsor on August 31, 1918, and transported to Camp Lee, Petersburg, Virginia. Assigned to this depot brigade. Honorably discharged at Camp Lee on December 17, 1918, having performed no overseas service.

## 156th DEPOT BRIGADE

## CAMP JACKSON, SOUTH CAROLINA

AUSTIN, JAMES CLAUDE, sergeant: Registered for Selective Service on June 5, 1917, at age 28; occupation - farmer. Inducted as a private at Windsor on October 22, 1917, and transported to Camp Jackson, Columbia, South Carolina. Assigned to this depot brigade. Promoted to saddler on July 1, 1918, and to sergeant on October 29, 1918. Honorably discharged at Camp Jackson on February 13, 1919, having performed no overseas service.

CASTELLOW, REDDEN ANTRY, private: Registered for Selective Service on June 5, 1918, at age 21; occupation – farmer. Inducted as a private at Windsor on August 26, 1918, and transported to Camp Jackson, Columbia, South Carolina. Assigned to this depot brigade. Honorably discharged on December 10, 1918, having performed no overseas service.

CASTELLOW, STARK LENFORD, private: Registered for Selective Service in Salem County, New Jersey on an undisclosed date, but likely on or about June 5, 1917, at age 23; occupation – munitions worker. Inducted as a private at Windsor on October 22, 1917, and transported to Camp Jackson, Columbia, South Carolina. Assigned to this depot brigade. Honorably discharged on May 30, 1919, having performed no overseas service.

CLARK, ISAAC*, private: Registered for Selective Service on June 5, 1917, at age 23; occupation – logging. Inducted as a private at Windsor on April 29, 1918, and transported to Camp Jackson, South Carolina. Assigned to this depot brigade. Died of lobar pneumonia on May 23, 1918.

CULLIPHER, MOODY TAYLOR, private: Registered for Selective Service on June 5, 1918, at age 21. Inducted as a private at Windsor on August 25, 1918, and transported to Camp Jackson, Columbia, South Carolina. Assigned to this depot brigade. Honorably discharged at Camp Jackson on December 10, 1918, having performed no overseas service.

CULLENS, WALTER HERBERT, private: Registered for Selective Service on June 5, 1918, at age 21. Inducted as a private at Windsor on August 26, 1918, and transported to Camp Jackson, Columbia, South Carolina. Assigned to this depot brigade until August 26, 1918, when he was transferred to the Field Artillery Replacement Draft, Camp Jackson. Transferred to the Automatic Replacement Draft on October 31, 1918. Honorably discharged at Camp Jackson on December 10, 1918, having performed no overseas service.

CONNER, MCKINLEY, private: Registered for Selective Service on June 5, 1918, at age 21; occupation – laborer. Inducted as a private at Windsor on August 26, 1918, and transported to Camp Jackson, Columbia, South Carolina. Assigned to this depot brigade. Honorably discharged at Camp Jackson on December 9, 1918, having performed no overseas service.

COREY, SAMUEL, private: Inducted as a private, reportedly in Bertie County, on August 15, 1918, at age 22, but no Selective Service registration found for this individual. Transported to Camp Jackson, Columbia, South Carolina, and assigned to this depot brigade. Honorably discharged at Camp Jackson on November 25, 1918, with a service-connected disability rated as 12 ½ percent. Performed no overseas service.

DAVIDSON, JESSE WILLARD, private: Previously served in Battery E, 316th Field Artillery Regiment, 156th Field Artillery Brigade, 81st Division. Transferred to this depot brigade on July 3, 1918. Transferred to the Utilities Detachment, Signal Corps at Camp Jackson on July 29, 1918. Honorably discharged at Camp Jackson on April 24, 1919, having performed no overseas service.

EARLY, CLYDE ROBERT., private first class: Registered for Selective Service as a resident of Aulander, Bertie County, in Detroit, Michigan on May 2, 1917, at age 22; occupation – street car conductor. Inducted as a private at Detroit on March 29, 1918, and transported to Camp Jackson, Columbia, South Carolina. Assigned to this depot brigade. Promoted to private first class on October 11, 1918. Honorably discharged at Camp Jackson on October 6, 1919, having performed no overseas service.

EARLY, SCARBOROUGH, private: Previously served in Battery A, 316th Field Artillery Regiment, 156th Field Artillery Brigade, 81st Division. Transferred to this depot brigade on July 25, 1918. Transferred to the Provost Guard Company, Camp Sevier, near Taylors, South Carolina on November 14, 1918.

EASON, HAYWARD*, corporal: Registered for Selective Service on June 5, 1917, at age 24; occupation – farmer. Inducted as a private at Windsor on April 29, 1918, and transported to Camp Jackson, Columbia, South Carolina. Assigned to this depot brigade. Promoted to corporal on September 7, 1918, and honorably discharged on an undisclosed date, having performed no overseas service.

GILLAM, THOMAS JR., private first class: Registered for Selective Service on June 5, 1917, at age 26; occupation – bank bookkeeper. Inducted as a private at Windsor on March 27, 1918, and transported to Camp Jackson, Columbia, South Carolina. Assigned to this depot brigade. Promoted to private first class on August 1, 1918. Honorably discharged at Camp Jackson on December 7, 1918, having performed no overseas service.

HARDEN, CALVIN CHARLES, private: Registered for Selective Service on June 5, 1917, at age 28; occupation – salesman. Inducted as a private at Windsor on June 28, 1918, and transported to Camp Jackson, Columbia, South Carolina. Assigned to this depot brigade and transferred to Camp Sevier, near Taylors, South Carolina on an undisclosed date. Honorably discharged on November 13, 1918, with a service-connected disability rated at 6 ¼ percent.

HARMON, JAMES REDDICK, private: Previously served in Company B, 306th Ammunition Train, 81st Division. Transferred to this depot brigade on June 21, 1918. Transferred to Company E, Ordnance Detachment of the Ordnance Department at Aberdeen Proving Ground, Aberdeen, Maryland on March 19, 1919.

HOGGARD, ARTHUR D., private: Previously served in Battery B, 316th Field Artillery Regiment, 156th Field Artillery Brigade, 81st Division. Transferred to this depot brigade on July 14, 1918. Transferred to 6th Ordnance Guard Company, Raritan Arsenal, Sparta, Wisconsin on September 16, 1918.

HOLLOMON, THAD W., private: Previously served in Battery E, 316th Field Artillery, 156th Field Artillery Brigade, 81st Division. Transferred to this depot brigade on July 3, 1918. Honorably discharged at Camp Jackson on December 7, 1918, having performed no overseas service.

JENKINS, ABRAM JACKSON, corporal: Registered for Selective Service on June 5, 1918, at age 21; occupation – farmer. Inducted as a private at Windsor on August 25, 1918, and transported to Camp Jackson, Columbia, South Carolina. Assigned to this depot brigade. Promoted to corporal on October 16, 1918. Honorably discharged at Camp Jackson on April 28, 1919, having performed no overseas service.

JONES, HOWARD*, private: Previously served in the 153rd Depot Brigade, Camp Dix, New Jersey. Transferred to this depot brigade on October 31, 1918. Honorably discharged on December 19, 1918, having performed no overseas service.

LAWRENCE, THOMAS RALEIGH, private: Registered for Selective Service on June 5, 1918, at age 21; occupation – laborer with cement company in Norfolk, Virginia. Inducted as a private at Windsor on August

25, 1918, and transported to Camp Jackson, Columbia, South Carolina. Assigned to this depot brigade. Honorably discharged at Camp Jackson on November 26, 1918, having performed no overseas service.

MILLER, ST. LEON, private: Registered for Selective Service on June 5, 1918, at age 21; occupation – farmer. Inducted as a private at Windsor on August 25, 1918, and transported to Camp Jackson, Columbia, South Carolina. Assigned to this depot brigade. Honorably discharged at Camp Jackson on December 11, 1918, having performed no overseas service.

NICHOLLS, WAYLAND, saddler: Registered for Selective Service on June 5, 1917, at age 29; occupation – farm laborer. Inducted as a private at Windsor on October 22, 1917, and transported to Camp Jackson, Columbia, South Carolina. Assigned to this depot brigade. Promoted to saddler on an undisclosed date. Honorably discharged on April 25, 1919, having performed no overseas service.

PARKER, OWEN WINFORD, private: Registered for Selective Service on June 5, 1917, at age 23; occupation – railroad clerk. Inducted as a private at Windsor on May 28, 1918, and transported to Camp Jackson, Columbia. South Carolina. Assigned to this depot brigade. Honorably discharged on December 19, 1918, having performed no overseas service.

PRITCHARD, JASON MITCHELL, sergeant: Registered for Selective Service in Wake County on an undisclosed date, but likely on or about June 5, 1917, at age 24; occupation – student. Inducted as a private at Windsor on May 28, 1918, and transported to Camp Jackson, Columbia, South Carolina. Assigned to this depot brigade. Promoted to corporal on August 1, 1918, and to sergeant on August 6, 1918. Honorably discharged on December 2, 1918, having performed no overseas service.

SKINNER, PETER*, private: Previously served in the 88th Prison Military Police, Camp Jackson, South Carolina. Transferred to this depot brigade March 25, 1919. Transferred to the Provost Guard on April 23, 1919, and to the Gas Prison Detachment Number 88, Camp Jackson, on July 29, 1919. Honorably discharged on November 3, 1919, having performed no overseas service.

STALLINGS, NOAH HENRY, JR., private: Previously served in Company L, 322nd Infantry Regiment, 161st Infantry Brigade, 81st Division. Transferred to this depot brigade on July 11, 1918. Honorably discharged on November 30, 1918, having performed no overseas service.

TARKENTON, HUBERT ROSS, private: Registered for Selective Service on June 5, 1918, at age 21; occupation – undisclosed. Inducted as a private at Windsor on August 25, 1918, and transported to Camp Jackson, Columbia, South Carolina. Assigned to this depot brigade. Honorably discharged on December 11, 1918, having performed no overseas service.

THOMAS, JAMES KELLY, private: Registered for Selective Service on June 5, 1917, at age 23; occupation – farmer. Inducted as a private at Windsor on May 28, 1918, and transported to Camp Jackson, Columbia, South Carolina. Assigned to this depot brigade. Honorably discharged on November 15, 1918, having performed no overseas service. Discharged with a service-connected disability rated as 25 percent.

THOMPSON, JOHN SAM, corporal: Registered for Selective Service on June 5, 1917, at age 27; occupation – farmer. Inducted as a private at Windsor on May 28, 1918, and transported to Camp Jackson, Columbia, South Carolina. Assigned to this depot brigade. Promoted to corporal on August 6, 1918. Honorably discharged on April 25, 1919, having performed no overseas service.

TODD, JOHN WASHINGTON, wagoner: Registered for Selective Service on June 5, 1917, at age 29; occupation – farmer. Inducted as a private at Windsor on October 22, 1917, and transported to Camp Jackson, Columbia, South Carolina. Assigned to this depot brigade. Promoted to wagoner on July 1, 1918. Honorably discharged on December 10, 1918, having performed no overseas service.

TRUMMEL, JOHN W., private: Previously served in Company M, 322nd Infantry Regiment, 161st Infantry Brigade, 81st Division. Transferred to this depot brigade on July 4, 1918. Honorably discharged on November 30, 1918, having performed no overseas service.

WALKE, WILLIAM CAPEHART, corporal: Registered for Selective Service on June 5, 1918, at age 22; occupation – salesman. Inducted as a private at Windsor on August 25, 1918, and transported to Camp Jackson, Columbia, South Carolina. Assigned to this depot brigade. Promoted to corporal on October 10, 1918. Transferred to the Port Utilities Detachment, Quartermaster Corps, Camp Hill, Newport News, Virginia on November 20, 1918.

WARD, JOHN RALEIGH, private: Registered for Selective Service on June 5, 1917, at age 30; occupation – filing saws. Inducted as a private at Windsor on May 28, 1918, and transported to Camp Jackson, Columbia, South Carolina. Assigned to this depot brigade. Honorably discharged on December 13, 1918, having performed no overseas service.

WARD, MILLIE, private: Registered for Selective Service on June 5, 1918, at age 21; occupation – undisclosed. Inducted as a private at Windsor on August 25, 1918, and transported to Camp Jackson, Columbia, South Carolina. Assigned to this depot brigade. Honorably discharged at Camp Jackson on March 5, 1919, having performed no overseas service.

WILLIAMS, EUGENIA*, private: Registered for Selective Service on June 5, 1917, at age 25; occupation – farmer. Inducted as a private at Windsor on April 29, 1918, and transported to Camp Jackson, Columbia, South Carolina. Assigned to this depot brigade. Honorably discharged on April 28, 1919, having performed no overseas service.

WOOD, JULIAN EDWARD, private first class: Registered for Selective Service on June 5, 1917, at age 30; occupation – farmer. Inducted as a private at Windsor on June 28, 1918, and transported to Camp Jackson, Columbia, South Carolina. Assigned to this depot brigade. Promoted to private first class on August 10, 1918. Transferred to the Central Officers Training School at Camp Gordon on September 11, 1918.

## 159th DEPOT BRIGADE

## CAMP TAYLOR, KENTUCKY

WALKER, PHILLIP*, private: Registered for Selective Service on June 5, 1917, at age 25; occupation – farmer. Inducted as a private at Windsor on June 21, 1918, and transported to Camp Taylor, Louisville, Kentucky. Assigned to this depot brigade. Honorably discharged on August 28, 1918, with a service-connected disability rated as 10 percent.

## 161st DEPOT BRIGADE

## CAMP GRANT, ILLINOIS

BAKER, ROLLAN, private: Previously served at the Evacuation Hospital No. 37, Camp Greenleaf, Fort Oglethorpe, Chickamauga Park, Georgia. Transferred to this depot brigade on October 17, 1918. Honorably discharged (location undisclosed) on December 31, 1918, having performed no overseas service.

BUNCH, ANDREW JACKSON*, private: Registered for Selective Service on June 5, 1917, at age 21; occupation – laborer for lumber company. Inducted as a private at Windsor on April 2, 1918, and transported to Camp Grant, Rockford, Illinois. Assigned to this depot brigade and honorably discharged on October 22, 1918, having performed no overseas service. Discharged due to service-connected disability rated as 33 1/3 percent.

CLARK, WILLIAM KNOWLEDGE*, private: Registered for Selective Service on June 5, 1917, at age 21; occupation – farmer. Inducted as a private at Windsor on April 28, 1918, and transported to Camp Grant, Rockford, Illinois. Assigned to this depot brigade. Honorably discharged on May 27, 1918, having performed no overseas service. Discharged due to service-connected disability rated as 33-1/3 percent.

COOPER, WILLIAM EDWARD*, private: Registered for Selective Service on June 5, 1917, at age 21; occupation – laborer. Inducted as a private at Windsor on April 28, 1918, and transported to Camp Grant, Rockford, Illinois. Assigned to Company A, Development Battalion, of this depot brigade. Honorably discharged at Camp Grant on November 21, 1918, having performed no overseas service. Discharged due to a service-connected disability rated as 33-1/3 percent.

DELOATCH, JAMES*, private: Registered for Selective Service on June 5, 1917, at age 22; occupation – farmer. Inducted as a private at Windsor on April 2, 1918, and transported to Camp Grant, Rockford, Illinois. Initially assigned to this depot brigade and transferred to Company B, 323rd Labor Battalion, Quartermaster Corps on May 26, 1918. Transferred back to this depot brigade on June 1, 1918, and to the 329th Labor Battalion on June 27, 1918, then back to this depot brigade on July 11, 1918. Honorably discharged at Camp Grant on October 21, 1918, having performed no overseas ser-

vice. Discharged due to a service-connected disability rated as 25 percent.

EARLY, LEWIS*, private: Registered for Selective Service on June 5, 1917, at age 24; occupation – public work. Inducted as a private at Windsor on April 28, 1918, and transported to Camp Grant, Rockford, Illinois. Assigned to this depot brigade in which he served until honorably discharged at Camp Grant on January 11, 1919, having performed no overseas service.

FREEMAN, LANG E.*, private: Registered for Selective Service on June 5, 1917, at age 26; occupation – farmer. Inducted as a private at Windsor on April 2, 1918, and transported to Camp Grant, Rockford, Illinois. Assigned to this depot brigade. Honorably discharged at Camp Grant on June 25, 1918, having performed no overseas service. Discharged due to a service-connected disability rated as 10 percent.

GILLAM, ARTHUR B., private first class: Enlisted as a private at Chicago, Illinois on August 5, 1918, at age 33. Assigned to this depot brigade at Camp Grant, Rockford, Illinois. Promoted to private first class on January 1, 1919, and honorably discharged at Camp Grant on February 9, 1919, having performed no overseas service.

LUTON, ISAIAH*, private: Registered for Selective Service on June 5, 1917, at age 23; occupation – farmer. Inducted as a private at Windsor on April 26, 1918, and transported to Camp Grant, Rockford, Illinois. Assigned to this depot brigade. Honorably discharged due to physical disability at Camp Grant on June 3, 1918.

SPELLER, HERBERT*, private: Registered for Selective Service on June 5, 1917, at age 24; occupation – farmer. Inducted as a private at Windsor on April 26, 1918, and transported to Camp Grant, Rockford, Illinois. Assigned to this depot brigade. Honorably discharged at Camp Grant on November 4,

1918, with a service-connected disability rated as 20 percent.

SPELLER, NOAH COOPER*, private: Registered for Selective Service on June 5, 1917, at age 28; occupation – farmer. Inducted as a private at Windsor on April 2, 1918, and transported to Camp Grant, Rockford, Illinois. Assigned to this depot brigade. Died of pneumonia at Camp Grant on April 14, 1918.

WALKER, GARFIELD*, private: Previously served in Headquarters Company, 365th Infantry Regiment, 183rd Infantry Brigade, 92nd Division. Transferred to this depot brigade on May 27, 1918. Arrested and jailed by Sheriff John W. Cooper in Bertie County on June 18, 1918, for being a "slacker." Released from jail and "carried to the Camp" on June 19, 1918. Transferred to Company A, 416th Service Battalion, on April 11, 1919.

WARD, CHARLIE*, private: Registered for Selective Service on June 5, 1917, at age 21; occupation – farmer. Inducted as a private at Windsor on April 28, 1918, and transported to Camp Grant, Rockford, Illinois. Assigned to this depot brigade. Honorably discharged on June 28, 1919, with a service-connected disability rated as 20 percent.

WILDER, THOMAS STEWART*, private: Previously served in the 329th Labor Battalion. Transferred to this depot brigade on July 11, 1918. Honorably discharged on January 11, 1919, having performed no overseas service.

## MEDICAL DEPARTMENT

BAKER, ROLLAN, private: Registered for Selective Service on June 5, 1917, at age 22; occupation – farmer. Inducted as a private at Windsor on July 5, 1918, and transported to Camp Greenleaf, Fort Oglethorpe, Chickamauga Park, Georgia. Initially assigned to Headquarters Battalion No. 15

and transferred to Evacuation Hospital No. 37 on July 22, 1918. Transferred to the 161st Depot Brigade, Camp Grant, Rockford, Illinois on October 17, 1918.

BUTLER, WALTER LAMAR, private: Registered for Selective Service on June 5, 1917, at age 27; occupation – farmer. Enlisted at Fort Thomas, Kentucky, on July 29, 1917, and was assigned to this department. Transferred to Camp Upton, Long Island, New York on August 1, 1918. Assigned to the July Automatic Replacement Draft on August 7, 1918, and subsequently to Medical Department, Base Hospital Number 2 (date of transfer and location of hospital undisclosed), with which he served until discharged. Served overseas from July 14, 1918, until February 3, 1919. Honorably discharged on July 12, 1919.

BUTLER, WILLIAM FOLK, private: Registered for Selective Service on June 5, 1917, at age 30; occupation – farmer. Inducted as a private at Windsor on July 12, 1918, and transported to Camp Greenleaf, at Fort Oglethorpe, Chickamauga Park, Georgia. Assigned to Evacuation Hospital Number 34 of this department. Transferred to Evacuation Hospital Number 41 on August 30, 1918, and to Evacuation Hospital Number 35 on September 20, 1918. Transferred to Camp Hospital Number 35 on May 10, 1919. Served overseas from November 10, 1918, until October 6, 1919. Honorably discharged at Camp Dix, near Trenton, New Jersey on October 11, 1919.

BUTTERTON, HENRY HUNTER, cook: Registered for Selective Service on June 5, 1918, at age 21; occupation – farmer. Inducted as a private at Windsor on August 26, 1918, and transported to Camp Jackson, Columbia, South Carolina. Initially assigned to the 156th Depot Brigade and transferred to Base Hospital Number 106, Camp Greenleaf, at Fort Oglethorpe, Chickamauga Park, Georgia on September 6, 1918. Promoted to cook on December 21, 1918. Served overseas from October

27, 1918, until July 10, 1919. Honorably discharged on July 21, 1919.

COBB, CHARLIE THOMAS, private first class: Registered for Selective Service on June 5, 1918, at age 21; occupation – laborer. Inducted as a private at Windsor on August 5, 1918, and transported to Camp Jackson, Columbia, South Carolina. Assigned to the base hospital at Camp Jackson. Promoted to private first class on December 9, 1918. Honorably discharged on February 11, 1919, having performed no overseas service.

COBB, THOMAS SPIVEY, sergeant: Enlisted at Fort Thomas, Kentucky on May 21, 1917, at age 30. Assigned to Field Hospital Number 24 until August 17, 1917, when he was transferred to Field Hospital Number 322. Promoted to sergeant on July 9, 1918. Served overseas from August 8, 1918, until June 20, 1919. Honorably discharged on June 29, 1919.

COOK, ARTHUR, Private first class: Enlisted at Fort Slocum, Davids Island, New York on June 23, 1914, at age 18. Assigned to this department and served at the base hospital at Fort Sill, Lawton, Oklahoma. Promoted to private first class on May 23, 1916. Transferred to Company M, 16th Infantry Regiment, 1st Infantry Brigade, 1st Division on July 4, 1918.

FAIRLESS, JOSEPH GRAHAM, private: Registered for Selective Service on June 5, 1918, at age 21; occupation – farmer. Inducted as a private at Windsor on August 25, 1918, and transported to Camp Jackson, Columbia, South Carolina. Assigned to the base hospital at Camp Jackson. Sent overseas on October 17, 1918, and transferred to Evacuation Hospital Number 26 on November 11, 1918. Returned from overseas on August 1, 1919, and honorably discharged on August 9, 1919.

FELTON, LEONIDAS POLK, private: Registered for Selective Service on June 5, 1917,

at age 22; occupation – farmer. Inducted as a private at Windsor on July 6, 1918, and transported to Camp Greenleaf, at Fort Oglethorpe, Chickamauga Park, Georgia. Assigned to Evacuation Hospital Number 35 and sent overseas on November 12, 1918. Transferred to Camp Hospital Number 35 on March 12, 1919. Returned from overseas on June 18, 1919, and honorably discharged on July 8, 1919.

JONES, JOHN P., private first class: Previously served in Medical Department of the 54th Infantry Regiment, 12th Infantry Brigade, 6th Division. Transferred as a private to United States General Hospital Number 14 (location not disclosed) on January 23, 1918. Promoted to private first class on July 15, 1918. Served overseas from October 27, 1918, until June 22, 1919. Honorably discharged on July 10, 1919.

LAWRENCE, ARTHUR FANNING, private first class: Registered for Selective Service on June 5, 1917, at age 26; occupation – laborer. Inducted as a private at Windsor on March 29, 1918, and transported to Camp Jackson, Columbia, South Carolina. Initially assigned to the 156th Depot Brigade and transferred to the base hospital at Camp Stuart, Newport News, Virginia on April 24, 1918. Promoted to private first class on January 1, 1919. Honorably discharged on March 22, 1919, having performed no overseas service.

LAWRENCE, FRANK, private: Registered for Selective Service on June 5, 1917, at age 22; occupation – farm laborer. Inducted as a private at Windsor on July 6, 1918, and transported to Camp Greenleaf at Fort Oglethorpe, Chickamauga Park, Georgia. Assigned to this department and served at Evacuation Hospital Number 49. Served overseas from October 17, 1918, until June 27, 1919. Honorably discharged on July 7, 1919.

LAWRENCE, PAUL SIMON, private first class: Registered for Selective Service on June 5, 1917, at age 27; occupation – farmer. Inducted as a private at Windsor on July 6,

1918, but failed to get the call "in time to leave" on his induction date. Subsequently transported to Camp Greenleaf at Fort Oglethorpe, Chickamauga Park, Georgia. Assigned to Base Hospital Number 105. Transferred to General Hospital Number 19 on August 20, 1918. Promoted to private first class on November 1, 1918. Honorably discharged on November 19, 1919, having performed no overseas service.

NEWSOME, JOSEPH MARTIN, sergeant: Registered for Selective Service as a Bertie County resident at Richmond, Virginia on June 5, 1917, at age 26; occupation – mechanic. Inducted as a private at Windsor on July 6, 1918, and transported to Camp Greenleaf, at Fort Oglethorpe, Chickamauga Park, Georgia. Served as a sergeant in Evacuation Hospital Number 36. No further information.

RHODES, GILBERT, wagoner: Enlisted as a private at Fort Thomas, Kentucky on July 29, 1917, at age 19. Assigned to this department. Promoted to private first class on October 2, 1917. Sent overseas on May 22, 1918. Promoted to wagoner on March 1, 1919. Returned from overseas on April 25, 1919, and honorably discharged on May 14, 1919.

SPEIGHT, LLOYD WOOD, private first class: Registered for Selective Service on June 5, 1917, at age 22; occupation – undisclosed. Enlisted as a private at Fort Thomas, Kentucky on August 1, 1917, at age 23. Initially assigned to Company C, Medical Officers Training Camp and transferred to Company A, Medical Detachment, Base Hospital, Camp Upton, Long Island, New York on an undisclosed date. Died at home in Bertie County on December 29, 1918; cause of death – "broncho pneumonia – influenza."

TARKENTON, EDWARD PERRY, sergeant fourth class: Enlisted at Washington, D.C. in the Enlisted Reserve Corps on May 19, 1917. Assigned to Section 513, Ambulance

Service. Promoted to sergeant on May 19, 1917. Sent overseas on December 26, 1917. Promoted to sergeant fourth class on December 3, 1918. Returned from overseas on April 20, 1919, and honorably discharged on April 22, 1919.

TAYLOE, JOHN W., private: Registered for Selective Service on June 5, 1917, at age 22; occupation – farmer. Inducted as a private at Windsor on May 28, 1918, and transported to Camp Jackson, Columbia, South Carolina. Initially assigned to the 156th Depot Brigade and transferred to the Ambulance Company Number 323, 308th Sanitary Train on June 2, 1918. Served overseas from August 8, 1918, until June 20, 1919. Honorably discharged on June 29, 1919.

WHITE, MARTIN HENRY, private: Enlisted as a private at Fort Thomas, Kentucky on September 23, 1917, at age 18. Assigned to the Medical Department, Camp Greenleaf, at Fort Oglethorpe, Chickamauga Park, Georgia. Transferred to the Medical Detachment, 3rd Trench Mortar Battalion on February 7, 1918.

WHITE, PETER R., private: Enlisted as a private at Fort Thomas, Kentucky on June 3, 1917, at age 23. Assigned to 310th Ambulance Company. Served overseas from June 4, 1918, until May 27, 1919. Honorably discharged on June 10, 1919.

WILLIFORD, GORDON CARLTON, private first class: Registered for Selective Service as a Bertie County resident in Philadelphia, Pennsylvania on May 29, 1917, at age 30; occupation – salesman. Inducted as a private at Windsor on September 28, 1917, and transported to Camp Jackson, Columbia, South Carolina. Assigned to the Medical Detachment, 321st Infantry Regiment, 161st Infantry Brigade, 81st Division. Transferred to 120th Field Hospital, 105th Sanitary Train on October 17, 1917. Promoted to private first class on an undisclosed date. Honorably discharged on May 2, 1918, due to "dependency."

## COAST ARTILLERY CORPS

## FORT AMADOR, PANAMA CANAL ZONE

BARNES, WILLIAM CLINGMAN, private: Enlisted as a private on an undisclosed date at Fort Grant, Panama Canal Zone. Served in this corps at Fort Amador, Panama Canal Zone, until May 2, 1918, when he was transferred to Student Company No. 8, Camp Johnston, Jacksonville, Florida. Honorably discharged as an enlisted soldier on June 13, 1918, to accept an officer's commission. Appointed second lieutenant in the Quartermaster Corps at Camp Johnston on June 1, 1918.

## FORT HOWARD, BALTIMORE COUNTY, MARYLAND

SLADE, CECIL E., sergeant: Enlisted as a private at Fort Hancock, Sandy Hook, New Jersey on May 25, 1914. Assigned to the 4th Company, Coast Artillery Corps, Fort Howard, Baltimore County, Maryland. Promoted to corporal on December 31, 1914, and to sergeant on August 1, 1916. Transferred to Truck Company F, 1st Ammunition Train, 1st Division on July 26, 1917.

## 103RD COMPANY, WASHINGTON, D.C.

BAZEMORE, TURNER FRANKLIN, corporal: Enlisted as a private on November 8, 1893, at age 22. Served as a cook in Battery I, 6th Artillery Regiment during the Spanish-American War. Discharged on an undisclosed date. Re-enlisted at Washington, D.C. on August 3, 1915, at age 44 and assigned to the 103rd Company, Coast Artillery Corps. Promoted to corporal on May 26, 1917. Transferred to Company F, 336th

Infantry Regiment, 168th Infantry Brigade, 84th Division on October 13, 1917.

## COAST DEFENSE COMMAND OF THE CAPE FEAR

## FORT CASWELL, NORTH CAROLINA

CHERRY, EDWARD GRAY, private first class: Enlisted as a private in the North Carolina National Guard at Raleigh on May 5, 1917, at age 22. Assigned to 1st Company, Coast Artillery Corps, North Carolina National Guard, Cape Fear, Fort Caswell. Transferred to the 7th Army Artillery Battery, Coast Artillery Corps at Fort Caswell on January 2, 1918. Promoted to private first class in July 1918. Served overseas from June 19, 1918, until March 7, 1919. Honorably discharged at Camp Lee, Petersburg, Virginia on March 21, 1919.

CHERRY, SOL, corporal: Enlisted as a private in the North Carolina National Guard at Raleigh on May 4, 1917, at age 24. Assigned to 1st Company, Coast Artillery Corps, North Carolina National Guard, Cape Fear, Fort Caswell on July 25, 1917. Promoted to corporal on December 18, 1917. Transferred to the 7th Army Artillery Battery, Coast Artillery Corps at Fort Caswell on January 2, 1918. Served overseas from June 10, 1918, until March 7, 1919. Honorably discharged at Camp Lee, Petersburg, Virginia on March 24, 1919.

OUTLAW, ALEXANDER BATES, first sergeant: Enlisted as a private in the North Carolina National Guard at Raleigh on May 28, 1917, at age 24. Assigned to the 1st Company, Coast Artillery Corps, North Carolina National Guard, Cape Fear, Fort Caswell. Transferred to the 7th Company, Coast Artillery Corps, Cape Fear, Fort Caswell on an undisclosed date. Promoted to corporal on September 14, 1917. Transferred to 2nd Trench Mortar Battery on

January 28, 1918. Promoted to sergeant on March 21, 1918. Transferred to the 11th Company, Coast Artillery Corps, Cape Fear, Fort Caswell on April 1, 1918. Promoted to first sergeant on July 10, 1918. Transferred as an unassigned non-commissioned officer to the Coast Artillery Corps on November 15, 1918, in which he served until honorably discharged on May 26, 1919.

PEELE, ROSCOE N., private first class: Enlisted as a private in the North Carolina National Guard at Raleigh on June 2, 1917, at age 24. Assigned to the 1st Company, Coast Artillery Corps, North Carolina National Guard, Cape Fear, Fort Caswell. Transferred to the 7th Company, Coast Artillery Corps, Cape Fear, Fort Caswell. Promoted to private first class on January 11, 1918, and to corporal on February 8, 1918. Transferred to Battery C, 2nd Trench Artillery on February 23, 1918. Sent overseas on May 28, 1918. Reduced to private on July 1, 1918, and promoted to private first class in December 1918. Returned from overseas on April 20, 1919, and honorably discharged on May 7, 1919.

PERRY, EDWARD SUTTON, first sergeant: Enlisted as a private in the North Carolina National Guard at Raleigh on July 25, 1917, at age 22. Assigned to the 1st Company, Coast Artillery Corps, North Carolina National Guard, Cape Fear, Fort Caswell. Transferred to the 7th Company, Coast Artillery Corps, Cape Fear, Fort Caswell. Promoted to private first class on December 1, 1917, to corporal on February 8, 1918, to sergeant on March 26, 1918, and to first sergeant on April 1, 1918. Honorably discharged at Camp Eustis, Virginia on December 7, 1918, having performed no overseas service.

POWELL, JUNIUS BISHOP, second lieutenant: Enlisted as a private in the North Carolina National Guard at Raleigh on May 5, 1917, at age 19. Assigned to the 1st Company, Coast Artillery Corps, North Carolina National Guard, Cape Fear, Fort Caswell. Transferred to the 7th Company, Coast Artillery Corps, Cape Fear, Fort Caswell. Honorably discharged on November 2, 1917, with a service-connected disability rated as 50 percent. Appointed second lieutenant on February 25, 1918, and assigned to the 61st Infantry Regiment, 9th Infantry Brigade, 5th Division.

SESSOMS, STANLEY B., corporal: Enlisted as a private in the North Carolina National Guard at Raleigh on May 24, 1917, at age 24. Assigned to the 1st Company, Coast Artillery Corps, North Carolina National Guard, Cape Fear, Fort Caswell. Transferred to the 7th Company, Coast Artillery Corps, Cape Fear, Fort Caswell Promoted to cook on January 7, 1918. Promoted to private first class on an undisclosed date and to corporal on May 11, 1918. Transferred to Battery F, 50th Artillery, Coast Artillery Corps, on July 18, 1918. Transferred to Headquarters Company, 45th Artillery, Coast Artillery Corps, on October 15, 1918. Served overseas from October 18, 1918, until March 17, 1919. Honorably discharged on April 15, 1919.

SKILES, STARK LAFAYETTE, sergeant: Registered for Selective Service on June 5, 1917, at age 24; occupation – farmer. Enlisted as a private in the North Carolina National Guard at Raleigh on July 22, 1917, at age 24. Assigned to the 1st Company, Coast Artillery Corps, North Carolina National Guard, Cape Fear, Fort Caswell. Transferred to the 7th Company, Coast Artillery Corps, Cape Fear, Fort Caswell. Promoted to cook on January 1, 1918, to corporal on February 26, 1918, and to sergeant on March 20, 1918. Sent overseas on September 25, 1918. Transferred to Battery A, 54th Artillery, Coast Artillery Corps on October 16, 1918. Returned from overseas on March 7, 1919, and honorably discharged on March 8, 1919.

SPIVEY, JOSEPH BRYAN, private first class: Enlisted as a private in the North Carolina National Guard at Raleigh on May 28, 1917, at age 26. Assigned to the 1st Company, Coast Artillery Corps, North Carolina

National Guard, Cape Fear, Fort Caswell. Transferred to the 7th Company, Coast Artillery Corps, Cape Fear, Fort Caswell. Promoted to private first class on December 1, 1917. Rated as a "1st class gunner" on December 19, 1917. Transferred to the 8th Anti-aircraft Battery, Coast Artillery Corps on January 2, 1918. Served overseas from June 10, 1918, until March 7, 1919. Honorably discharged on March 24, 1919.

THOMPSON, WILLIAM C., sergeant: Enlisted as a private in the North Carolina National Guard at Raleigh on June 2, 1917, at age 28. Assigned to the 1st Company, Coast Artillery Corps, North Carolina National Guard, Cape Fear, Fort Caswell. Transferred to the 7th Company, Coast Artillery Corps, Cape Fear, Fort Caswell. Promoted to corporal on February 8, 1918, and to sergeant on May 1, 1918. Transferred to Battery E, 47th Artillery, Coast Artillery Corps, on August 26, 1918. Served overseas from October 14, 1918, until February 18, 1919. Honorably discharged on February 22, 1919.

## MISCELLANEOUS

HUGHES, ZACK ODELL, private: Registered for Selective Service on June 5, 1917, at age 23; occupation – farmer. Enlisted as a private at Windsor on July 26, 1918. Transported to Camp Screven, Georgia, where he was assigned to a recruit company. Transferred to Battery D, 51st Artillery, Coast Artillery Corps. Served overseas from September 25, 1918, until January 14, 1919. Honorably discharged at Camp Gordon, Augusta, Georgia on February 1, 1919.

MARSH, CLARENCE TALMAGE, lieutenant colonel: A resident of Aulander, Bertie County, and a career officer in the regular army. Served in the Coast Artillery Corps. Served overseas from August 9, 1918, until April 27, 1919.

Nicholls, Levy H., mechanic: Enlisted as a private at Fort Monroe, Hampton, Virginia on February 9, 1915, at age 30. Assigned to the

6th Company, Coast Artillery Corps. Promoted to mechanic on February 12, 1916. Honorably discharged for re-enlistment on June 17, 1919, having performed no overseas service.

## MILITARY POLICE

## 6th MILITARY POLICE

## Company A

THOMAS, CLYDE P., private first class: Previously served in Company M, 54th Infantry Regiment, 12th Infantry Brigade, 6th Division. Transferred to this company on April 24, 1918. Served overseas from July 7, 1918, until July 2, 1919. Honorably discharged on July 18, 1919.

## 208th MIITARY POLICE COMPANY

TARKENTON, JOSEPH R., private first class: Previously served in Company A, 1st Army Corps Headquarters Regiment. Transferred as a private to his company on September 25, 1918, while serving overseas. Promoted to private first class on December 4, 1918. Returned from overseas on June 28, 1919, and honorably discharged on July 13, 1919.

## 287th MILITARY POLICE COMPANY

BURKETT, ERNEST EARL, private first class: Previously served in Company E, 321st Infantry Regiment, 161st Infantry Brigade, 81st Division. Transferred as a corporal to this unit on May 30, 1919, while serving overseas. Reduced in rank to private first class on May 20, 1919. Returned from overseas on August 20, 1919. Honorably discharged on September 8, 1919, for the purpose of re-enlisting. No information found relative to that action.

## 88th PRISON MILITARY POLICE

SKINNER, PETER*, private: Previously served in Company A, 328th Service Battalion. Transferred to this unit at Camp Jackson, Columbia, South Carolina on July 22, 1918. Transferred to the 156th Depot Brigade, Camp Jackson, on March 25, 1919.

## CENTRAL OFFICERS TRAINING SCHOOLS

CASTELLOE, OBED, second lieutenant: Previously served in Company E, 321st Infantry, 161st Infantry Brigade, 81st Division. Transferred as a sergeant to the Central Officers Training School at Camp Gordon, Augusta, Georgia on March 19, 1918. Honorably discharged on August 25, 1918, to accept an officer's commission. Appointed second lieutenant on August 26, 1918 and assigned to the 62nd Pioneer Infantry Regiment at Camp Wadsworth, Spartanburg, South Carolina on an undisclosed date.

GATLING, JOHN MORRIS, corporal: Registered for Selective Service on June 5, 1917, at age 22; occupation – attorney. Inducted as a private at Windsor on June 28, 1918, and transported to Camp Jackson, Columbia, South Carolina. Assigned to the 156th Depot Brigade until transferred to Central Officers Training School at Camp Taylor, Louisville, Kentucky. Honorably discharged at Camp Taylor on December 20, 1918, having performed no overseas service.

SITTERSON, THADDEUS BERKLEY, sergeant: Registered for Selective Service as a Bertie County resident at Norfolk, Virginia on June 1, 1917, at age 26; occupation – clerk. Inducted as a private at Windsor on March 27, 1918, and transported to Camp Jackson, Columbia, South Carolina. Initially assigned to the 156th Depot Brigade. Promoted to sergeant on July 16, 1918, and transferred to the Central Officers Training School, Camp Gordon, Augusta, Georgia,

on July 18, 1918. Sent overseas on October 26, 1918. Transferred to Headquarters, 3rd Army Corps, American Expeditionary Forces, France on November 11, 1918.

WOOD, JULIAN EDWARD, private first class: Previously served in the 156th Depot Brigade, Camp Jackson, South Carolina. Transferred to the Central Officers Training School at Camp Gordon on September 11, 1918. Honorably discharged on November 28, 1918, having performed no overseas service.

## VETERINARY CORPS

BURDEN, HENRY VERNON, private: Registered for Selective Service on June 5, 1917, at age 21; occupation – medical student. Inducted as a private at Windsor on March 29, 1918, and transported to Camp Jackson, Columbia, South Carolina. Initially assigned to the 156th Depot Brigade and transferred to the Veterinary Corps at Camp Jackson on April 16, 1918. Honorably discharged on May 27, 1919, having performed no overseas service.

## REPLACEMENT DRAFTS

## ENGINEERS

BURDEN, WALTER JACKSON, private: Previously served in the October Automatic Replacement Draft at Washington Barracks, Washington, D.C. Transferred to the 116th Engineers Regiment, 41st Division on September 30, 1918.

BOWEN, EDWARD WORLEY, private: Registered for Selective Service on June 5, 1918, at age 21; occupation – supervisor of township roads. Inducted as a private at Windsor on August 26, 1918, and transported to Camp Jackson, Columbia, South Carolina. Initially assigned to Company A, 3rd Provisional Regiment, 156th Depot Brigade and transferred to the 1st Company, Engineers

October Automatic Replacement Draft at Camp Forrest, Fort Oglethorpe, Chickamauga Park, Georgia. on October 2, 1918. Transferred to Company B, 5th Engineers Training Regiment at Camp Forrest on November 22, 1918. Honorably discharged on December 30, 1918, having performed no overseas service.

CARTER, RHODES TAYLOR*, private first class: Registered for Selective Service on June 5, 1917, at age 21; occupation – farmer. Inducted as a private at Windsor on August 23, 1918, and slated to be transported to Camp Greene, Charlotte, but failed to report to military authorities. Inducted a second time on August 31, 1918, and transported to Camp Lee, Petersburg, Virginia. Initially assigned to the 155th Depot Brigade and transferred to the 110th Provisional Company, Automatic Replacement Draft at Camp Lee on November 8, 1918. Promoted to private first class on December 10, 1918, and honorably discharged at Camp Lee on January 27, 1919, having performed no overseas service.

# FIELD ARTILLERY

BAGGETT, JAMES ALLEN, private: Registered for Selective Service on June 5, 1918, at age 21; occupation - farmer. Inducted as a private at Windsor on August 26, 1918, and transported to Camp Jackson, Columbia, South Carolina. Initially assigned to the 156th Depot Brigade and transferred to Battery C, 8th Field Artillery Regiment Replacement Draft, at Camp Jackson on August 31, 1918. Transferred to the 16th Battery, October Automatic Replacement Draft, at Camp Jackson on October 31, 1918. Transferred to Battery B, 2nd Field Artillery Regiment Replacement Draft on November 30, 1918. Honorably discharged (location undisclosed, but likely Camp Jackson) on December 11, 1918, having performed no overseas service.

BAKER, HIRAM STANLEY, private: Registered for Selective Service on June 5, 1918, at age 21; occupation – farmer. Inducted as

a private at Windsor on August 26, 1918, and transported to Camp Jackson, Columbia, South Carolina. Initially assigned to Company A, Provisional Regiment, 156th Depot Brigade and transferred to Battery C, 8th Field Artillery Regiment Replacement Draft on August 1, 1918. Transferred to Battery D, 307th Field Artillery Regiment, 153rd Field Artillery Brigade, 78th Division on October 15, 1918.

BEASLEY, JOHN CECIL, PRIVATE: REGISTERED FOR SELECTive Service on June 5, 1917, at age 21; occupation - chauffer. Inducted as a private at Windsor on August 26, 1918, and transported to Camp Jackson, Columbia, South Carolina. Initially assigned to the 156th Depot Brigade and transferred to Battery C, 8th Field Artillery Regiment Replacement Draft on August 31, 1918. Transferred to Battery B, 307th Field Artillery Regiment, 153rd Field Artillery Brigade, 78th Division, on an undisclosed date.

BAZEMORE, JAMES LANG, private: Registered for Selective Service on June 5, 1917, at age 22; occupation – farmer. Inducted as a private at Windsor on August 26, 1918, and transported to Camp Jackson, Columbia, South Carolina. Initially assigned to Company A, 3rd Provisional Regiment, 156th Depot Brigade and transferred to Battery E, 1st Field Artillery Regiment Replacement Draft at Camp Jackson on September 6, 1918. Transferred to the 19th Battery, October Automatic Replacement Draft on October 3, 1918. Transferred to the 3rd Battery, Field Artillery Replacement Regiment, on an undisclosed date. Served overseas from October 28, 1918, until May 21, 1919, and honorably discharged at Camp Lee, Petersburg, Virginia on May 26, 1919.

BUTLER, CURTIS, private: Registered for Selective Service on June 5, 1917, at age 24; occupation – farmer. Inducted as a private at Windsor on September 11, 1918, and transported to Camp Jackson, Columbia, South Carolina. Initially assigned to the 156th Depot Brigade and transferred to the Field Artillery Replacement Draft on September

15, 1918. Honorably discharged on December 9, 1918, at Camp Jackson, having performed no overseas service.

COWAND, ALLCY, private: Registered for Selective Service on June 5, 1917, at age 24; occupation – car repair. Inducted as a private at Windsor on May 28, 1918, and transported to Camp Jackson, Columbia, South Carolina. Initially assigned to the 156th Depot Brigade and transferred to Battery A, 2nd Battalion, Field Artillery Replacement Draft, Camp Jackson, on June 15, 1918. Sent overseas on July 2, 1918, and transferred to Battery F, 113th Field Artillery Regiment, 55th Field Artillery Brigade, 30th Division on July 13, 1918.

DUNLOW, JOHN THOMAS, private: Registered for Selective Service on June 5, 1917, at age 23; occupation – farmer. Inducted as a private at Windsor on September 11, 1918, and transported to Camp Jackson, Columbia, South Carolina. Initially assigned to the 156th Depot Brigade and transferred to the November Automatic Replacement Draft on November 16, 1918. Transferred to Battery A, 13th Field Artillery Replacement Draft on November 21, 1918. Honorably discharged at Camp Jackson on December 7, 1918, having performed no overseas service.

EARLY, JOSEPH MERRILL, private: Registered for Selective Service on June 5, 1917, at age 25; occupation – farmer. Name appears on a list of Bertie County men inducted on August 5, 1918, who were transported to Camp Wadsworth, Spartanburg, South Carolina, but the entry for Early was lined through. Inducted as a private at Windsor on August 25, 1918, and transported to Camp Jackson, Columbia, South Carolina. Assigned to Battery C, 8th Field Artillery Regiment Replacement Draft. Transferred to Battery 14, October Automatic Replacement Draft, Field Artillery on October 15, 1918. Sent overseas on October 28, 1918. Transferred to Battery C, 307th Field Artillery Regiment, 153rd Field Artillery Brigade, 78th Division on an undisclosed date.

EVANS, ESSIE CLARENCE, private: Registered for Selective Service on June 5, 1918, at age 21; occupation – laborer. Inducted as a private at Windsor on September 11, 1918, and transported to Camp Jackson, Columbia, South Carolina. Assigned to Battery A, 13th Field Artillery Regiment Replacement Depot Group. Honorably discharged at Camp Jackson on December 9, 1918, having performed no overseas service.

FLOYD, WOODY, private: Registered for Selective Service on June 5, 1918, at age 21; occupation – laborer. Inducted as a private at Windsor on August 25, 1918, and transported to Camp Jackson, Columbia, South Carolina. Assigned to the Field Artillery Replacement Draft at Camp Jackson until honorably discharged on December 11, 1918, having performed no overseas service.

HOGGARD, JAMES FRANCIS, private: Registered for Selective Service on June 5, 1918, at age 21; occupation – laborer. Inducted as a private at Windsor on August 25, 1918, and transported to Camp Jackson, Columbia, South Carolina. Assigned to Battery F, 9th Field Artillery Regiment Replacement Draft at Camp Jackson. Transferred to Battery 11, October Replacement Draft at Camp Hill, Newport News, Virginia. Honorably discharged on February 14, 1919, having performed no overseas service.

KENNEDY, ALFRED FORBES, JR., private: Registered for Selective Service on June 5, 1918, at age 21; occupation – laborer. Inducted as a private at Windsor on August 26, 1918, and transported to Camp Jackson, Columbia, South Carolina. Initially assigned to the 156th Depot Brigade and transferred to Battery C, Field Artillery Replacement Draft on August 31, 1918. Transferred to the 16th Battery, October Automatic Replacement Draft on October 31, 1918. Honorably discharged on December 13, 1918, having performed no overseas service.

LASSITER, DAVE W., private: Registered for Selective Service on June 5, 1918, at age 21; occupation – laborer. Inducted as a private at Windsor on August 26, 1918, and transported to Camp Jackson, Columbia, South Carolina. Initially assigned to the 156th Depot Brigade and transferred to the Camp Jackson Field Artillery Replacement Draft on September 8, 1918. Honorably discharged at Camp Jackson on December 13, 1918, having performed no overseas service.

LAWRENCE, GEORGE ERNEST, private: Registered for Selective Service on June 5, 1918, at age 21; occupation – laborer. Inducted as a private at Windsor on August 26, 1918, and transported to Camp Jackson, Columbia, South Carolina. Initially assigned to the 156th Depot Brigade and transferred to Battery A, Field Artillery Replacement Draft on an undisclosed date. Honorably discharged on December 26, 1918, having performed no overseas service.

LOWE, JAMES EMMET, private: Registered for Selective Service as a Bertie County resident in Salem County, New Jersey on an undisclosed date, but likely on or about June 5, 1917, at age 26; occupation – munitions worker. Inducted as a private at Windsor on October 30, 1918, and transported to Camp Jackson, Columbia, South Carolina. Assigned to the Field Artillery Replacement Draft. Honorably discharged on December 23, 1918, having performed no overseas service.

MIZELL, THOMAS FRANKLIN, private: Registered for Selective Service on June 5, 1917, at age 28; occupation – automobile mechanic. Inducted as a private at Windsor on May 28, 1918, and transported to Camp Jackson, Columbia, South Carolina. Initially assigned to the 156th Depot Brigade and transferred to the Field Artillery Replacement Draft, Camp Jackson on June 25, 1918. Transferred to Company K, 137th Infantry Regiment, 69th Infantry Brigade, 35th Division on July 10, 1918.

ODER, WILLIAM H., private: Registered for Selective Service as a Bertie County resident in Salem County, New Jersey on June 5, 1917, at age 25; occupation – munitions worker. Inducted as a private at Windsor on May 28, 1918, and transported to Camp Jackson, Columbia, South Carolina. Initially assigned to the 156th Depot Brigade and transferred to the July Automatic Replacement Draft, Camp Jackson on July 8, 1918. Transferred to Battery B, 316th Field Artillery Regiment, 161st Infantry Brigade, 81st Division on an undisclosed date, but likely prior to July 22, 1918.

PERRY, JOSEPH CLEE, bugler: Previously served in Company B, 1st Infantry Regiment, Louisiana National Guard, from which he was honorably discharged on April 27, 1917. Registered for Selective Service in Bertie County on June 5, 1917, at age 21; occupation – undisclosed. Inducted as a private at Windsor on August 25, 1918, and transported to Camp Jackson, Columbia, South Carolina. Initially assigned to the 156th Depot Brigade and assigned to Battery C, 8th Field Artillery Replacement Draft, Camp Jackson, on an undisclosed date. Promoted to bugler on November 10, 1918. Honorably discharged on December 9, 1918, having performed no overseas service.

PERRY, LONNIE*, private: Registered for Selective Service on June 5, 1917, at age 21; occupation – laborer, log woods. Arrested and jailed by Sheriff John W. Cooper in Bertie County on June 18, 1918, for being a "slacker." Released from jail and inducted as a private at Windsor on June 19, 1918, and transported to Camp Jackson, Columbia, South Carolina. Initially assigned to the 156th Depot Brigade and transferred to the 20th Battery, August Automatic Replacement Draft (Field Artillery) on August 9, 1918. Sent overseas on August 20, 1918. Transferred to Company F, 365th Infantry Regiment, 183rd Infantry Brigade, 92nd Division on September 24, 1918.

PERRY, ROSVILLE, W., private: Registered for Selective Service on June 5, 1918, at age

21; occupation – undisclosed. Inducted as a private at Windsor on August 25, 1918, and transported to Camp Jackson, Columbia, South Carolina. Assigned to the Field Artillery Replacement Draft, Camp Jackson. Honorably discharged on December 7, 1918, having performed no overseas service.

PIERCE, LUTHER MATTHEW, private: Registered for Selective Service on June 5, 1918, at age 21; occupation – undisclosed. Inducted as a private at Windsor on August 25, 1918, and transported to Camp Jackson, Columbia, South Carolina. Assigned to the 156th Depot Brigade and subsequently to Battery B, 9th Field Artillery Regiment Replace Draft. Honorably discharged at Camp Jackson on December 9, 1918, having performed no overseas service.

PRITCHARD, LLOYD ERNEST, private: Registered for Selective Service on June 5, 1918, at age 21; occupation – undisclosed. Inducted as a private at Windsor on August 25, 1918, and transported to Camp Jackson, Columbia, South Carolina. Initially assigned to the 156th Depot Brigade and transferred to the Field Artillery Replacement Draft, Camp Jackson on August 31, 1918. Transferred to the October Automatic Replacement Draft on October 15, 1918. Sent overseas on October 28, 1918, and transferred to Headquarters Company, 309th Field Artillery Regiment, 153rd Field Artillery Brigade, 78th Division on December 9, 1918.

SPEIGHT, FRANCIS WAYLAND, private: Registered for Selective Service on June 5, 1918, at age 21; occupation – undisclosed. Inducted as a private at Windsor on September 11, 1918, and transported to Camp Jackson, Columbia, South Carolina. Assigned to the 156th Depot Brigade. Transferred to the November Automatic Replacement Draft, Camp Jackson on November 8, 1918. Honorably discharged at Camp Jackson on December 9, 1918, having performed no overseas service.

TODD, FRANK CRAIG, private: Registered for Selective Service on June 5, 1918, at age 21; occupation – undisclosed. Inducted as a private at Windsor on August 25, 1918, and transported to Camp Jackson, Columbia, South Carolina. Initially assigned to the 156th Depot Brigade and transferred to the Field Artillery Replacement Draft, Camp Jackson on August 31, 1918. Transferred to Battery C, 309th Field Artillery Regiment, 153rd Field Artillery Brigade, 78th Division on October 15, 1918.

VAN NORTWICK, DAVID, private: Registered for Selective Service on June 5, 1917, at age 24; occupation – farmer. Inducted as a private at Windsor on May 28, 1918, and transported to Camp Jackson, Columbia, South Carolina. Initially assigned to the 156th Depot Brigade. Sent overseas on May 26, 1918, and transferred to the Camp Jackson Automatic Replacement Draft (field artillery) on July 8, 1918. Transferred to Battery F, 113th Field Artillery Regiment, 55th Field Artillery Brigade, 30th Division on August 27, 1918.

## INFANTRY

WATFORD, JERRY*, private: Registered for Selective Service on June 5, 1917, at age 22; occupation – farmer. Inducted as a private at Windsor on August 31, 1918, and transported to Camp Lee, Petersburg, Virginia. Assigned to Company D, 13th Battalion, Infantry Replacement and Training Camp. Transferred to 117th Provisional Company, December Automatic Replacement Draft on November 18, 1918. Honorably discharged at Camp Lee on December 17, 1918, having performed no overseas service.

## MACHINE GUN

FREEMAN, JOSEPH JOHN, private: Registered for Selective Service on June 5, 1917, at age 21; occupation – farmer. Inducted as a private at Windsor on July 22, 1918, and transported to Camp Hancock, near Augusta, Georgia. Assigned to the Main Training Depot, Machine Gun Training Center. Transferred to the Camp Hancock October Automatic Replacement Draft (machine gun) on October 21, 1918. Sent overseas on November 10, 1918 and transferred to the Machine Gun Company, 331st Infantry Regiment, 166th Infantry Brigade, 83rd Division on November 24, 1918.

HOGGARD, JOSEPH ROGER, private: Previously served in the 51st Company, Motor Transport Division, Camp Hancock, Georgia. Transferred to the Camp Hancock October Automatic Replacement draft (machine gun) on October 21, 1918. Served overseas from November 10, 1918, until March 11, 1919. Honorably discharged at Camp Lee, Petersburg, Virginia on March 24, 1919.

MIZELL, GEORGE TIMOTHY, private: Registered for Selective Service on June 5, 1917, at age 29; occupation – farmer. Inducted as a private at Windsor on July 22, 1918, and transported to Camp Hancock, near Augusta, Georgia. Assigned to the Machine Gun Training Center. Transferred to the October Automatic Replacement Draft, Camp Hancock on October 21, 1918. Sent overseas on November 1, 1918. Transferred to Company D, 324th Machine Gun Battalion, 166th Infantry Brigade, 83rd Division on November 23, 1918.

RAWLS, CLARENCE, private: Previously served in the 53rd Depot Brigade, Camp Hancock, near Augusta, Georgia. Transferred to the Camp Hancock Automatic Replacement Draft (machine gun) on October 21, 1918. Sent overseas on November 10, 1918, and transferred to Company G, 159th Infantry Regiment, 80th Infantry Brigade, 40th Division on November 24, 1918.

WADSWORTH (WARDSWORTH), JAMES B., private: Registered for Selective Service on June 5, 1917, at age 24; occupation – farmer. Inducted as a private at Windsor on July 22, 1918, and transported to Camp Hancock, near Augusta, Georgia. Assigned

to the Main Training Depot, Machine Gun Training Center. Transferred to the Camp Hancock October Automatic Replacement Draft on October 31, 1918. Sent overseas on November 9, 1918, and transferred to Company E, 4th Provisional Regiment on November 23, 1918.

## MISCELLANEOUS

HILL, WILLIE JOE*, private: Registered for Selective Service on June 28, 1918, at age 21; occupation – laborer. Inducted as a private at Windsor on August 31, 1918, and transported to Camp Lee, Petersburg, Virginia. Assigned to the 155th Depot Brigade and transferred to the 117th Provisional Company, December Automatic Replacement Draft on November 8, 1918. Honorably discharged at Camp Lee on December 17, 1918, having performed no overseas service.

## CASUAL DEPOT, ARMY POST OFFICE 910

DAVIS, CHARLIE*, private: Previously served in Company B, 344th Labor Battalion. Transferred to the Casual Depot, Army Post Office (APO) 910 on October 26, 1918, while serving overseas. Returned from overseas on June 9, 1919, and honorably discharged on July 14, 1919.

## TRANSPORTATION TRAIN MEAL SERVICE, ARMY POST OFFICE 717

WINSTON, MOSES C.*, private: Previously served in Company B, 344th Labor Battalion, Quartermaster Corps. Transferred to Transportation Train Meal Service, Quartermaster Corps, Army Post Office (APO) 717 on an undisclosed date. Served overseas from September 20, 1918, until October 6, 1919. Honorably discharged on October 14, 1919.

## MACHINE GUN TRAINING CENTER

## CAMP HANCOCK, GEORGIA

BRINKLEY, RAYMOND MILES, private: Registered for Selective Service on June 5, 1917, at age 26; occupation – farmer. Inducted as a private at Windsor on July 22, 1918, and transported to Camp Hancock, near Augusta, Georgia. Assigned to the 3rd Recruit Company, Receiving Depot, Machine Gun Training Corps. Transferred to the 51st Company, 8th Group, Machine Gun Training Corps on August 23, 1918. Transferred to the School for Bakers and Cooks on August 27, 1918. Transferred to the 123rd Company, Engineers Training Detachment, Machine Gun School on October 13, 1918. Transferred to the 125th Company, Engineers Training Detachment in December 1918, and to the 20th Company, 3rd Provisional Group, Machine Gun Training Detachment, in which he served until he died on January 10, 1919, of "broncho pneumonia." All service apparently performed at Camp Hancock.

COBB, BRUCE LLOYD, mess sergeant: Registered for Selective Service on June 5, 1917, at age 27; occupation – salesman. Inducted as a private at Windsor on July 22, 1918, and transported to Camp Hancock, near Augusta, Georgia. Assigned to the 51st Company, Main Training Depot, Machine Gun Training Center. Promoted to cook on June 25, 1918, and to mess sergeant in August 1918. Honorably discharged at Camp Hancock in December 1918, having performed no overseas service.

COBB, DAVID HENRY, private: Registered for Selective Service on June 5, 1917, at age 30; occupation – farmer. Name appears on a list of Bertie County men inducted on May 28, 1918, July 6, 1918, who were transported to Camp Jackson, Columbia, South Carolina, but the entry for Cobb was lined through. Inducted as a private at Windsor on July 22,

1918, and transported to Camp Hancock, near Augusta, Georgia. Assigned to the 51st Company, 5th Group, Main Training Depot, Machine Gun Training Center. Transferred to the 1st Company, Development Battalion, Machine Gun Training Center on November 11, 1918. Transferred to 1st Provisional regiment, Ordnance Training Camp, Camp Hancock, on November 20, 1918. Transferred to the United States Nitrate Plant, Sheffield, Alabama on December 16, 1918. Transferred to the 16th Ordnance Guard Company, Muscle Shoals, Alabama on an undisclosed date and served in this unit until honorably discharged at Muscle Shoals on March 27, 1919, having performed no overseas service.

LASSITER, JAMES W., private: Registered for Selective Service on June 5, 1917, at age 30; occupation – farmer. Inducted as a private at Windsor on July 22, 1918, and transported to Camp Hancock, near Augusta, Georgia. Assigned to the Main Training Depot, Machine Gun Training Center. Promoted to corporal on October 24, 1918, and reduced to private on October 27, 1918. Honorably discharged on December 20, 1918, having performed no overseas service.

MOUNTAIN, JAMES T.*, private: Registered for Selective Service as a Bertie County resident at Windsor, Connecticut, on June 1, 1917, at age 21; occupation – farmer. Inducted as a private at Windsor, North Carolina on June 30, 1918, and transported to Florida Agriculture and Mechanical College, Tallahassee. Assigned to the Training Detachment at the college. Transferred to the Main Training Depot, Machine Gun Training Center, Camp Hancock, near Augusta, Georgia on August 27, 1918. Sent overseas on September 29, 1918. Transferred to the 26th Company, Depot Service, Army Service Corps on November 7, 1918.

WADSWORTH (WARDSWORTH), JAMES B., private: Previously served in the Camp Hancock Automatic Replacement Draft (machine gun). Transferred to Company E, 4th Provisional Regiment on November 23, 1918, while serving overseas. Transferred to the Depot Service Company, 85th Division on March 30, 1919.

WHITE, ERNEST, private: Registered for Selective Service on June 5, 1917, at age 22; occupation – farmer. Inducted as a private at Windsor on July 22, 1918, and transported to Camp Hancock, near Augusta, Georgia. Assigned to the Machine Gun Training Camp. Honorably discharged on May 12, 1919, having performed no overseas service.

WHITE, JESSE EDWARD, corporal: Registered for Selective Service on June 5, 1917, at age 24; occupation – farmer. Inducted as a private at Windsor on July 22, 1918, transported to Camp Hancock, near Augusta, Georgia. Assigned to the 51st Company, 5th Group, Motor Transport Detachment, Machine Gun Training Center. Honorably discharged at Camp Hancock on December 20, 1918, having performed no overseas service.

## RECRUIT CAMPS, BATTALIONS, AND UNSPECIFIED UNITS

## CAMP GREENE, CHARLOTTE

CHERRY, JOSEPH BLOUNT, private: Registered for Selective Service on June 5, 1917, at age 28; occupation – insurance agent. Inducted as a private at Windsor on August 23, 1918, and transported to Camp Greene, Charlotte. Served in the 2nd Company, Development Battalion and honorably discharged at Camp Greene on January 3, 1919, having performed no overseas service.

DAVIS, PERCY BOGGS, private: Registered for Selective Service on June 5, 1917, at age 21; occupation – automobile mechanic. Inducted as a private at Windsor on August 31, 1918, and transported to Camp Greene, Charlotte. Assigned to Recruit Camp Num-

ber 4 at Camp Greene until honorably discharged on December 21, 1918.

DUNSTAN, SHEPHARD W.*, private: Registered for Selective Service on June 5, 1917, at age 29; occupation – laborer, log woods. Inducted as a private at Windsor on August 23, 1918, and transported to Camp Greene, Charlotte. Assigned to the 2nd Development Battalion. Honorably discharged at Camp Greene on December 18, 1918, having performed no overseas service.

HARDY, TOM HENRY*, private: Registered for Selective Service on June 5, 1917, at age 22; occupation – farm laborer. Inducted as a private at Windsor on August 23, 1918, and transported to Camp Greene, Charlotte. Assigned to Recruit Camp Number 3 and transferred to the Development Battalion, Camp Greene, on September 27, 1918. Honorably discharged at Camp Greene on January 29, 1919, having performed no overseas service.

HARGROVE, JULIAN*, private: Registered for Selective Service on June 5, 1917, at age 27; occupation – carrier. Inducted as a private at Windsor on July 29, 1918, and transported to Camp Greene, Charlotte. Assigned to Recruit Camp Number 3 and transferred to Recruit Camp Number 5 on November 4, 1918. Deserted at Camp Greene on December 10, 1918.

HOLLEY, ATLAS J.*, private: Registered for Selective Service on June 5, 1917, at age 21; occupation – farmer. Inducted as a private at Windsor on August 23, 1918, and transported to Camp Greene, Charlotte. Served in an undisclosed infantry regiment and discharged on December 26, 1918.

HOLLEY, THEODORE*, private: Registered for Selective Service on June 5, 1917, at age 21; occupation – public laborer. Inducted as a private at Windsor on July 29, 1918, and transported to Camp Greene, Charlotte. Assigned first to Recruit Camp Number 1, then to Recruit Camp Number 3 on September 27, 1918, and subsequently to the

5th Company, Development Battalion on an undisclosed date. Honorably discharged on November 6, 1918, having performed no overseas service. Discharged due to service-connected disability rated as 40 percenT.

JENKINS, HUGHEY M.,* private: Registered for Selective Service on June 5, 1917, at age 25; occupation – farmer. Inducted as a private at Windsor on August 23, 1918, and transported to Camp Greene, Charlotte. Served in an unspecified infantry unit. Honorably discharged on January 13, 1919, having performed no overseas service.

NEWSOME, HEZ*, private: Registered for Selective Service on June 5, 1917, at age 21; occupation – farm laborer. Inducted as a private at Windsor on August 23, 1918, and transported to Camp Greene, Charlotte. Unassigned until honorably discharged at Camp Greene on December 26, 1918, having performed no overseas service.

RIDDICK, ROBERT*, private: Registered for Selective Service on June 5, 1917, at age 26; occupation – farmer. Inducted as a private at Windsor on August 23, 1918, and transported to Camp Greene, Charlotte. Honorably discharged at Camp Greene on September 10, 1918. Reason for discharge not disclosed.

SESSOMS, ST. ELMO*, private: Registered for Selective Service on June 5, 1917, at age 21; occupation – undisclosed. Inducted as a private at Windsor on August 23, 1918, and transported to Camp Greene, Charlotte. Unit(s) to which assigned and date(s) assigned not disclosed in military record. Honorably discharged on December 10, 1918.

## ORDNANCE DEPARTMENT

EVANS, CHARLES SPURGEON, private: Registered for Selective Service on June 5, 1918, at age 21; occupation – laborer. Inducted as a private at Windsor on August 25, 1918, and transported to Camp Jackson, Columbia, South Carolina. Initially assigned to the 156th Depot Brigade and transferred to the Ordnance Supply Company, Camp Jackson on November 21, 1918. Honorably discharged at Camp Jackson on March 29, 1919, having performed no overseas service.

HARMON, JAMES REDDICK, private: Previously served in the 156th Depot Brigade, Camp Jackson, South Carolina. Transferred to Company E, Ordnance Detachment of the Ordnance Department at Aberdeen Proving Ground, Aberdeen, Maryland on March 19, 1919. Honorably discharged at Aberdeen Proving Ground on November 10, 1919, having performed no overseas service.

HOGGARD, ARTHUR D., private: Previously served in the 156th Depot Brigade, Camp Jackson, South Carolina. Transferred to the 6th Ordnance Guard Company, Raritan Arsenal, Sparta, Wisconsin on September 16, 1918. Transferred to the Sparta General Ordnance Department on February 4, 1919. Honorably discharged at Raritan Arsenal on March 20, 1919, having performed no overseas service.

KEETER, BEN, private: Registered for Selective Service on June 5, 1917, at age 27; occupation – farmer. Inducted as a private at Windsor on June 28, 1918, and transported to Camp Jackson, Columbia, South Carolina. Initially assigned to the 156th Depot Brigade and transferred to an unspecified ordnance company on July 30, 1918. Honorably discharged on January 27, 1919, having performed no overseas service.

MYERS, DAVID E., sergeant: Enlisted as a private at Fort Thomas, Kentucky, on April 27, 1917, at age 22. Assigned to the Ordnance Department, Aberdeen Proving Ground, Aberdeen, Maryland. Promoted to corporal on November 1, 1918, and to sergeant on January 1, 1919. Honorably discharged on April 10, 1919, having performed no overseas service.

## CHEMICAL WARFARE SERVICE

ODER, GEORGE R., private: Registered for Selective Service as a Bertie County resident in Salem County, New Jersey on June 5, 1917, at age 22; occupation – munitions worker. Inducted as a private at Windsor on May 28, 1918, and transported to Camp Jackson, Columbia, South Carolina. Assigned to the Chemical Warfare Service, Edgewood Arsenal, Maryland. Honorably discharged on December 14, 1918, having performed no overseas service.

## MISCELLANEOUS UNITS

HOLLEY, ERNEST A.*, private: Registered for Selective Service on June 5, 1917, at age 25; occupation – farm laborer. Inducted as a private at Windsor on August 31, 1918, and transported to Camp Lee, Petersburg, Virginia. Assigned to an unspecified sanitation unit. Honorably discharged at Camp Lee on February 24, 1919, having performed no overseas service.

JOHNSON, THOMAS GILBERT, private: Registered for Selective Service on June 5, 1917, at age 22; occupation – farm laborer. Inducted as a private at Windsor on May 28, 1918, and transported to Camp Jackson, Columbia, South Carolina. Initially assigned to the 156th Depot Brigade and subsequently served in Company I, Salvage Division, at an undisclosed location. Honorably discharged on January 24, 1919, having performed no overseas service.

MORRIS, TOMMIE T., private: Registered for Selective Service on June 5, 1917, at age 21; occupation – clerk. Inducted as a private at Windsor on March 27, 1918, and transported to Camp Jackson, Columbia, South Carolina. Initially assigned to the 156th Depot Brigade and transferred to Company F, Casual Battalion at Camp Merritt, New Jersey on April 25, 1918. Transferred to Company E, 351st Infantry Regiment, 176th Infantry Brigade, 88th Division on August 10, 1918.

PERRY, WILLIE G.*, private first class: Registered for Selective Service on June 5, 1917, at age 21; occupation – farmer. Inducted as a private at Windsor on April 2, 1918, and transported to Camp Grant, Rockford, Illinois. Unit to which assigned not disclosed in military record. Sent overseas on an undisclosed date in July 1918. Promoted to private first class on August 1, 1918. Returned from overseas on July 4, 1919, and honorably discharged on July 10, 1919.

THOMAS, ISAIAH W., private first class: Previously served as a private in Battery B, 19th Field Artillery Regiment, 5th Field Artillery Brigade, 5th Division. Transferred as a private to the 5th Trench Mortar Battalion (corps troops) on December 20, 1917. Promoted to private first class on July 6, 1918. Honorably discharged on April 7, 1919, having performed no overseas service.

TODD, ARTHUR LEE, private: Registered for Selective Service on June 5, 1917, at age 22; occupation – foreman at a cement plant. Inducted as a private at Windsor on April 26, 1918, and transported to Camp Jackson, Columbia, South Carolina. Initially assigned to the 156th Depot Brigade and transferred to Company M, 524th Infantry Regiment. Served overseas from August 5, 1918, until June 18, 1919. Honorably discharged on June 25, 1919.

VEALE, WINCE*, private: Registered for Selective Service on June 5, 1917, at age 21; occupation – farmer. Inducted as a private at on April 29, 1918, and transported to Camp Jackson, Columbia, South Carolina. Assigned to a sanitation company. Honorably discharged at Charleston, South Carolina on December 24, 1918, having performed no overseas service.

WALKE, WILLIAM CAPEHART, sergeant: Previously served in the 156th Depot Brigade, Camp Jackson, Columbia, South Carolina. Transferred as a corporal to the Port Utilities Detachment, Quartermaster Corps, Camp Hill, Newport News, Virginia on November 20, 1918. Promoted to sergeant on April 12, 1919. Honorably discharged on May 26, 1919, having performed no overseas service.

MINTON, PATRICK WINSTON, private: Previously served the 309th Auxiliary Remount Depot. Transferred to the 104th Motor Ordnance Repair Depot on December 1, 1917. Sent overseas on June 29, 1918. Promoted to cook in August 1918 and reduced to private on November 11, 1918. Returned from overseas on May 2, 1919, and honorably discharged on May 30, 1919.

WHITE, MARTIN HENRY, private first class: Previously served in the Medical Department, Camp Greenleaf, at Fort Oglethorpe, Chickamauga Park, Georgia. Transferred as a private to the Medical Department, 3rd Trench Mortar Battalion (corps troops) on February 7, 1918. Promoted to private first class on May 3, 1918. Served overseas from July 14, 1918, until January 18, 1919. Honorably discharged on January 27, 1919.

WILDER, ANDREW JACKSON*, private: Registered for Selective Service on June 5, 1917, at age 23; occupation – laborer. Inducted as a private at Windsor on April 29, 1918, and transported to Camp Jackson, Columbia, South Carolina. Unit(s) to which assigned not disclosed in military record. Honorably discharged on December 30, 1918, having performed no overseas service.

WILLIFORD, WILLIE*, private: Registered for Selective Service on June 5, 1917, at age 23; occupation – farmer. Inducted as a private at Windsor on April 26, 1918, and transported to Camp Grant, Rockford, Illinois. Assigned to the 358th Casual Detachment. Transferred to Company C, 323rd Labor Battalion, Quartermaster Corps on an undisclosed date.

## INDUCTED AND REJECTED OR REPORTEDLY INDUCTED BUT NO AVAILABLE RECORD OF SERVICE PERFORMED

ARMSTRONG, TOMMIE*, private: Registered for Selective Service on June 5, 1917, at age 23; occupation – laborer. Name appears on a Bertie County Local Board Report of Inducted Men. Name also appears on Bertie County Local Board's "Final List of Delinquents and Deserters" with the notation "Classified after desertion 4A", reported to North Carolina Adjutant General on February 5, 1919.

BARNES, J. G., private: Registered for Selective Service on June 5, 1917, at age 21; occupation - farmer. Inducted as a private at Windsor on May 28, 1918, and transported to Camp Jackson, Columbia, South Carolina where he was rejected by military authorities.

BELL, LOUIS*: Registered for Selective Service on June 5, 1917, at age 27; occupation – farmer. Name appears on a list of Bertie County men inducted on August 14, 1918, who were transported to Camp Greene, Charlotte, but the entry for Bell was lined through. Name appears on Bertie County Local Board's "Final List of Delinquents and Deserters" with the notation "Classified after desertion 1X 6-17-1918", reported to North Carolina Adjutant General on February 5, 1919.

BENN, HENRY*, private: Registered for Selective Service in Rockland County, New York on June 5, 1917, at age 27; occupation – bricklayer. Inducted as a private at Windsor on July 16, 1918, and transported to Camp Dix, near Trenton, New Jersey, where he was rejected by military authorities. However, his name appears on Bertie County Local Board's "Final List of Delinquents and Deserters" with the notation "Address unknown"; reported to District Attorney on February 18, 1919.

BOND, HAYWOOD JR.*, private: Registered for Selective Service on June 5, 1917, at age 27; occupation — farmer. Inducted as a private at Windsor on August 23, 1918, and transported to Camp Greene, Charlotte. Discharged from the draft on September 11, 1918, by reason of "disability."

BOYETTE, ROBERT FRANCIS, private: Registered for Selective Service on June 5, 1917, at age 28; occupation — lumber inspector. Inducted as a private at Windsor on October 4, 1917, and transported to Camp Jackson, Columbia, South Carolina, where he was rejected by military authorities on October 12, 1917.

BURNETT, STARLING*, private: Registered for Selective Service on June 5, 1917, at age 21; occupation — farmer. Reportedly inducted as a private at Windsor on August 14, 1918, and "sent [the] next day" to Camp Greene, Charlotte, but the entry for Burnett was lined through. Name appears on Bertie County Local Board's "Final List of Delinquents and Deserters" with the notation "Classified after desertion 1A[,] delinquent order suspended: Sec. 135."

BYRD, THOMAS J., private: Registered for Selective Service on June 5, 1917, at age 29; occupation — powder maker. Inducted as a private at Windsor on July 2, 1918, and transported to Camp Hancock, near Augusta, Georgia, where he was rejected by military authorities.

CHERRY, JAMES ANDREW*: Registered for Selective Service on June 5, 1918, at age 21; occupation — laborer. Name appears on a list of Bertie County men inducted on August 26, 1918, who were transported to Camp Jackson, Columbia, South Carolina, but the entry for Cherry was lined through.

CHERRY, JAMES EDWARD*, private: Registered for Selective Service on June 5, 1917, at age 22; occupation — farmer. Inducted as a private at Windsor on August 31, 1918, and transported to Camp Lee, Petersburg, Virginia. Name appears on Bertie County Local Board's "Final List of Delinquents and Deserters" with the notation "Address unknown"; reported to District Attorney on February 18, 1919.

CHERRY, WALTER*, private: Registered for Selective Service on June 5, 1917, at age 21; occupation — farmer laborer. Inducted as a private at Windsor on August 23, 1918, and transported to Camp Greene, Charlotte. Name appears on Bertie County Local Board's "Final List of Delinquents and Deserters" with the notation "Address unknown"; reported to District Attorney on February 18, 1919.

COGGINS, LUTHER MORRIS*, private: Registered for Selective Service on June 21, 1918, at age 21; occupation — farmer. Name appears on a list of Bertie County men inducted on August 31, 1918, who were transported to Camp Lee, Petersburg, Virginia, but the entry for Coggins was lined through. Inducted as a private at Windsor on September 4, 1918, and transported to Camp Lee where he was rejected by military authorities.

COOPER, WILLIAM HENRY*, private: Registered for Selective Service on June 5, 1917, at age 29; occupation — farmer. Name appears on a list of men inducted at Windsor on April 26, 1918, who were transported to Camp Grant, Rockford, Illinois, but he was reported as "sick" and did not enter service. Subsequently, inducted as a private on July 16, 1918, and transported to Camp Dix, near Trenton, New Jersey. May have served as a private in Battery D, Casual Detachment at Camp Jackson, Columbia, South Carolina, based on information contained in an application for a military headstone for a William Henry Cooper who died on September 29, 1931.

GILLAM, WILLIAM LENTON*, private: Registered for Selective Service on June 5, 1917, at age 21; occupation — laborer. Inducted as a private at Windsor on April

2, 1918, and transported to Camp Grant, Rockford, Illinois. Rejected by military authorities on May 3, 1918.

HARMON, RALEIGH*, private: Registered for Selective Service on June 5, 1917, at age 21; occupation – farmer. Inducted as a private at Windsor on April 29, 1918, and transported to Camp Jackson, Columbia, South Carolina, where he was rejected by military authorities.

HARRELL, CLYDE ESTON, private: Registered for Selective Service on June 5, 1917, at age 21; occupation – farmer. Inducted as a private at Windsor on March 27, 1918, and transported to Camp Jackson, Columbia, South Carolina. Rejected by military authorities.

HAUGHTON, SHERMAN*: Registered for Selective Service on June 5, 1917, at age 21; occupation – farm laborer. Name appears on a list of Bertie County men inducted on April 29, 1918, who were transported to Camp Jackson, Columbia, South Carolina, but the entry for Haughton was lined through.

KEETER, CHARLES NORMAN, private: Registered for Selective Service on June 5, 1917, at age 27; occupation – farmer. Inducted as a private at Windsor on March 27, 1918, and transported to Camp Jackson, Columbia, South Carolina. No military service record found, but Keeter's enumeration in the 1930 Federal census of Bertie County indicates that he was a World War veteran.

MITCHELL, JUDGE*, private: Registered for Selective Service on June 5, 1917, at age 21; occupation – public work. Inducted as a private at Windsor on April 29, 1918, and transported to Camp Jackson, Columbia, South Carolina. Rejected by military authorities.

NEWSOME, TOM*, private: Registered for Selective Service on June 5, 1917, at age 25; occupation – farmer. Inducted as a private at

Windsor on December 18, 1917, and transported to Camp Jackson, Columbia, South Carolina. Rejected by military authorities on December 31, 1917.

NOWELL, PETER*, private: Registered for Selective Service on June 5, 1917, at age 21; occupation – laborer. Inducted as a private at Windsor on April 26, 1918, and transported to Camp Grant, Rockford, Illinois. Served until August 12, 1918, when he was "released" (discharged).

PIERCE, JOHN HOBBS, Private: Registered for Selective Service on June 5, 1917, at age 25; occupation – farmer. Inducted as a private at Windsor on April 26, 1918, and transported to Camp Jackson, Columbia, South Carolina, where he was rejected by military authorities.

PUGH, PAUL*, private: Registered for Selective Service on June 5, 1917, at age 28; occupation – farmer. Inducted as a private at Windsor on June 21, 1918, and transported to Camp Taylor, Louisville, Kentucky. Rejected by military authorities.

SIMONS, MARTIN, Registered for Selective Service on September 12, 1918, at age 19; occupation – undisclosed. Name appears on a list of men inducted at Windsor on August 31, 1918, and transported to Camp Lee, Virginia, but the entry for Simons was lined through with the notation "bad finger."

SKILES, EDDIE MILES, private: Registered for Selective Service as a Bertie County resident in Salem, New Jersey on or about June 5, 1917, at age 26; occupation – powder worker. Inducted as a private at Windsor on May 28, 1918, and transported to Camp Jackson, Columbia, South Carolina. Rejected by military authorities.

SMALLWOOD, EDWARD*, private: Registered for Selective Service on June 5, 1917, at age 24; occupation – farmer. "Ordered to report" and inducted as a private at Windsor on December 25, 1917, and transported to Camp Jackson, Columbia, South Carolina.

Rejected by military authorities on December 31, 1917. Reason for rejection – "heart trouble".

SMITH, BROGIE*, private: Registered for Selective Service on June 5, 1917, at age 26; Windsor; occupation – farmer. Inducted as a private at Windsor on June 21, 1918, and transported to Camp Taylor, Louisville, Kentucky. Rejected by military authorities.

STALLINGS, WALTER TUNIS, private: Registered for Selective Service on June 5, 1917, at age 21; occupation – farmer. Inducted as a private at Windsor on April 26, 1918, and transported to Camp Jackson, Columbia, South Carolina, where he was rejected by military authorities.

SWAIN, JOHN*, private: Registered for Selective Service on June 5, 1917, at age 21; occupation – farmer. Inducted as a private at Windsor on December 29, 1917, and transported to Camp Jackson, Columbia, South Carolina. Rejected by military authorities on December 31, 1917.

TEASTER, WILLIE CHERRY; private: Registered for Selective Service on June 5, 1917, at age 28; occupation – merchant and farmer. Inducted as a private at Windsor on May 10, 1918, and transported to Camp Screven, Georgia. Rejected by military authorities.

TWINE, SANSBERRY*, private: Registered for Selective Service on June 5, 1917, at age 22; occupation – farmer. Inducted as a private at Windsor on June 21, 1918, and transported to Camp Taylor, Louisville, Kentucky. Rejected by military authorities.

TYNER, JOE P.*: Registered for Selective Service on June 5, 1917, at age 21; occupation – farmer. Name appears on a list of Bertie County men inducted on August 31, 1918, who were transported to Camp Lee, Petersburg, Virginia, but the entry for Tyner was lined through with the notation "broken arm."

WATSON, AUSTON JR.*, private: Registered for Selective Service on June 5, 1917, at age 21; occupation – laborer. Inducted as a private at Windsor on June 21, 1918, and transported to Camp Taylor, Louisville, Kentucky. Rejected by military authorities.

WHITE, ARTHUR CLYDE, private: Registered for Selective Service on June 5, 1917, at age 23; occupation – laborer, log woods. Inducted as a private at Windsor on July 22, 1918, and transported to Camp Hancock, near Augusta, Georgia. Rejected by military authorities.

# UNITED STATES MARINE CORPS

SPEIGHT, JAMES ALEXANDER, private: Enlisted as a private at Norfolk, Virginia on June 23, 1917. Assigned to the 77th Company, 7th Machine Gun Battalion, Quantico, Virginia on July 29, 1917. Sent overseas on December 31, 1917. Wounded on July 19, 1918. Admitted to hospital on November 18, 1918. Returned from overseas on February 19, 1919. Transferred to Personnel Detachment at New York City on March 1, 1919, and transferred to Marine Barracks Detachment, Norfolk, Virginia on March 24, 1919. Honorably discharged on June 25, 1919.

# UNITED STATES NAVY

ANDERSON, MARY JORDAN, nurse: Appointed nurse at the Navy Recruiting Station, St. Louis, Missouri on April 18, 1912, at age 30. Served at the Naval Hospital, Philadelphia, Pennsylvania (April 6, 1917 [date of the United States' war declaration] – December 2, 1917), the Naval Hospital, Norfolk, Virginia (December 2, 1917 – June 12, 1918), and the Naval Hospital, New York City (June 12, 1918 – November 11, 1918). Honorably discharged at the Naval Hospital, Great Lakes, Illinois on April 7, 1920.

BARKER, ROBERT EDWARD, machinist's mate first class: Enrolled in the United States Navy Reserves at the Navy Recruiting Station, Norfolk, Virginia on June 3, 1918, at age 21. Assigned to the Naval Unit, Columbia University, New York City, as a machinist's mate second class on August 26, 1918. Honorably discharged as a machinist's mate first class at Columbia University on April 11, 1919.

BASS, JAMES AUGUSTUS, seaman second class: Registered for Selective Service on June 5, 1917, at age 27; occupation – farmer. Enrolled in the United States Navy Reserves at the Navy Recruiting Station, Norfolk, Virginia on June 8, 1918. Appointed seaman second class. Assigned to the Naval Training Station, Norfolk on July 17, 1918. Transferred to the USS Pennsylvania (a battleship) on August 30. 1918. Placed on inactive duty by Headquarters, 5th Naval District, Norfolk on December 27, 1918.

BAZEMORE, JOHN LESLIE, fireman first class: Registered for Selective Service as a Bertie County resident in Prince George County, Virginia on June 5, 1917, at age 22; occupation – oiler. Enlisted at the Navy Recruiting Station, Norfolk, Virginia on December 13, 1917. Appointed fireman third class and assigned to receiving ship at Norfolk. Transferred to the Naval Operating Base, Norfolk on February 9, 1918 and served as a fireman second class. Transferred to the USS Alabama (a patrol boat) March 7, 1918. Transferred to receiving ship at Norfolk on April 19, 1918 and to receiving ship at New York City on April 28, 1918. Transferred to the USS Pastores (a stores ship) on May 6, 1918. Transferred to receiving ship at Norfolk on August 28, 1918. Honorably discharged as a fireman first class at Norfolk on June 6, 1919.

BELL, ELLA RUBY, yeoman second class (female): Enrolled in the United States Navy Reserves at the Navy Recruiting Station, Norfolk, Virginia on August 10, 1918, at age 20. Appointed yeoman third class (female). Assigned to the Navy Yard, Norfolk on Au-

gust 22, 1918. Placed on inactive duty by Headquarters, Norfolk as a yeoman second class (female) on July 23, 1919.

BROWN, JULIUS EARL, seaman second class: Registered for Selective Service on June 5, 1918, at age 21; occupation – laborer. Enrolled in the United States Navy Reserves at the Navy Recruiting Station, Norfolk, Virginia on July 8, 1918. Appointed seaman second class. Assigned to the Naval Air Station, Hampton Roads, Virginia on October 8, 1918. Placed on inactive duty while serving at Hampton Roads on September 3, 1919.

BURDEN, MARION CLYDE, electrician third class – radio: Registered for Selective Service on June 5, 1917, at age 21; occupation – telegraph operator. Enrolled in the United States Navy Reserves at the Enrolling Office, Norfolk, Virginia on November 28, 1917. Appointed electrician third class – radio and assigned to the Naval Radio School, Cambridge, Massachusetts. Transferred to the USS Supply (a stores ship) June 14, 1918. Placed on inactive duty while serving aboard the USS Solace (a hospital ship) at Norfolk on January 23, 1919.

CASTELLOE, COLA, lieutenant – assistant surgeon: Registered for Selective Service at the University of Pennsylvania, Philadelphia on May 30, 1917, at age 30; occupation – medical student. Appointed lieutenant – assistant surgeon on August 17, 1917. Assigned to the Naval Hospital, Philadelphia on August 31, 1917. Transferred to the USS Siboney (a troop transport) on April 28, 1918. Transferred on temporary duty to receiving ship at Norfolk, Virginia on June 26, 1918. Transferred to the USS Susquehanna (a troop transport) on July 24, 1918. Date of discharge not disclosed in extant military service record, but Castelloe was still on active duty on July 1, 1920.

CASTELLOE, DWIGHT MOODY, hospital apprentice first class: Enlisted at the Navy Recruiting Station, Raleigh on April 9, 1917, at age 17. Appointed hospital apprentice second class. Assigned to the Naval Training

Station, Newport, Rhode Island on April 9, 1917. Transferred to the Naval Hospital, Norfolk, Virginia on November 20, 1917. Promoted to hospital apprentice first class on an undisclosed date. Transferred to the USS Florida (a battleship) on November 20, 1917, and to receiving ship at New York City on March 25, 1918. Honorably discharged at New York City on April 16, 1918. Registered for Selective Service on September 12, 1918; occupation – brakeman.

CHERRY, LINEAR*, mess attendant third class: Enrolled in the United States Navy Reserves at the Navy Recruiting Station, Norfolk, Virginia on April 22, 1918, at age 23. Appointed mess attendant third class. Assigned to Headquarters, 5th Naval District on April 24, 1918, and transferred to the Naval Operating Base, Norfolk on May 3, 1918. Honorably discharged at Norfolk on June 8, 1918.

COLLINS, ALFRED MAGRUDER*, mess attendant first class: Registered for Selective Service on June 5, 1917, at age 24; occupation - farmer. Enrolled in the United States Navy Reserves at the Navy Recruiting Station, Plymouth, North Carolina on May 20, 1918. Appointed mess attendant third class. Assigned to the Naval Training Station, Norfolk, Virginia on May 28, 1918. Transferred to the Naval Air Station, Hampton Roads, Virginia on June 3, 1918, where he was honorably discharged on August 11, 1919, at the rank of mess attendant first class.

HARRELL, JESSE JAMES, fireman first class: Registered for Selective Service on June 5, 1917, at age 22; occupation – farmer. Enlisted at the Navy Recruiting Station, Norfolk, Virginia on December 14, 1917. Appointed apprentice seaman and assigned to receiving ship at Norfolk. Transferred to the Naval Operating Base, Norfolk on February 9, 1918, and promoted to fireman third class on an undisclosed date. Transferred to the USS Alabama (a patrol boat) on March 7, 1918. Promoted to fireman second class on an undisclosed date. Transferred to receiving ship, Norfolk on April 19, 1918, and to

receiving ship, New York City, on April 25, 1918. Transferred to the USS Princess Matoika (a troop transport) on May 1, 1918. Honorably discharged while serving aboard the USS Koningin De Nederlanden (a troop transport) at Newport News, Virginia on June 4, 1919, at the rank of fireman first class.

HARRELL, MYRON LEE, seaman: Enrolled in the United States Navy Reserves at Navy Recruiting Station, Norfolk, Virginia on June 14, 1918, at age 19. Appointed seaman second class and assigned to the Naval Operating Base, Norfolk. Admitted to the Naval Hospital at Norfolk or Hampton Roads, Virginia on September 23, 1918, and released on September 28, 1918. Transferred to the USS Eastern Chief (a cargo ship) on October 4, 1918. Promoted to seaman on an undisclosed date and placed on inactive duty while serving at Hampton Roads on August 28, 1919.

HECKSTALL, THOMAS JULIAN, seaman: Registered for Selective Service on June 5, 1918, at age 21; occupation – farmer. Enlisted at the Navy Recruiting Station, Raleigh on July 20, 1918. Appointed apprentice seaman and assigned to the Naval Training Station, Hampton Roads, Virginia. Promoted to seaman second class and seaman on undisclosed dates. Honorably discharged at Hampton Roads on June 9, 1919.

HOGGARD, JOSEPH THOMAS, chief water tender: Enlisted at Norfolk, Virginia on March 1, 1917, at age 41. Appointed oiler. Promoted to water tender and chief water tender on undisclosed dates. Assigned to the USS Downes (a destroyer) on April 8, 1917. Transferred to the USS Virginia (a battleship) on May 15, 1917, and to receiving ship at Philadelphia, Pennsylvania on March 21, 1918. Transferred to receiving ship at Boston, Massachusetts on October 24, 1918. Retired from active duty on April 1, 1935.

HOGGARD, WILLIAM VANCE, chief pharmacist's mate: Enlisted at the Navy Recruiting Station, Baltimore, Maryland on January 19, 1917, at age 25. Appointed pharmacist's mate second class. Assigned to, or was serving aboard, the *USS Beale* (a destroyer) on April 6, 1917 (date of the United States' war declaration). Transferred to the *USS Melville* (a destroyer tender) on May 8, 1917. Promoted to pharmacist's mate first class and chief pharmacist's mate on undisclosed dates. Transferred to the USS Parker (a destroyer) on July 10, 1917. Honorably discharged on May 24, 1927.

LUTON, CHARLES EDWARD*, mess attendant third class: Enlisted at the Navy Recruiting Station, Norfolk, Virginia on June 15, 1918, at age 20. Appointed mess attendant third class. Assigned to the Naval Air Station, Queenstown, Ireland on August 12, 1918. Honorably discharged at Philadelphia, Pennsylvania on December 30, 1919.

MITCHELL, ZACK PERRY, hospital apprentice first class: Registered for Selective Service in Salem County, New Jersey on June 5, 1917, at age 28; occupation – munitions worker. Enrolled in the United States Navy Reserves at the Navy Recruiting Station, Raleigh on December 8, 1917, at age 28. Appointed hospital apprentice first class. Assigned to the Naval Unit, Medical College of Virginia, Richmond. Honorably discharged at the college on December 22, 1918.

NORFLEET, JOSEPH PUGH, lieutenant commander: Appointed as a midshipman to the United States Naval Academy, Annapolis, Maryland, on May 7, 1906. Promoted to lieutenant on March 7, 1915. Transferred to the *USS Melville* (a destroyer tender) on January 2, 1916. "Under instruction in dirigibles" at Goodyear Tire and Rubber Company, Akron, Ohio from June 30, 1917 until October 11, 1917. Under treatment as a patient at the Naval Hospital, Washington, D.C. from October 24, 1917, until January 24, 1918. Served in the Office of Chief of Naval Operations, Navy Department, Washington, D.C. from January 24, 1918, until September 8, 1918. Transferred to Naval Aviation Forces Abroad, United States Naval Headquarters, London, England on September 30, 1918. On duty with Naval

Forces (Aviation) Brest, France from October 13, 1918, until November 24, 1918. Retired from military service in 1923.

NORFLEET, LESLIE GRAHAM, engineman first class: Registered for Selective Service on June 5, 1917, at age 22; occupation – farmer. Enlisted at Norfolk, Virginia on September 4, 1917, at age 22. Appointed apprentice seaman. Assigned to receiving ship at Norfolk until transferred to the Naval Training Station, Norfolk on October 12, 1917. Transferred to the *USS Kentucky* (a battleship) on January 11, 1918. Transferred to receiving ship at New York City on February 15, 1918. Transferred to the *USS Zeelandia* (a troop transport) on April 1, 1918, and to receiving ship at Norfolk on September 7, 1918. Transferred to receiving ship at Philadelphia, Pennsylvania on October 25, 1918. Promoted to fireman third class and fireman first class on undisclosed dates. Honorably discharged at Constantine, Turkey, while serving aboard the *USS Chattanooga* (a cruiser) on September 1, 1920.

PHELPS, WILLIAM BRYAN, machinist's mate second class: Registered for Selective Service on June 5, 1917, at age 23; occupation – chauffer. Enrolled in the United States Navy Reserves at the Navy Recruiting Station, Norfolk, Virginia on December 14, 1917, at age 24. Appointed machinist's mate second class. Transferred to the *USS Maggie* (a patrol vessel) on April 3, 1918, and to the *USS Dixie* (a destroyer tender) on April 11, 1918. Transferred to the *USS Granite State* (a naval hospital receiving ship) on May 1, 1918, and to receiving ship at Pensacola, Florida on May 22, 1918. Honorably discharged at Pensacola on March 8, 1919.

PHELPS, WOODSON SPRUILL, seaman: Enlisted at Norfolk, Virginia on October 23, 1916, at age 17. Appointed apprentice seaman. Assigned to, or was serving aboard, the *USS Sampson* (a destroyer) on April 6, 1917 (date of the United States' war declaration). Transferred to the *USS Santee* (a freighter) on December 23, 1917. Promoted to seaman on an undisclosed date. Transferred to receiving ship at Boston, Massachusetts on April 8, 1918. Admitted to the Naval Hospital, Chelsea, Massachusetts on September 7, 1918, and released on October 30, 1918. Honorably discharged while serving aboard the USS McDermut (a destroyer) at San Diego, California on February 23, 1920.

PRUDEN, CHARLES ROY, seaman second class: Enrolled in the United States Navy Reserves at the Navy Recruiting Station, Norfolk, Virginia on June 4, 1918, and registered for Selective Service the next day in Bertie County at age 21; occupation – farmer. Appointed seaman second class and assigned to the Naval Operating Base, Hampton Roads, Virginia. Admitted to the Naval Hospital, Hampton Roads on September 24, 1918, and released on October 2, 1918. Placed on inactive duty by Headquarters, 5th Naval District, Norfolk on June 25, 1919.

PRUDEN, WALTER GRADY, water tender: Enlisted at the Navy Recruiting Station, Richmond, Virginia on February 6, 1915, at age 23. Appointed coal passer. Assigned to, or was serving aboard, the USS Kansas (a battleship) on April 6, 1917 (date of the United States' war declaration). Transferred to the USS Fanning (a destroyer) on May 10, 1917. Promoted to fireman second class, fireman first class, and water tender on undisclosed dates. Honorably discharged while serving aboard the USS Fanning at Brest, France on February 5, 1919.

RASCOE, LEWIS TAYLOE, machinist's mate second class: Registered for Selective Service on June 5, 1917, at age 21; occupation – salesman. Enrolled in the United States Navy Reserves at the Navy Recruiting Station, Norfolk, Virginia on June 11, 1918, at age 22. Appointed seaman second class. Assigned to Headquarters, Norfolk. Transferred to the USS Myrtle (a patrol vessel) on October 19, 1918. Promoted to machinist's mate second class on an undisclosed date. Honorably discharged at Norfolk on December 3, 1918.

RAYNER, JOSEPH REUBIN, ship's cook second class: Enrolled in the United States Navy Reserves at the Navy Recruiting Station, Norfolk, Virginia on February 7, 1918, at age 26. Appointed seaman second class and assigned to Headquarters, Norfolk. Promoted to ship's cook third class and ship's cook second class on undisclosed dates. Placed on inactive duty while serving at Norfolk on December 22, 1918.

RAYNOR, KENNETH TYSON, seaman second class: Registered for Selective Service on June 5, 1917, at age 26; occupation – grade school superintendent. Enrolled in the United States Navy Reserves at the Navy Recruiting Station, Norfolk, Virginia on June 22, 1918, at age 27. Appointed seaman second class and assigned to Headquarters, Norfolk. Placed on inactive duty while serving at Norfolk on December 21, 1918.

SAUNDERS, DONALD EUGENE, chief quartermaster: A Bertie County resident attending Trinity College in Durham when he enrolled in the United States Navy Reserves at the Navy Recruiting Station, Raleigh on May 25, 1918, at age 21. Appointed chief quartermaster aviation. Assigned to the Massachusetts Institute of Technology, Cambridge, Massachusetts on July 17, 1918. Placed on inactive duty by Headquarters, 5th Naval District, Norfolk on December 9, 1918.

SMITH, HELEN TILLERY, yeoman second class (female): Enrolled in the United States Navy Reserves at the Navy Recruiting Station, Norfolk, Virginia on August 27, 1918, at age 19. Appointed yeoman third class (female). Assigned to the Navy Yard, Norfolk on September 5, 1918. Promoted to yeoman second class (female) on an undisclosed date. Placed on inactive duty by the 5th Naval District, Hampton Roads, Virginia on July 26, 1919.

SMITH, MARY GLADYS, yeoman third class (female): Enrolled in the United States Navy Reserves at the Navy Recruiting

Station, Norfolk, Virginia on August 27, 1918, at age 22. Appointed yeoman third class (female). Assigned to the Navy Yard, Norfolk on September 5, 1918. Promoted to yeoman second class (female) on an undisclosed date. Placed on inactive duty by Headquarters, 5th Naval District, Norfolk on July 26, 1919.

SPIVEY, WILLIAM BRYANT, seaman: Registered for Selective Service as a Bertie County resident at Philadelphia, Pennsylvania on May 26, 1917, at age 23; occupation – machinist. Enlisted at Norfolk, Virginia on August 9, 1917. Appointed apprentice seaman. Assigned to receiving ship at Norfolk and transferred to the USS Neptune (a collier), September 28, 1917. Promoted to seaman second class and seaman on undisclosed dates. Honorably discharged at Norfolk on May 9, 1919.

SPRUILL, LATHAM OTIS, seaman second class: Enrolled in the United States Navy Reserves at the Navy Recruiting Station, Edenton on May 13, 1918, at age 18. Appointed seaman second class. Assigned to the Naval Operating Base, Norfolk, Virginia. Admitted to the Naval Hospital, Norfolk on November 2, 1918, and released on an undisclosed date. Placed on inactive duty while serving on receiving ship at Hampton Roads, Virginia on August 20, 1919.

SUTTON, EARNEST TEEN*, mess attendant third class: Enlisted at the Navy Recruiting Station, Philadelphia, Pennsylvania on December 18, 1917, at age 18. Appointed mess attendant third class. Assigned to receiving ship at Norfolk, Virginia. Transferred to the Naval Operating Base, Norfolk on January 9, 1918. Transferred to the Naval Air Station, Miami, Florida on January 29, 1918. Honorably discharged at New York City on June 19, 1919.

TARKENTON, ERIC LEE, seaman second class: Registered for Selective Service on June 5, 1918, at age 21; occupation – farmer. Enrolled in the United States Navy Reserves at

the Navy Recruiting Station, Norfolk, Virginia on June 14, 1918. Appointed seaman second class. Assigned to the Naval Operating Base, Norfolk on July 26, 1918. Admitted to the Naval Hospital, Hampton Roads, Virginia on October 2, 1918, where he died of pneumonia on October 8, 1918.

TAYLOR, JESSE POWELL, pharmacist's mate second class: Enlisted at the Navy Recruiting Station, Raleigh on April 9, 1917, at age 21. Appointed hospital apprentice second class. Was home in Bertie County awaiting orders until April 14, 1917, when assigned to the Naval Training Station, Newport, Rhode Island. Transferred to the Naval Hospital, Norfolk, Virginia on April 20, 1917. Transferred to the USS Charleston (a cruiser) on November 12, 1917. Transferred to the Naval Operating Base, Norfolk on December 17, 1917. Transferred to Naval Hospital, Norfolk on January 24, 1918. Promoted to hospital apprentice first class, pharmacist's mate third class and pharmacist's mate second class on undisclosed dates. Honorably discharged at the Naval Hospital, Norfolk on September 19, 1919.

THOMAS, DELL, fireman third class: Enlisted at Norfolk, Virginia on April 21, 1915, at age 23. Appointed coal passer. Was serving at the Naval Hospital, Chelsea, Massachusetts on April 6, 1917 (date of the United States' war declaration). Promoted to fireman third class on an undisclosed date. Honorably discharged at the Naval Hospital, Chelsea, on March 8, 1918. Registered for Selective Service on October 3, 1918; occupation – farmer.

THOMPSON, GEORGE BERTICE, fireman first class: Enlisted aboard the USS Nevada (a battleship) at Norfolk, Virginia on April 14, 1917, at age 21. Appointed fireman third class. Served aboard the USS Nevada until transferred to the USS Missouri (a battleship) on May 9, 1917. Transferred back to the USS Nevada on May 25, 1917, and transferred to the USS Sultana (a patrol craft) on May 29, 1917. Admitted to Naval Base Hospital Number 5, Brest, France on May 12, 1918, and released on June 7, 1918. Again admitted to Naval Hospital Number 5 on July 8, 1918, and released on September 17, 1918. Promoted to fireman second class and fireman first class on undisclosed dates. Honorably discharged at Norfolk on June 30, 1919.

TYLER, LODWICK LLOYD, boatswain's mate second class: Enlisted at the Navy Recruiting Station, Richmond, Virginia on May 22, 1917, at age 20. Appointed apprentice seaman. Served aboard receiving ship at Norfolk, Virginia, until transferred to the USS Ohio (a battleship) on July 15, 1917. Promoted to seaman second class, seaman, coxswain, and boatswain's mate second class on undisclosed dates. Honorably discharged while serving aboard the USS Ohio at Philadelphia, Pennsylvania on July 22, 1920.

TYNES, LOUIS CARRELL, ship's fitter first class: Enrolled in the United States Navy Reserves at the Navy Recruiting Station, Norfolk, Virginia on July 23, 1917, at age 18. Appointed seaman second class. Assigned to the USS Bulgaria, upon which he served until transferred to the Maryland State Rifle Range, Glen Burnie, Maryland, on August 3, 1917. Transferred to the Virginia Beach Rifle Range on September 20, 1917. Placed on inactive duty on September 25, 1917, and recalled to active duty on October 29, 1917 at the Virginia Beach Rifle Range. Transferred to the Naval Overseas Transportation Service, Norfolk on July 26,

1918. Transferred to Headquarters, 5th Naval District, Norfolk on November 9, 1918, and to the USS Western Chief (a cargo ship) later on the same day. Promoted to plumber and fitter, then ship's fitter first class on undisclosed dates. Honorably discharged at Norfolk on August 16, 1921.

WHITE, WILLIAM ERNEST, seaman second class: Registered for Selective Service on June 5, 1918, at age 21. Enrolled in the United States Navy Reserves at the Navy Recruiting Station, Norfolk, Virginia on July 16, 1918. Appointed apprentice seaman. Assigned to the Naval Training Station, Hampton Roads, Virginia on September 4, 1918. Admitted to the Naval Hospital, Hampton Roads on October 4, 1918, and released on October 25, 1918. Promoted to seaman second class on an undisclosed date. Placed on inactive duty while serving at Hampton Roads on December 22, 1918.

WILLIAMS, JAMES WORLEY, engineman second class: Enlisted at Norfolk, Virginia on March 3, 1915, at age 22. Appointed coal passer. Assigned to, or was serving aboard, the USS Arkansas (a battleship) on April 6, 1917 (date of the United States' war declaration). Transferred to the USS Mississippi (a battleship) on June 24, 1918. Promoted to fireman first class and engineman second class on undisclosed dates. Honorably discharged at Philadelphia, Pennsylvania on February 20, 1919.

# APPENDIX 2

## BERTIE COUNTY CITIZENS CIVIC INVOLVEMENT DURING WORLD WAR I[1]

The citizens of Bertie County, both adults and children, answered the nation's and North Carolina's calls for service in various capacities in support of the overall war efforts during 1917 and 1918. Dozens of people contributed their time to organize, oversee, and administer various war-supportive functions, including food production, fundraising, assisting military personnel, and administering Selective Service processes. As Chairman of the Bertie County Council of Defense, the influential Windsor lawyer, John Hilary Matthews, marshalled, organized, and oversaw the county-wide endeavors, which contributed significant resources. The following table lists county citizens who served in various capacities (exclusive of active military service).

| Name | Address | Service |
|------|---------|---------|
| Adams, Solomon Benjamin | Merry Hill | Member, Bertie County Soldiers Business Committee; White's Township, District 5 food administration committee; Selective Service registrar, September 12, 1918. |
| Andrew, Prof. J. M. | Colerain | Colerain Township, District 1 food administration committee. |
| Austin, Owen Griffin | Kelford | Roxobel Township, District 6 food administration committee. |
| Baggett, W. E. | Windsor | Windsor Township, District 2 food administration committee. |
| Baker, John | Colerain | Colerain Township, District 2 food administration committee. |
| Baker, W. L. | Windsor | Windsor Township, District 13 food administration committee. |
| Barnes, Mrs. Ham | Kelford | Roxobel Township, District 3 food administration committee. |
| Barnes, Moses R. | Aulander | Mitchell's Township, District 5 food administration committee; Selective Service registrar, June 5, 1917. |

| Barnes, Mrs. Moses R. | Aulander | Mitchell's Township, District 5 food administration committee. |
| Bazemore, Arthur | Kelford | Roxobel Township, District 5 food administration committee. |
| Bazemore, Charles H. | Kelford | Roxobel Township, District 4 food administration committee. |
| Bazemore, Goldie | Kelford | Roxobel Township, District 5 food administration committee. |
| Bazemore, H. Lewis | Windsor | Snakebite Township, District 3 food administration committee; Selective Service registrar, September 12, 1918. |
| Bazemore, H. S. | Aulander | Snakebite Township, District 5 food administration committee. |
| Bazemore, L. T. | Aulander | Snakebite Township, District 5 food administration committee. |
| Bazemore, Mrs. Langley | Aulander | Snakebite Township, District 6 food administration committee. |
| Bazemore, Scott | Aulander | Snakebite Township, District 4 food administration committee. |

| | | |
|---|---|---|
| Bazemore, Van Deventer | Kelford | Roxobel Township, District 5 food administration committee. |
| Bell, Holley Mack | Windsor | Selective Service registrar, June 5, 1917, June 5, 1918, and September 12, 1918. |
| Bell, John Cartwright | Windsor | Bertie County treasurer; Selective Service registrar, June 5, 1917, and September 12, 1918. |
| Bond, Mary W. | Quitsna | Indian Woods Township, District 1 food administration committee. |
| Bond, Turner Carter | Windsor | Selective Service registrar, September 12, 1918. |
| Bowen, Mrs. Thomas E. | Merry Hill | Merry Hill Township, District 4 food administration committee. |
| Bracey, Walter Preston | Kelford | Roxobel Township, District 3 food administration committee. |
| Brette, Belle | Windsor | Chairwoman, Bertie County Woman's Liberty Loan Committee. |
| Bridger, Mrs. T. H. | Lewiston | Woodville Township, District 1 food administration committee. |

| | | |
|---|---|---|
| Brinkley, Mrs. Javan | Colerain | Colerain Township, District 3 food administration committee. |
| Britt, Miss Willie | Merry Hill | Merry Hill Township, District 2 food administration committee. |
| Britton, Daniel Roy | Colerain | Chairman, Bertie County Board of Commissioners and overseer of identification and cultivation of vacant farm land within the county; Selective Service registrar, September 12, 1918. |
| Bryant, Arthur C. | Kelford | Roxobel Township, District 3 food administration committee. |
| Bryant, Goldie D. | Powellsville | Windsor Township, District 11 food administration committee. |
| Bunch, Andrew | Lewiston | Woodville Township, District 3 food administration committee. |
| Butler, Frank | Askewville | Windsor Township, District 7 food administration committee. |
| Bynum, John Robert | Windsor | Windsor Township, District 4 food administration committee. |

| | | |
|---|---|---|
| Cale, John Thomas | Windsor | Windsor Township, District 5 food administration committee. |
| Capehart, George W. | Avoca | Merry Hill Township, District 5 food administration committee. |
| Capehart, William Rhodes | Merry Hill | Merry Hill Township, District 4 food administration committee. |
| Castelloe, Allen Thurman | Aulander | Selective Service registrar, September 12, 1918. |
| Castellow, Albert Fulton | Windsor | Windsor Township, District 13 food administration committee. |
| Castellow, George Whidbee | Windsor | Windsor Township, District 14 food administration committee. |
| Castellow, Grover Cephas | Windsor | Selective Service registrar, September 12, 1918. |
| Cobb, Albert Valentine | Windsor | Bertie County Food Administration executive committee; Snakebite Township, District 2 food administration committee; Selective Service registrar, June 5, 1917, and September 12, 1918. |
| Cobb, Connaughton | Avoca | Merry Hill Township, District 5 food administration committee. |

| | | |
|---|---|---|
| Cobb, David Lee | Windsor | Windsor Township, District 14 food administration committee. |
| Cobb, George H. | Merry Hill | White's Township, District 2 food administration committee. |
| Cobb, Sue | Merry Hill | Merry Hill Township, District 3 food administration committee. |
| Cobourn, Elisha | Windsor | Windsor Township, District 3 food administration committee. |
| Cooper, Annie | Woodville | Woodville Township, District 2 food administration committee. |
| Cooper, George B. | Windsor | Indian Woods Township, District 2 food administration committee. |
| Cooper, John Wheeler | Windsor | Bertie County sheriff; chairman, Bertie County Board of Registration. |
| Cooper, Mary | Windsor | Indian Woods Township, District 2 food administration committee. |
| Cowan, John T. | Windsor | Windsor Township, District 6 food administration committee. |
| Cowan, Mrs. John T. | Aulander | Snakebite Township, District 6 food administration committee. |

| | | |
|---|---|---|
| Cowan, Nona | Powellsville | Colerain Township, District 4 food administration committee. |
| Cowan, Worley | Windsor | Windsor Township, District 6 food administration committee. |
| Cullipher, Eddie | Merry Hill | White's Township, District 5 food administration committee. |
| Daniel, Edward E. | Colerain | White's Township, District 4 food administration committee. |
| Davis, Rev. M. P. | Aulander | Mitchell's Township, District 1 food administration committee. |
| Drake, Julian Claude | Ahoskie | Mitchell's Township, District 3 food administration committee; Selective Service registrar, June 5, 1917, and September 12, 1918. |
| Dunning, Andrew Jackson Jr. | Windsor | Secretary of Bertie County Exemption Board ("local board"); Selective Service registrar, June 5, 1917, June 5, 1918, August 24, 1918, and September 12, 1918. |
| Dunning, J. C. | Quitsna | Indian Woods Township, District 1 food administration committee. |

| Early, Allie J. | Cremo | Colerain Township, District 6 food administration committee. |
| Early, Ethel | Aulander | Mitchell's Township, District 1 food administration committee. |
| Early, Gladys | Woodard | Windsor Township, District 12 food administration committee. |
| Early, Hosea Leander | Aulander | Selective Service registrar, June 5, 1917. |
| Early, John A. | Aulander | Mitchell's Township, District 4 food administration committee. |
| Early, Josiah | Aulander | Mitchell's Township, District 3 food administration committee. |
| Early, Whitmel Franklin | Aulander | Selective Service registrar, June 5, 1917. |
| Early, Mrs. Whitmel Franklin | Aulander | Home demonstration agent, Bertie County Food Administration; Snakebite Township, District 5 food administration committee. |
| Eaton, Lucille | Woodard | Windsor Township, District 12 food administration committee. |

| | | |
|---|---|---|
| Edwards, Claire | Powellsville | Colerain Township, District 6 food administration committee. |
| Edward, P. W. | Aulander | Mitchell's Township, District 7 food administration committee. |
| Evans, George W. | Colerain | White's Township, District 1 food administration committee. |
| Evans, W. C. | Kelford | Bertie County Food Administration executive committee. |
| Evans, W. T. D. | Merry Hill | White's Township, District 3 food administration committee. |
| Fore, David Archie | Roxobel | Selective Service registrar, June 5, 1917. |
| Freeman, Leon H. | Cremo | Colerain Township, District 6 food administration committee; Selective Service registrar, June 5, 1917, and September 12, 1918. |
| Freeman, Lecausey P. | Colerain | Colerain Township, District 5 food administration committee. |
| Freeman, Revel Laton | Powellsville | Colerain Township, District 4 food administration committee. |

| | | |
|---|---|---|
| Freeman, Samuel B. | Colerain | Colerain Township, District 2 food administration committee. |
| Gaskins, Eugene Virgil | Windsor | Windsor Township, District 5 food administration committee. |
| Gatling, John Morris | Windsor | Chairman, Bertie County Legal Advisory Board |
| Gillam, Helen | Windsor | Windsor Township, District 1 food administration committee. |
| Gillam, Moses Braxton | Windsor | Chairman, Bertie County Exemption Board ("local board"). |
| Godwin, Mrs. | Ahoskie | Mitchell's Township, District 6 food administration committee. |
| Godwin, Charles S. | Ahoskie | Mitchell's Township, District 6 food administration committee; Selective Service registrar, September 12, 1918. |
| Godwin, Levy Junius | Ahoskie | Selective Service registrar, September 12, 1918. |
| Gray, Edward Watson | Windsor | Selective Service registrar, September 12, 1918. |
| Griffin, Mrs. Thomas Whitmel | Woodville | Woodville Township, District 2 food administration committee. |

| Hale, Joseph J. | Kelford | Roxobel Township, District 6 food administration committee. |
| Hale, Mrs. Perry | Aulander | Mitchell's Township, District 2 food administration committee. |
| Hale, Peter | Aulander | Snakebite Township, District 4 food administration committee. |
| Hall, J. H. | Kelford | Roxobel Township, District 5 food administration committee. |
| Harden, Mrs. George A. | Merry Hill | Merry Hill Township, District 3 food administration committee. |
| Harrell, Edward Cary | Aulander | Selective Service registrar, September 12, 1918. |
| Harrell, J. W. | Colerain | Colerain Township, District 3 food administration committee. |
| Harrington, Henry Grady | Lewiston | Member of Bertie County Legal Advisory Board; Selective Service registrar, June 5, 1917, and September 12, 1918. |
| Harris, J. L. | Aulander | Mitchell's Township, District 8 food administration committee. |

| | | |
|---|---|---|
| Helleman, Herbert | Powellsville | Mitchell's Township, District 8 food administration committee. |
| Helleman, Mrs. Herman | Merry Hill | White's Township, District 3 food administration committee. |
| Helleman, Mrs. T. E. | Aulander | Mitchell's Township, District 5 food administration committee. |
| Hobbs, Charles E. | Windsor | Indian Woods Township, District 2 food administration committee; Selective Service registrar, September 12, 1918. |
| Hoggard, Mrs. Archie Clifton | Merry Hill | White's Township, District 5 food administration committee. |
| Hoggard, Jesse | Aulander | Mitchell's Township, District 4 food administration committee. |
| Hoggard, Jesse W. | Windsor | Snakebite Township, District 1 food administration committee. |
| Hoggard, John Thomas | Merry Hill | White's Township, District 1 food administration committee, Selective Service registrar, September 12, 1918. |

| Hoggard, Linwood Levy | Windsor | Snakebite Township, District 3 food administration committee; Selective Service registrar, September 12, 1918. |
|---|---|---|
| Hoggard, Marrietta | Windsor | Snakebite Township, District 1 food administration committee. |
| Howard, J. R. | Aulander | Mitchell's Township, District 2 food administration committee. |
| Hughes, Charles Crayton | Merry Hill | White's Township, District 1 food administration committee. |
| Hughes, Simeon T. | Colerain | Colerain Township, District 3 food administration committee. |
| Jacobs, Jacob Madison, Dr. | Roxobel | Member, Bertie County Council of Defense; Roxobel Township, District 1 food administration committee; Selective Service registrar, September 12, 1918. |
| Jenkins, Charles H. | Aulander | Member, Bertie County Council of Defense; chairman, Third Liberty Loan Campaign in Bertie County. |
| Jenkins, Charles M. | Aulander | Mitchell's Township, District 1 food administration committee. |

| | | |
|---|---|---|
| Jenkins, James S. | Aulander | Mitchell's Township, District 2 food administration committee. |
| Jenkins, Mamie | Kelford | Roxobel Township, District 2 food administration committee. |
| Jernigan, Ethel | Aulander | Snakebite Township, District 4 food administration committee. |
| Jernigan, G. D. | Merry Hill | White's Township, District 2 food administration committee. |
| Jernigan, Mrs. J. A. | Aulander | Snakebite Township, District 5 food administration committee. |
| Jernigan, William Mills | Ahoskie | Mitchell's Township, District 6 food administration committee. |
| Jernigan, William P. | Powellsville | Windsor Township, District 11 food administration committee. |
| Jernigan, William Roy | Powellsville | Windsor Township, District 11 food administration committee. |
| Jilcott, Carew | Kelford | Roxobel Township, District 3 food administration committee. |

| | | |
|---|---|---|
| Joyner, Daylee | Aulander | Mitchell's Township, District 7 food administration committee. |
| Keeter , Fannie | Avoca | Merry Hill Township, District 5 food administration committee. |
| Kenney, Stephen White | Windsor | Bertie County Registrar of Deeds and de facto Selective Service registrar. |
| Lassiter, Alexander | Aulander | Selective Service registrar, June 5, 1917, and September 12, 1918. |
| Lassiter, Bessie | Windsor | Windsor Township, District 9 food administration committee. |
| Lassiter, Mrs. Fannie J. | Colerain | Colerain Township, District 1 food administration committee. |
| Lawrence, James H. | Merry Hill | Colerain Township, District 4 food administration committee. |
| Lazar, Prof. James T. | Aulander | Mitchell's Township, District 1 food administration committee. |
| Leicester, George E. | Merry Hill | Merry Hill Township, District 2 food administration committee. |

| | | |
|---|---|---|
| Leggett, C. D. | Windsor | Indian Woods Township, District 3 food administration committee. |
| Leggett, Ebenezer | Windsor | Indian Woods Township, District 3 food administration committee. |
| Lineberry, Rev. R. B. | Colerain | Colerain Township, District 1 food administration committee. |
| Liverman, Mattie | Kelford | Roxobel Township, District 2 food administration committee. |
| Livermon, Carl Raby | Roxobel | Selective Service registrar, June 5, 1917. |
| Lyon, William Llewelyn | Windsor | Clerk of Bertie County Superior Court; member, Bertie County Council of Defense; member, Bertie County Board of Registration; treasurer, Bertie County Chapter of the American Red Cross. |

| Matthews, John Hilary | Windsor | Representative, North Carolina General Assembly; chairman, Bertie County Council of Defense; Bertie County Food Administrator; Bertie County Government Appeal Agent; chairman, Bertie County War Savings Stamp Committee; chairman, Bertie County Chapter of the American Red Cross. |
|---|---|---|
| McGraw, Mack | Windsor | Windsor Township, District 3 food administration committee. |
| Miller, E. H. | Windsor | Windsor Township, District 13 food administration committee. |
| Miller, Solomon Moore | Powellsville | Windsor Township, District 11 food administration committee. |
| Miller, Starkey T. | Merry Hill | Selective Service registrar, September 12, 1918. |
| Minton, W. H. | Kelford | Roxobel Township, District 4 food administration committee. |

| | | |
|---|---|---|
| Mitchell, Arthur Cleveland | Windsor | Clerk, Bertie County Exemption Board ("local board"); Selective Service registrar, June 5, 1917. |
| Mitchell, C. W. | Windsor | Merry Hill Township, District 1 food administration committee. |
| Mitchell, Clingman Webster [Sr.] | Aulander | Industrial and agricultural advisor, North Carolina Eastern District (Goldsboro). |
| Mitchell, Clingman Webster, Jr. | Aulander | Member, Bertie County Board Exemption Board ("local board"); Selective Service registrar, September 12, 1918; co-chairman, War Savings Campaign in Bertie County. |
| Mitchell, Gaither Wingate | Ahoskie | Mitchell's Township, District 3 food administration committee; Selective Service registrar, September 12, 1918. |
| Mitchell, J. B. | Powellsville | Colerain Township, District 4 food administration committee. |
| Mitchell, James G. | Windsor | Windsor Township, District 7 food administration committee. |

| | | |
|---|---|---|
| Mitchell, John W. | Windsor | Windsor Township, District 9 food administration committee. |
| Mitchell, W. M. | Ahoskie | Mitchell's Township, District 6 food administration committee. |
| Mitchell, Dr. Wayland | Lewiston | Member of Bertie County Council of Defense. |
| Mitchell, Mrs. Wayland | Lewiston | Woodville Township, District 1 food administration committee. |
| Mizell, Charles Wesley | Windsor | Windsor Township, District 14 food administration committee. |
| Mizell, Lee | Windsor | Windsor Township, District 3 food administration committee. |
| Mizell, Lera | Windsor | Windsor Township, District 6 food administration committee. |
| Mizell, Wayland Alexander | Windsor | Windsor Township, District 8 food administration committee. |
| Mizell, Mrs. William H. | Merry Hill | Merry Hill Township, District 3 food administration committee. |

| | | |
|---|---|---|
| Mizell, William Joseph | Windsor | Windsor Township, District 9 food administration committee. |
| Mizell, W. T. | Windsor | Windsor Township, District 6 food administration committee. |
| Montague, Merle Rice | Colerain | Selective Service registrar, September 12, 1918. |
| Morris, Charles Bell | Colerain | Selective Service registrar, June 5, 1917, and September 12, 1918. |
| Morris, J. P. | Aulander | Mitchell's Township, District 4 food administration committee. |
| Myers, Mrs. Samuel | Aulander | Mitchell's Township, District 4 food administration committee. |
| Newbern, Herbert Ethelbert | Askewville | Windsor Township, District 7 food administration committee. |
| Newell, J. L. | Kelford | Roxobel Township, District 4 food administration committee. |
| Nowell, Dr. L. A. | Colerain | Member, Bertie County Council of Defense. |

| | | |
|---|---|---|
| Nowell, Mrs. L. A. | Colerain | Colerain Township, District 1 food administration committee. |
| Oder, T. R. | Merry Hill | Windsor Township, District 10 food administration committee. |
| Outlaw, Walton B. | Colerain | White's Township, District 4 food administration committee. |
| Parker, George Thomas | Kelford | Roxobel Township, District 2 food administration committee; Selective Service registrar, June 5, 1917, and September 12, 1918. |
| Parker, Rowland Wood | Kelford | Roxobel Township, District 6 food administration committee. |
| Parker, Samuel | Windsor | Snakebite Township, District 1 food administration committee. |
| Paschal, Prof. H. R. | Lewiston | Woodville Township, District 1 food administration committee. |
| Peele, Joseph Jackson | Lewiston | Selective Service registrar, September 12, 1918. |
| Peele, Mary | Aulander | Snakebite Township, District 4 food administration committee. |

| | | |
|---|---|---|
| Perry, J. E. R. | Powellsville | Colerain Township, District 6 food administration committee. |
| Perry, James H. | Colerain | White's Township, District 4 food administration committee. |
| Perry, Mrs. James Monroe | Colerain | Colerain Township, District 2 food administration committee. |
| Perry, John T. | Windsor | Windsor Township, District 9 food administration committee. |
| Perry, Matthew Blunt | Colerain | Colerain Township, District 2 food administration committee. |
| Perry, Philip T. | Windsor | Selective Service registrar, June 5, 1917, and September 12, 1918. |
| Perry, Mrs. W. B. | Colerain | White's Township, District 4 food administration committee. |
| Phelps, Mae | Merry Hill | Merry Hill Township, District 2 food administration committee. |
| Phelps, John R. | Windsor | Merry Hill Township, District 1 food administration committee. |

| | | |
|---|---|---|
| Phelps, P. W. | Askewville | Windsor Township, District 8 food administration committee. |
| Phelps, T. H. | Merry Hill | White's Township, District 3 food administration committee. |
| Phelps, William S. | Windsor | Windsor Township, District 5 food administration committee. |
| Pierce, Charlie | Colerain | Colerain Township, District 5 food administration committee. |
| Pierce, James | Windsor | Windsor Township, District 5 food administration committee. |
| Pierce, James P. | Windsor | Windsor Township, District 4 food administration committee. |
| Pierce, William Edward | Merry Hill | Merry Hill Township, District 3 food administration committee. |
| Pigg, Nannie E. | Colerain | Colerain Township, District 5 food administration committee. |
| Powell, Kader | Aulander | Roxobel Township, District 7 food administration committee. |

| | | |
|---|---|---|
| Pritchard, John | Windsor | Selective Service registrar, June 5, 1917, and September 12, 1918. |
| Pritchard, Dr. John Lamb | Windsor | County physician; member, Bertie County Board of Registration and Bertie County Exemption Board ("local board"). |
| Pritchard, Calvin | Aulander | Mitchell's Township, District 7 food administration committee. |
| Pritchard, Lewis | Windsor | Windsor Township, District 2 food administration committee. |
| Pruden, Chloe M. | Aulander | Snakebite Township, District 6 food administration committee. |
| Raney, E. R. | Windsor | Farm demonstrator, Bertie County Food Administration; Windsor Township, District 1 food administration committee. |
| Rascoe, Aaron Spivey | Windsor | Appointed Chairman, Bertie County Board of Registration by Gov. Thomas Bickett (tenure of service, if any, appears to have been quite short). |

| | | |
|---|---|---|
| Rawls, David Walter | Aulander | Roxobel Township, District 7 food administration committee. |
| Rawls, W. L. | Aulander | Roxobel Township, District 7 food administration committee. |
| Rayner, Prof. Kenneth Tyson | Windsor | Windsor Township, District 1 food administration committee. |
| Rick, Mrs. Burden | Windsor | Snakebite Township, District 3 food administration committee. |
| Ruffin, C. S. | Cremo | Mitchell's Township, District 5 food administration committee. |
| Ruffin, Dr. Joseph Blunt | Powellsville | Bertie County Food Administration executive committee. |
| Sallenger, William Henry | Merry Hill | Windsor Township, District 10 food administration committee. |
| Saunders, John Barrett | Lewiston | Woodville Township, District 1 food administration committee. |
| Sawyer, Foy Allen (Mrs. Charles J. Sawyer) | Windsor | Chairwoman, Bertie County Woman's Liberty Loan Committee |

| | | |
|---|---|---|
| Shields, Emma | Merry Hill | Windsor Township, District 10 food administration committee. |
| Shields, Mrs. Robert J. | Windsor | Merry Hill Township, District 1 food administration committee. |
| Simons, Walter L. | Colerain | Colerain Township, District 3 food administration committee. |
| Smith, H. R. | Merry Hill | White's Township, District 3 food administration committee. |
| Smith, Mrs. R. L. | Merry Hill | Merry Hill Township, District 4 food administration committee. |
| Smith, William Richard | Merry Hill | Selective Service registrar, September 12, 1918. |
| Smithwick, Alfred Duncan | Windsor | Selective Service registrar, September 12, 1918. |
| Smithwick, Mrs. Alfred Duncan | Windsor | Merry Hill Township, District 1 food administration committee. |

| | | |
|---|---|---|
| Smithwick, Thomas Allen | Merry Hill | Bertie County Food Administration executive committee; Merry Hill Township, District 2 food administration committee; Selective Service registrar, June 5, 1917, and September 12, 1918. |
| Speelman, Prof. G. C. | Woodville | Woodville Township, District 2 food administration committee. |
| Speight, Tulie | Windsor | Snakebite Township, District 2 food administration committee. |
| Speller, Charles Broomfield | Windsor | Indian Woods Township, District 3 food administration committee. |
| Speller, C. D. | Windsor | Indian Woods Township, District 3 food administration committee. |
| Spruill, Charles Wayland | Windsor | Snakebite Township, District 3 food administration committee; Selective Service registrar, September 12, 1918. |
| Spruill, Elmer Duke | Quitsna | Indian Woods Township, District 1 food administration committee; Selective Service registrar, June 5, 1917, and September 12, 1918. |

| | | |
|---|---|---|
| Spruill, M. L. | Windsor | Windsor Township, District 2 food administration committee. |
| Tadlock, William Andrew | Woodard | Windsor Township, District 12 food administration committee. |
| Tarkenton, Robert Edward | Woodard | Windsor Township, District 12 food administration committee. |
| Tayloe, J. R. | Powellsville | Mitchell's Township, District 8 food administration committee. |
| Thomas, Jeppie | Windsor | Windsor Township, District 4 food administration committee. |
| Thompson, William Luther | Merry Hill | Windsor Township, District 10 food administration committee. |
| Todd, Mrs. T. S. | Windsor | Snakebite Township, District 1 food administration committee. |
| Todd, William Riley | Windsor | Windsor Township, District 13 food administration committee. |
| Tyler, Charles Cotton | Roxobel | Roxobel Township, District 1 food administration committee. |
| Tyler, Ernest Rudolph | Roxobel | Selective Service registrar, September 12, 1918. |

| | | |
|---|---|---|
| Tyler, Mrs. Ernest Rudolph | Roxobel | Roxobel Township, District 1 food administration committee. |
| Tyler, Joseph Eugene | Kelford | Roxobel Township, District 2 food administration committee; Selective Service registrar, September 12, 1918. |
| Urquhart, Richard Alexander | Woodville | Selective Service registrar, June 5, 1917, and September 12, 1918. |
| Urquhart, Mrs. Richard Alexander | Woodville | Woodville Township, District 2 food administration committee. |
| Vaughn, Mrs. J. Clyde | Powellsville | Mitchell's Township, District 8 food administration committee. |
| Veale, Joseph Turner | Woodville | Selective Service registrar, September 12, 1918. |
| Vick, L. P. | Kelford | Roxobel Township, District 4 food administration committee. |
| Vinson, Bota | Ahoskie | Mitchell's Township, District 3 food administration committee. |
| Wadsworth, Samuel | Lewiston | Woodville Township, District 3 food administration committee. |

| | | |
|---|---|---|
| Walke, Mrs. E. H. | Avoca | Merry Hill Township, District 5 food administration committee. |
| Ward, E. E. | Windsor | Snakebite Township, District 2 food administration committee. |
| Ward, H. J. | Merry Hill | Member, Bertie County Council of Defense. |
| Ward, Mrs. James | Windsor | Snakebite Township, District 2 food administration committee. |
| Ward, Jordan | Merry Hill | White's Township, District 1 food administration committee. |
| Warly, H. W. | Windsor | Bertie County Food Administration executive committee. |
| White, A. J. | Askewville | Windsor Township, District 7 food administration committee. |
| White, Alpheus Durant | Colerain | Selective Service registrar, June 5, 1917, and September 12, 1918. |
| White, James Allie | Windsor | Windsor Township, District 14 food administration committee. |
| White, J. J. | Colerain | Colerain Township, District 5 food administration committee. |

| White, Mrs. J. W. | Merry Hill | Merry Hill Township, District 4 food administration committee. |
| White, Janie | Aulander | Windsor Township, District 4 food administration committee. |
| White, John T. | Merry Hill | White's Township, District 2 food administration committee. |
| White, M. L. | Aulander | Snakebite Township, District 6 food administration committee. |
| White, William D. | Windsor | Windsor Township, District 8 food administration committee. |
| White, Mrs. William Gilbert | Askewville | Windsor Township, District 8 food administration committee. |
| Williams, William Thomas | Merry Hill | White's Township, District 5 food administration committee. |
| Williford, Gordon Carlton | Aulander | Selective Service registrar, September 12, 1918. |
| Winston, Francis Donell | Windsor | Member, Bertie County Legal Advisory Board; chairman, Second Liberty Loan Campaign in Bertie County. |

| Winston, Rosa K. (Mrs. Francis Donell Winston) | Windsor | Chair, Woman's Committee, Bertie County Council of Defense; Bertie County Food Administration executive committee; Windsor Township, District 1 food administration committee; chair and secretary, Bertie County Chapter of the American Red Cross. |
| Winston, Prof. Marcellus Eaton | Roxobel | Roxobel Township, District 1 food administration committee. |

1. The author compiled the names of the individuals presented in this appendix from various records and documents primarily found in, but not limited to, World War I Selective Service System Draft Registration Cards (Bertie County) (microfilm), Record Group 163, National Archives; County War Records, North Carolina Council of Defense, Liberty Loan Campaigns, Local Draft Boards and Recruiting in the State, and Food Administration Papers, Military Collection, World War I Papers, 1903-1933, State Archives; Minute Book, Bertie County Chapter American Red Cross, Minutes Executive, and Red Cross volume (untitled), Bertie County Register of Deeds Office, Windsor.

# BIBLIOGRAPHY

## Bertie County Register of Deeds Office, Windsor, N.C.

Death Certificates

Jail Record

Minute Book, Bertie County Chapter of the American Red Cross

Minute Book, Bertie County Chapter American Red Cross (unlabeled), 1917–1918
— First World War

Record of Soldiers from Bertie County in the World War, 1917-1918

Soldiers and Sailors Discharge Records (9 vols.)

Special Report, 1914, Bertie County


## Department of the Navy, Washington, D.C.

U.S. Navy Casualties Books, 1776-1941. Officers and Enlisted Men, 1917–1918


## National Archives, Washington, D.C. and Atlanta, Georgia

Appeals to the President and Correspondence from the Provost Marshal's Office,
Selective Service System (World War 1), 1917–1918, Mississippi, North Carolina.
Record Group 163.

Applications for Headstones for U.S. Military Veterans, 1925-1941 (microfilm).
Records of the Office of the Quartermaster General. Record Group 92.

Fifteenth Census of the United States, 1930 (microfilm). Bertie County, North
Carolina. Records of the Bureau of the Census. Record Group 29.

Fourteenth Census of the United States, 1920 (microfilm). Bertie County, North
Carolina. Records of the Bureau of the Census. Record Group 29.

List of Delinquents and Deserters for Military Duty: Form 4003, Selective Service System, Provost Marshal General's Office Records of Local Boards, 1917-1919 (Bertie County, North Carolina), Record Group 163, National Archives, Atlanta, GA.

*Pamphlet Describing M1509, World War I Selective Service System Draft Registration Cards.* Record Group 163.

Records of the Council of National Defense. Finding Aid. Record Group 62.

Records of the United States Food Administration. Finding Aid. Record Group 4.

Sixteenth Census of the United States, 1940 (microfilm). Bertie County, North Carolina. Records of the Bureau of the Census. Record Group 29.

Thirteenth Census of the United States, 1910 (microfilm). Bertie County, North Carolina. Records of the Bureau of the Census. Record Group 29.

War Department, Office of the Provost Marshal General, Selective Service System, 1917–July 15, 1919. Lists of Men Ordered to Report to Local Board for Military Duty, 1917–1918. North Carolina (Bertie County). Records of the Selective Service System (World War 1). Record Group 163.

World War I Selective Service System Draft Registration Cards (microfilm). Record Group 163.


## North Carolina State Archives, Office of Archives and History, Raleigh, N.C.

Bertie County Commissioners Minutes, 1896–1933 (microfilm)

Bertie County Elections, Record of, 1878–1932 (microfilm)

Bickett, Thomas W., Governors Papers

Military Collection. Adjutant General – World War I Service Cards (microfilm)

Military Collection. World War I Papers.
    County War Records
    Food Administration Papers and Finding Aid

Liberty Loan Campaigns – Finding Aid and General Records

Local Draft Boards and Recruiting (Bertie County folder)

North Carolina Council of Defense

## Library of Congress

Woodrow Wilson, *Message to Congress*. 63rd Cong., 2d Sess., 1914, Senate Doc. No. 566.

## Newspapers

*Alamance Gleaner* (Graham)

*Bertie Ledger-Advance* (Windsor)

*Courier* (Asheboro)

*Daily Times* (Wilson)

*Enterprise* (Williamston)

*Hickory Democrat*

*Mebane Leader*

*News and Observer* (Raleigh)

*New York Times*

*New York Tribune*

*Raleigh Times*

*Review* (High Point)

*Roanoke Beacon* (Plymouth)

*Roanoke News* (Weldon)

*Washington Post*

*Windsor Ledger*

## Books, Pamphlets, Articles, and Other Published Material

*Annual Report of the Adjutant General of the State of North Carolina, 1917–1918*. Raleigh:Edwards & Broughton Printing Co., State Printers, 1920.

*Annual Report of the Auditor of the State of North Carolina for the Fiscal Year Ending November 30, 1917*. Raleigh: Edwards & Broughton Printing Co., State Printers, 1919.

Breen, William J. "The North Carolina Council of Defense During World War I, 1917-1918." *North Carolina Historical Review*, 50 (January 1973): 1-31.

Cheney, John L., Jr. ed. *North Carolina Government, 1585–1974: A Narrative and Statistical Abstract*. Raleigh: North Carolina Department of the Secretary of the State, 1975.

Connor, R. D. W. comp. & ed. *North Carolina Manual*, 1919. Raleigh: Edwards & Broughton, 1918.

*Final Report of the Provost Marshal General to the Secretary of War on the Operations of the Selective Service System to July 15, 1919*. Washington: Government Printing Office, 1920.

Fries, F. H., comp. *History of War Savings Campaign of 1918 in North Carolina*. Winston-Salem: n.p., n.d.

Halpern, Paul G. "The War at Sea," in Hew Strachan, ed., *The Oxford Illustrated History of the First World War*. Oxford and New York: Oxford University Press, 1998.

Haulsee, W. M., F. G. Howe and A. C. Doyle, comps. *Soldiers of the Great War*, 3 vols. Washington: Soldiers Record Publishing Association, 1920.

Hilton, George W. *American Narrow Gauge Railroads*. Stanford, California: Stanford University Press, 1990.

*History, 119th Infantry, 60th Brigade, 30th Division, U.S.A., Operations in Belgium and France, 1917–1919*. Wilmington: Wilmington Chamber of Commerce, 1920.

Lemmon, Sarah McCulloh and Nancy Smith Midgette. *North Carolina and the Two World Wars*. Raleigh: Office of Archives and History, 2013.

Link, Arthur S., et al., eds. *The Papers of Woodrow Wilson*, 69 vols. Princeton, New Jersey: Princeton University, 1966-1994.

*The Literary Digest 55* (July 1917 – December 1917). New York: Funk & Wagnalls Company.

Martin, Santford, comp., and R. B. House, ed. *Public Letters and Papers of Thomas Walter Bickett, Governor of North Carolina, 1917–1921*. Raleigh: Edwards & Broughton, 1923.

McGrath, John J. *The Other End of the Spear: The Tooth-to-Tail Ratio (T3R) in Modern Military Operations*. Fort Leavenworth, Kansas: Combat Studies Institute Press, 2007.

McKercher, B. J. C. "Economic Warfare," in Hew Strachan, ed. *The Oxford Illustrated History of the First World War*. Oxford and New York: Oxford University Press, 1998.

Navy Department, Historical Section, comp. *American Ship Casualties of the World War, including Naval Vessels, Merchant Ships, Sailing Vessels and Fishing Craft*. Washington: Government Printing Office, 1923.

Neiberg, Michael S. *Fighting the Great War: A Global History*. Cambridge and London: Harvard University Press, 2005.

*The Official Record of the United States' Part in the Great War*. Washington: Government Printing Office, 1920.

*Order of Battle of the United States Land Forces in the World War*, 3 vols. Washington: Government Printing Office, 1931–1949; repr., Washington, Center of Military History, 1988.

Patterson, Thomas G., J. Gary Clifford, Shane J. Maddock, Deborah Kisatsky, and Kenneth J. Hagan. *American Foreign Relations: A History, Volume 2 Since 1895*. Boston: Cengage Learning, 2009.

Rinaldi, Richard A., comp. *The United States in World War I, Orders of Battle, Ground Units, 1917–1919*. (Publication fact missing) Tiger Lily Publications, LLC, the compiler, 2005.

*Second Report of the Provost Marshal General to the Secretary of War on the Operations of the Selective Service System to December 20, 1918*. Washington: Government Printing Office, 1919.

*Selective Service Regulations Prescribed by the President Under the Authority Vested in Him by the Terms of the Selective Service Law (Act of Congress Approved May 18, 1917)*. Washington: Government Printing Office, 1917.

Strachan, Hew. *The First World War*. New York: Penguin Group, 2003.

Trask, David F. *The War with Spain in 1898*. Lincoln and London: University of Nebraska Press, 1981.

*United States Statutes at Large*.

Venzon, Anne Cipriano, ed. *The United States in the First World War: An Encyclopedia*. New York and London: Garland Publishing, Inc., 1995.

Walker, Maj. John O., et al. *Official History of the 120th Infantry, "3rd North Carolina" 30th Division, From August 5, 1917, to April 17, 1919*. Lynchburg, Virginia: J. P. Bell Co., 1919.

Williamson, Samuel R. Jr. "The Origins of the War," in Hew Strachan, ed., *The Oxford Illustrated History of the First World War*. Oxford and New York: Oxford University Press, 1998.

Willmott, H. P. *World War I*. New York: Dorling Kindersley Publishing, 2003.

*World Book Encyclopedia*. 2000 edition.

Yockelson, Mitchell. "They Answered the Call: Military Service in the United States Army during World War I, 1917–1919." *Prologue*, vol. 30, no. 3 (Fall 1998).

## Other Sources

American Battle Monuments Commission, www.abmc.gov. Website.

American Presidency Project. Presidential Executive Orders. University of California, Santa Barbara, www.presidency.ucsb.edu. Website.

American Red Cross. www.redcross.org. Website.

"Assassination of Archduke Ferdinand, 1914." Eyewitness to History. www.eyewitnesstohistory.com. Website.

*A Brief History of the Quartermaster Corps*. Quartermaster Museum, Fort Lee, Virginia. www.qmmuseum.lee.army.mil. Website.

Brigham Young University Library. http://net.lib.byu/estu/wwi/bio/p/princip.html. Website.

Byrd, Joseph Levy, Letters and Papers (courtesy of Carolyn Dail, Buck Sitterson and Sue Byrd Sitterson).

Doughboy Center. www.worldwar1.com. Website.

Great Pandemic, 1918-1919. http://www.flu.gov/pandemic/history/1918. Website.

Leicester, Nova Asbell. "Tales Told to Me by My Mother When I Was a Child," (unpublished research report, 1977 ca.).

Military headstones, World War 1 veterans. Bertie County cemeteries (various).

NCpedia. http://ncpedia.org/history/health/influenza. Website.

Phelps, William Miles, letter (undated) (courtesy of Dennis Phelps).

"Secrets of World War I," 2006, History Channel.

United States Navy website, www.history.navy.mil. Website.

Made in the USA
Middletown, DE
04 November 2021